BUDDY

BUDDY

*How
a Rooster
Made Me
a Family
Man*

Brian McGrory

CROWN PUBLISHERS

New York

Copyright © 2012 by Brian McGrory

Published in the United States by Crown Publishers, an imprint of
the Crown Publishing Group, a division of Random House, Inc.,
New York.
www.crownpublishing.com

CROWN and the Crown colophon are registered trademarks of
Random House, Inc.

Library of Congress Cataloging-in-Publication Data
McGrory, Brian.
Buddy : how a rooster made me a family man / Brian McGrory.
— 1st ed.
1. McGrory, Brian—Family.   2. Authors, American—Biography.
3. Human-animal relationships.   4. Roosters.   I. Title.
PS3563.C36814Z46 2012
813'.6—dc23
[B]
2012011720

ISBN 978-0-307-95306-3
eISBN 978-0-307-95308-7

Printed in the United States of America

Jacket photograph: Tamara Staples
Additional jacket photographs: (frames) Robert Kirk, (photo of
family) Sam Edwards, (golden retriever) courtesy of the author
Author photograph: Suzanne Kreiter

10 9 8 7 6 5 4 3 2 1

First Edition

To Pam, Abigail, and Caroline
(as well as Baker, Walter, Charlie, Tigger, Lily, Dolly, Mokey,
Lala, Smurf, Chaz, and the nameless frog—what a house)

> 1 <

Try as you might, you never forget that first time a rooster announces the dawn of a new day from your very own yard.

In my case, I jerked awake to find myself in a place I had never been, on a bed that wasn't mine, in a room I didn't know. There were windows where there had never been windows, and outside those windows, the first hint of morning light revealed the outline of tall trees I had never seen before.

I pressed and poked at the unfamiliar alarm clock until I realized it wasn't the source of the sound. No, the noise in question was somewhere else, somewhere out of reach, somewhere outside of this room.

"Cock-a-doodle-doo! Cock-a-doodle-doo!"

It seemed to be getting closer, louder, clearer.

"Dammit." I whirled toward the origin of the profanity, a figure that had suddenly stirred beside me in bed, a woman with a raspy voice still choked by sleep. She tossed off the thick comforter and lunged toward her side of the room.

In the darkness, I caught a glimpse of the yellow sweatshirt and blue surgical scrubs worn by this mysterious, fleeting figure. Hey, wait a minute. This wasn't any unknown blonde. It was my fiancée, Pam. What was she doing here? I watched as she paused in the murky expanse, apparently gathering her bearings, and then vanished through an open door.

"Cock-a-doodle-doo! Cock-a-doodle-doo!"

I looked at the alarm clock on the bedside table: 4:55 A.M. Clarity was making a comeback. Memories were returning, gaps filling in. I had moved the day before. Yes, right, moved. It wasn't a small move. I'd left the city I love, Boston, where I had lived for most of the last twenty-two years, for a distant and leafy place known as suburbia. I'd left a classic 150-year-old brick town house loaded with character and charm for a rambling new suburban home surrounded by this thing I was told was a lawn. I'd left a life of total freedom and independence—the only thing resembling a familial obligation was my golden retriever, who never felt obligatory at all—to live with Pam, her two daughters, their two rabbits, and their dog, Walter, in a new house that, as of the previous day, I think I even co-owned.

"Cock-a-doodle-doo!"

Oh, and how could I forget their rooster? Otherwise known as my wake-up call. That was Buddy screaming outside, Buddy waking me up, Buddy announcing, with singular style, that my life would never again be the same. Just as I had spent my first night in a new house, so had he, in his case a grossly expensive shed that Pam had custom-built in the side yard, with tall double cedar doors, insulated walls, a shingled roof, a shelf that served as his high perch, and windows that had yet to be installed, which explained the penetrating predawn alert. Buddy had awakened to the sounds of potential predators outside his house, which meant that the rest of the street awoke to Buddy's war cry. Good morning, new neighbors!

I heard footsteps downstairs, then the happy yelps and little barks of the relieved chicken undoubtedly being carried in Pam's arms. I had this rush of fear that she was bringing him up to bed until I heard the cellar door open, steps, silence. Moments later, the darkness giving way to more light, Pam fell into bed next to me.

"Poor guy is scared and confused," she said sleepily.

"I'll be okay," I said.

"No. I mean Buddy."

As Pam drifted back to sleep, I lay in bed trying to get my head around how all this was going to work. I'm not talking about this new, grand, crowded life filled with spasms of drama lurking around the most seemingly complacent corners, or the constant cacophony of girls, dogs, and chicken, or the long commute to work, or the neighbor inevitably leaning over my back fence to tell me when to flip my burgers, or the fact that my new walk to the coffee shop led me along a highway and to a strip mall. No, I just mean getting up, getting ready, getting out. In my old life, as in yesterday, I'd accompany my golden retriever on a quiet walk through a tranquil park known as the Esplanade set along the banks of the Charles River in Boston. The river flowed on one side, surprisingly clean. The highrises of Back Bay towered on the other. We'd loop through the Public Garden, where swan boats awaited the day's riders and the colorful palette of fat tulips signaled the start of better things. We'd mosey up Newbury Street, past the stores and boutiques that had yet to come to life for the day, the dog happily slurping water from any shopkeepers who happened to be hosing down their sidewalks. We'd stop at a coffee shop where the nice counter clerk knew what I wanted and always seemed happy that I was there, and wind up on my front stoop, where I'd read the paper and the tired dog would laze in the sun.

Now I had the finite space of a yard. Now I had a car to get to Dunkin' Donuts. And now I had an eight-year-old in the house named Caroline who had learned from her older cousin the prior summer how to pick a lock with a bobby pin. She was excellent at it, a talent that would result in uncharacteristically short and uncommonly tense showers for me.

"Mommy! Mommy! Mommy!"

The kids, two girls, raced into the room at that very minute, dived through the air, and landed on the bed between Pam and myself, the older of the daughters, Abigail, rolling into me, giggling loudly as she gave me the once-over from her vantage point on the pillow, and declaring "Your hair is sticking straight up."

Good to know. Pam rolled over, and the three of them hugged and talked about their first night in their new bedrooms. The two dogs had stirred and began wrestling on the bedroom floor. Buddy began crowing again from two floors below.

"He's in the basement," Pam told the kids, who were looking quizzical, and it was as if she had lit the fuse of a rocket. They roared out of the room as fast as they had arrived, followed more slowly by their mother, who was followed by the two dogs, leaving me alone with my hopes and fears—my hopes being that this whole big venture would work out as it was supposed to, my fears being about every possible way that my twisted little mind could devise to screw things up.

I took the quickest shower of my life. Downstairs, every living creature in the house had gathered in the kitchen. The dogs were lying in wait, though out of their element and unclear on the agenda. "I get it, guys," I told them. The rabbit cage had somehow shown up next to the kitchen table with two creatures named Dolly and Lily inside, though I wouldn't pass a test on which was which. Pam was dicing fruit and cooking pancakes on a stovetop griddle that had appeared out of nowhere and that I hadn't known we owned. How had she even found it in this sea of boxes? Ten years in my old condo and I don't think I opened the oven door, let alone cooked breakfast.

And Buddy. Big, white, proud, and round, with a rubbery red comb and a matching red wattle, he was clucking around the floor, high-stepping between the dogs, cooing at the kids who were on their knees doing their very best to make him feel at home. "You are the best rooster in town," Abigail told him. Caroline swooped him into her thin arms so he could watch her mother make the pancakes. "Oh, poor Boo-Boo, don't be scared," she whispered in his ear. "We all love you."

What followed were twenty or so minutes of orchestrated pandemonium during which I was every inch, at every moment, the uninvited guest. To intrude would have been like tossing a butter knife into the blades of a whirring fan. Food was furiously eaten. Dishes were swept away in a clack of noise, yet still found their way to the dishwasher. Kids raced upstairs to get dressed for school. Countdown clocks were yelled. Kids argued about what they were going to wear. Lunches were made and recess snacks prepared in separate bags. Soon enough, I found myself standing on the front porch watching the three women of Sawmill Lane heading toward Pam's car, the two girls lugging backpacks as their little ponytails bounced with every step. Did they really do this every morning?

"Hey, Brian," Caroline said in her squeaky little voice as she rolled down the back window on their way out of the driveway. Acknowledgment! "Don't eat all the cupcakes that Mom bought." And they were off.

Alone, I stepped out into the yard, which was more weeds than grass, but I'd take care of that. I looked back at the barn red house, and I had to admit, it was pretty handsome, everything brand-new, never lived in before, meaning that every day spent here, every memory made here, would be all and only ours, and if this morning was any indication, the memories would be plentiful. Pam and I would be married soon in this house. The kids would grow from girls to teenagers to young women in this house. They'd return from college, surrounded by their pasts, to contemplate where in this world they wanted to go. Everything was set for a wonderful narrative filled with unique characters that would unfold over the many years ahead, hopefully more comedy than drama.

That first day in a new house, there are no bad places, no unpleasant recollections of arguments or phone calls or knocks on the door that could send your world spinning out of control in a whispered moment. There were only possibilities. The floors shone. The windows glistened. The counters sparkled. It was all new—as new as my new life had ever been—and it was ours, mine and Pam's, together.

As I emerged from my reverie, I walked back onto the porch admiring the craftsmanship and the details that had gone into the house. And that's when I heard him, his long, raspy groan, as if his emotions—specifically, anger— were billowing up inside his barrel chest. I looked down to see Buddy emerge from behind a pillar, almost comically corpulent from the copious amounts of food that the kids constantly fed him. The Roman philosopher Cicero once wrote that a chicken approaching from the left is always good luck. I have no idea whether or not that's true, but I do know that Buddy was decidedly approaching from my right, if only to make the point completely moot, perhaps meaningfully so.

All of this would have been nothing more than wallpaper to this incredibly pretty and memorable day but for one key point: Buddy didn't like me. Well, actually, that's not the whole truth. No, the whole truth is, Buddy hated my guts. He didn't understand the actual point of me. If he was there to watch over his kingdom of pretty, blond hens, why was this frivolous little man around as well? Add to that the fact that he was probably just smart enough to know that I would have roasted him as fast as he would fit into an oversized pan. The result was a relationship far less than idyllic.

Though he could chirp and play with the kids and bat his beady little eyes at Pam as she talked to him in her high chicken voice ("You're the most handsome Boo-Boo in the whole big world!"), he thought nothing, absolutely nothing, of extending and flapping his wings at me while charging with a mix of disdain and fury on his otherwise vacuous chicken face. His goal: to jam his sharp beak into the fleshiest parts of my legs. When I batted him away, he would leap into the air, as if trying to castrate me. I swear he spent quiet nights on his perch plotting my demise.

So there I was, first day at this new house, having my moment on the porch, and I froze. I remembered Pam's warning that sudden movements would put him into full attack mode. Likewise, I recalled her advice that standing my ground too firmly could be seen as a challenge and provoke an attack anyway. And then there was the helpful advice that if I backed away, even subtly, he would sense weakness and really go for it. So I stood there, trying to look strong but not threatening, tense as a tuning fork though trying to hide it, willing myself to the door without actually moving, when my dog, Baker, came walking right between us, dropped the ball at my feet, and stared up at my face.

"Good boy," I said, in my deep dog voice. "Very good boy." I picked up the ball and walked to the door, Baker following me with his eyes, the net effect being that Buddy was boxed out in a way that would have made my old high school basketball coach proud.

I tossed the ball. Baker bounded after it, leaving me and Buddy and an expanse of about a dozen feet of beautiful, unblemished deck between us. He could probably cover that distance in a matter of a moment, but I now had the confidence of someone with an escape clause—my hand, firmly on the door. I began turning the knob ever so slowly.

He assessed the situation, his face twitching, his comb flopping on his head, little clucks coming from his throat, when finally, mercifully, he turned away and hopped down the two steps onto the brick walkway and into the front yard. Before he did that, though, he paused just long enough to drop a massive ring of white and black chicken turd that landed on the wood of my brand-new front porch with an almost sickening thwack.

He scratched at my grass, such as it was, let out a loud crow, as if saying he had plenty of time to deal with me, and waddled around the side of the house.

> 2 <

The story of this rooster actually begins with a dog.

His name was Harry, and if it's true that you get just one truly wonderful animal in your time on this earth, then without a flicker of a doubt, he was mine. He arrived in the cargo hold of a then-USAir jet bound from Philadelphia to Boston a week before Christmas in 1994. Maybe it's bizarre, even embarrassing, to say a dog could change your life, but he did.

Harry was anything but an impulsive acquisition, pretty much the opposite of a Hey-I've-got-an-idea-why-don't-we-get-a-dog decision. My then wife and I talked about dogs endlessly, imagining the morning walks through a quiet city, the days on the beach, the nights with him lying between us watching TV. We were so starry-eyed that we used to wander the pet aisle of the Stop & Shop when we were buying groceries, fantasizing about what it would be like to be picking up bags of food and boxes of treats for our very own retriever. We would all but slam the brakes on the car when we drove by a particularly regal golden retriever padding down a city street, then gawk in envious amazement. The problem was, there was always a roadblock to our dream, whether an apartment lease that barred animals, the fact that we were living in two separate cities for a while, or just the long, dog-unfriendly hours that we were putting in at our respective jobs.

But the first lesson I learned from Harry came before he even arrived: if you wait for perfection, it'll probably never come, and what will fill the void is regret. When my wife and I were finally living in the same city, Boston, following her move from Washington, D.C., I came up with a plan. We worked a lot, she as a political strategist, me as a reporter for the *Boston Globe,* but it wasn't unbearable. And my landlord was eminently reasonable when I nervously picked up the phone one evening and offered a higher security deposit if he'd waive the no-pets clause in our lease. After that I spent days secretly researching breeders, reading training books, and accosting dog owners on the street for insight into their animals—secretly because I wanted it to be a surprise.

By the time I walked through the nearly empty Prudential Center Mall in Boston's Back Bay early on a Saturday morning in December to send a check by express mail to the breeder in Pennsylvania who said she had one last golden retriever puppy left, I was so excited I thought my knees might buckle and I'd just collapse on the floor amid the holiday decorations and the canned Christmas music, helped to my feet by wary shoppers as I kept mumbling "A puppy. I'm getting a puppy."

Harry was supposed to arrive on Christmas Eve day, thus keeping the extraordinary surprise to my wife intact until just the right time. But once the breeder got my check in her mailbox, she apparently just wanted the dog out of her hands. My phone rang in the *Boston Globe* newsroom at about noon that Tuesday. The dog—my dog— was at the Philadelphia airport, she said. He would be on a flight arriving in Boston at 5:15 P.M. I needed to be there to claim him.

Panic. Paralyzing terror. Years of imagining, months of planning, weeks of executing, but I had no food, no crate, no toys, no bowls, no nothing. I paced around my desk. I took long, deep breaths. I steadied myself from a bout of dizziness. Name a cliché, I was immersed in it. I had never before experienced the responsibility of dependents, probably for good reason, and now I had this living, breathing creature arriving unexpectedly early and was in a prime position to completely screw up the entire endeavor.

My nerves were only slightly calmer when I pulled into the cargo terminals at Logan International Airport as dark was falling on a cold December afternoon. The wind off Boston Harbor was damp and merciless. Jet engines roared in the near distance. I climbed the few concrete steps to the entrance of the warehouse-style building and walked into a small reception area with cement floors, a Formica counter, and a couple of burly men in dark shirts with

USAir patches on their chests, the heavy metal door shutting loudly behind me.

"I'm here to pick up a dog," I said, faux casual, as if it were no big deal, as if I were picking up shirts at the dry cleaners.

One of the guys glided his pen up and down a clipboard in silence, shaking his head in an almost imperceptible way. "No, I don't see any dog deliveries," he replied. "You know the flight number?"

It was at that moment that a massive garage door opened at the far end of the warehouse with a clack and a gush of cold air. A truck backed in with a flurry of high-pitched beeps. A man I couldn't see shouted, "Animal crate in the shipment!"

"I guess this is it," the guy at the counter said, unemotional at this turning point in my life. He disappeared for a moment and returned with a small plastic container, which he put on the counter with a thud that made me wince.

If there was a previous moment in my thirty-two years on this Earth as thick with anticipation, I couldn't remember it—not my wedding (I had already met the bride), not college graduation (it felt more like an end than a beginning), probably not even my first day at the *Globe* (I was conceited enough to assume I'd do well). I peered through the metal grates and saw golden fur but nothing else, so I fidgeted nervously with the springs until the door swung open and the dog came triumphantly out for a memorable introduction that we would both cherish forever.

Except he didn't. I waited, and waited some more, and

my reporter friend, Tony, who had driven me there and had just come inside, was now standing behind me waiting as well. So were the guys at the counter, passively curious, if only to see whether I got a manly breed or some sort of white puffball with bulging eyes and a shrill bark. I peered inside the carrier and saw that the fur was shaking. The frightened puppy was scared and trembling amid the shredded paper that filled the base of the crate and this bizarre series of events in his life. His little water bottle was still filled, meaning he had been too scared to drink on his hours-long journey. So I reached in, groped around for his shoulders, and gingerly pulled him out, maneuvering and manipulating his various parts to get him through the small opening.

And there he was, aloft in front of me, his four legs dangling in midair, his luxuriant blond fur tousled in a way that would later become his trademark, his jowls loose, his jet-black nose set off against deep brown eyes that carried a mix of fear and—I swear I saw this—relief. The very sight of him nearly made me cry, and I'm not a crier by nature, except at the end of *Planes, Trains, and Automobiles* and, okay, sometimes *Home Alone*. All those years, all those hopes, so many false starts, too many reasons not to make it happen, and here he was in front of me, softer and more handsome than I ever would have allowed myself to imagine. As I pulled him tight and pressed his face against mine, the airline workers, who couldn't have been more bored a few minutes before, had come out from behind the counter and were waiting to stroke him. "Hey, Jimmy, you've got to see this!" one of them shouted. And then there were more workers and more still, workers exhausted from the day, workers with knee pads on, tough men, men's men, gathered around in a loose circle cooing at this ridiculously charming dog.

It gave me my first realization that dogs, like people, either have charisma or they don't. Some men and women can stand in a room and never be noticed. If they are, it may not be for the reasons they'd like. Other people are like magnets. I don't know if it's the look in their eyes or the shape of their face or the aura and tone they project to the world around them. But this yet-to-be-named puppy was an absolute traffic stopper in every possible way.

What was odd was that he didn't squirm. He didn't whine. He didn't squeak or squeal or really express any immediate needs or desires at all. What he did was rest passively—or peacefully—in my arms, his eyes constantly glued to mine with the oddest look of trust. For my part, I couldn't take my eyes off him, his wispy ears that were darker than the rest of his face, his fleeting whiskers, his blocky midsection. I didn't know then, couldn't know then, just how amazing the whole thing would be, but I already knew I would love it.

I knew he wasn't a child. I knew he wasn't my own likeness, carrying my blood, my genes, my hopes. But he was what I had, what I'd always wanted to have, and in that moment, in many future moments, he was what I needed.

I cradled the pup in my arms, Tony grabbed his small crate, and we made for the door amid a flurry of good-byes and good wishes.

"You two be good to each other," one of the men called out. He had no idea.

*   *   *

He planted his little puppy behind on the carpet of the vestibule of my town house condominium building and, with his ears pressed tight against his head, looked at me as though I were completely out of my mind. The grand staircase above him was wide and steep, and there was no way he planned to climb it to my third-floor apartment.

"All right, already," I said, swooping him up in one arm, balancing the crate and a hatbox in the other, trying not to make any noise. Upstairs, Caitlin, my wife of a little more than a year, had utterly no idea what was about to walk through the door.

On the dimly lit third-floor landing, I gently placed the puppy inside the box and slowly covered it, whispering "Only for a minute, honest." He didn't like it, but he didn't fight it. I left the crate in the hall, unlocked the door, and let myself in.

The television was on, the volume playing softly. Our Christmas tree was illuminated in the windows. Caitlin was on the couch reading magazines and drinking Diet Coke, unwinding after work. She knew something was up from the moment she saw me, not only because I was home abnormally early for me or any other reporter but also because I wore what must have been the goofiest look any man has ever had. I don't do secrets particularly well, even less well when the secret changes pretty much every part of my entire life. And also, there was the matter of a box I was gripping with both hands as if I were carrying a heart to a transplant operation.

"I couldn't wait to give you your Christmas present," I said, without the benefit of any salutation. Even the tone of my voice, the very words, were absurd. She looked at me funny, got up off the couch, and said, "Aw, you got me a hat."

"You'll see."

She took the box. "Be careful," I said reflexively.

"Heavy," she said. She put it down on the coffee table and regarded it for a long moment before pulling off the top. In that brief span, as if on cue, as if he had been rehearsing this moment all eleven weeks of his young life, the puppy pushed his golden head up, pushing the top off the box, and meeting her stunned gaze. He clumsily began climbing out of the box, all rumpled fur and oversized paws. She looked at him and then at me and then at him again and then at me, and finally she picked him up and hugged him tight, her face against his just as mine had been. And when she sat down on the couch, the content dog still in her arms, her cheeks were soaked by a stream of silent tears.

If you could bottle a moment, relive it, borrow against

it, grow from it, things might have turned out different in the months and years ahead. But for us, for Caitlin and me, it wouldn't get any better than that Tuesday night in the throes of a pine-scented Christmas season in our Back Bay apartment with a brand-new dog that represented a life together we would never have. The shame—and regret—stayed with us both for a long time to come.

> 3 <

We named him Harry, partly for my favorite children's storybook, *Harry the Dirty Dog,* but also because he just looked like a Harry, thoughtful and dignified, with a tendency to furrow his brow and become snaggle-toothed as he tried to get his very large brain around the rare situations that didn't quite make sense. Sometimes, staring at me as I got my coat, his analytic mind working at a hundred miles a minute to figure out if we were going for a walk or a ride, he would squint and take on the appearance of a well-preserved older man reading a dinner menu in a dimly lit bistro.

More often, he was as centered and serene as any creature—human or animal—that I had ever met, fully immersed in what he nearly always regarded as a very worthwhile moment. He was a city dog who never required a leash, a characteristic that gave him the aura of celebrity in my Boston neighborhood, sashaying, as he did, down

busy sidewalks or along the tree-lined pedestrian promenade on the Commonwealth Avenue mall, pretty satisfied
with who he was and doing little not to let people know it.

When he was a puppy, we worked at that, mostly because I regarded a leash as beneath him, a choke on his
freedom, and soon enough so did he. First, still on leash,
I made him stop and sit for several long moments at every
curb, curb after curb, week after week, until he got into
the routine of it. Then we would rise especially early for
training exercises. We'd walk along the curb, Harry in a
training collar, and I'd casually toss a dog treat into the
road. The first time I did it, he stepped off the curb after
it. I snapped him back with the leash. He looked at me
annoyed. I did it again, and he tepidly made a motion as
though he was going to retrieve it. I snapped. He looked at
me. The third treat I tossed he regarded absently and kept
walking. He wouldn't have gotten more praise from me if
he had just won the Nobel Prize for tennis ball retrieval.

Speaking of which, that was the next step, because he
was a much bigger fan of the ball than he ever was of food.
I'd toss a ball into the road. He'd go up to the curb and virtually quiver, he was so tempted, but ultimately he'd look
back at me for the permission he knew he wasn't going to
get. We did it again and again. The final exam occurred
at a little after six on a gorgeous Sunday morning in May.
There were no cars at that hour, so I pulled off the leash
and, when he least expected it, bounced a brand-new shiny
green tennis ball that still had that fresh can smell into
the street. He tensed up, watched it roll teasingly along the

sun-splashed pavement to the opposite curb, and finally put his head down and walked toward me.

"Good boy! You good, good boy!" I rubbed him all over. He squeezed between my legs. He looked at the ball out of the corner of his eye as we kept walking. We did it again and then again, and when we got home that day, I declared to Caitlin that we had an off-leash dog, and I was right. I don't think that Harry stepped off a curb without me ever again.

I learned just how disciplined he was a couple of months later. Newbury Street is the Back Bay's main shopping avenue, Boston's Rodeo Drive or Worth Avenue, filled with trendy boutiques and upscale national chain stores. It was one of those delightfully warm days when the sidewalks were swarmed, and Harry and I were running errands—more of the hardware store variety than anything else.

We were stopped at a curb, waiting for the traffic light to change, and when it did, we walked. Except when I looked for him as I stepped onto the opposite curb, Harry wasn't with me. Panicked, I looked ahead, but no dog. I whirled around, and there he was, still sitting on the curb I had just left, his eyes bulging with fear, searching through the mass of humanity for me, almost willing me to show up, but never lifting his tail off the ground. When I went back to get him, he tried to act casual about it, but we both knew we had given each other a world-class scare.

Harry's calling card was his sheer dignity, manifest in his calm, methodical gait, more a tail-swishing swagger than anything else. Whenever I stopped to talk to a neighbor or acquaintance, Harry would sit patiently beside me, as if part of the·conversation, or, if he realized from my tone that it could go on for a while, he'd find a stick, sprawl in the grass, and chew on it. He had just two demands in life: always count him in, and make sure I had a tennis ball at all times. When he spied someone he knew, he would turn to me expectantly with a look that said, "Give me the damned ball." And when I placed it in his jaw, he would just hold it in his teeth, as if the passerby would have somehow been disappointed if it wasn't there.

On every walk, at every stop, Harry attracted the kind of crowd that was foreshadowed in the USAir cargo terminal that December afternoon, partly for his looks but more for his demeanor. If he was appreciative of the attention, he wasn't always demonstrative in return. Truth is, Harry could be a pretty aloof dog, and with some people, he literally looked past them as they rubbed his head or talked baby talk or made frantic motions as if they were trying to play. He would often just gaze at me with an expression that said, "What an idiot."

Others, he liked, especially women, and he would subtly circle around them, ball in his mouth, before calmly moving on. His one doglike indulgence: squirrels. He could spy one from a hundred yards away in the early-morning light of the Public Garden. He'd freeze, slowly lift his front leg in pointing fashion, and squint toward the rodent with his restaurant-menu face ("Maybe I'll try the steak frites tonight with a whimsical Pinot Noir"), breaking the reverie long enough to slowly turn in my direction for the sign—a simple nod—that it was okay to engage in pursuit. If I shook my head no, he broke the trance and resumed real life.

What I found in this dog was a capacity—my capacity— for unadulterated love. I'd shoot out of bed in the morning looking forward to the solitude and serenity of our hour-long romp in the Public Garden. I'd race home from work at day's end so that Harry, Caitlin, and I could walk the Commonwealth Avenue mall as a trio, Harry in his glory striding between us, the journey being as good as any destination. Before I got a dog, I knew well the various buildings of my Boston neighborhood, the stores, and the restaurants. Once I got a dog, I got to know the people, and they were better than I would have imagined—the brilliant, eccentric woman named Marie whose mane of gray hair blew in the breeze as she rode her bike, the kindly neighbor named Frank who not only looked exactly like his yellow lab, but also had the same side-to-side gait as his dog. It was pure joy, all of it: Harry on walks, Harry beside me as I wrote newspaper stories or pecked at a novel at home, Harry curled up between the couch and the coffee table as we watched TV, Harry climbing slowly onto our bed and falling asleep at day's end with a long, satisfied sigh. There is nothing in this world warmer than a bed with an exhausted dog in it.

Yet, amid the joy, something was going wrong, something that I either didn't grasp or, more likely, didn't want to. Work couldn't have been better. The *Globe* had promoted me to the position of roving national reporter, a journalistic dream job, my only charge being to jet around the United States in pursuit of interesting and offbeat stories that would splash color on our front page. I was in the Pacific Northwest writing about a flock of sea lions that was eating all the salmon, in El Paso writing about Mexican train bandits, in Montana writing about cattle ranchers facing falling beef prices. But at home, in our apartment, amid the spates of happiness, there was too much silence too often broken by trivial arguments. Caitlin became moody. Instead of addressing it head-on, I lived more and more on the road, away for a week, in Boston for a week. When I was home, she wasn't there as much. The whole thing, the uncertainty, fed on itself.

Harry emerged, among other great things, as the sinecure—so much joy in one hilarious package, single-handedly able to ward off the growing pit in my stomach with his ritualistic dances over a pig's ear, his boundless enthusiasm chasing a tennis ball, or the way he slept so deeply and completely at my feet. He made it impossible to feel lonely. I loved that dog even as my life was taking some strange and unsettling turns.

* * *

I sat in a room at the Fairmont hotel in San Francisco one Saturday morning arriving at the stark realization that things were not going as I had planned and that I was at least partly to blame. Caitlin and I were missing—not missing each other, just missing, as in not connecting, and that disconnect was beneath us. It felt as though the only thing we held in common was our mutual refusal to address it. Maybe I wasn't fit to be married, or maybe she wasn't. Maybe there was a reason it had taken us seven years of dating to tie the knot. Why's everyone always in such a rush, I used to joke; now it didn't seem all that funny. Regardless, picking at a room service breakfast on the other side of the country, feeling lonelier than I could ever remember yet unclear what I was lonely for, I decided it was time to confront it.

I wasn't scheduled to fly back until Sunday morning, giving me plenty of time to file my story for the Sunday paper. But I woke up before dawn Saturday, wrote as fast as my fingers would skim across the keyboard of my laptop, and rushed to the airport to catch a morning flight heading east with a connecting flight through Philadelphia. I would surprise her, but, more important, I would insist that we face whatever awkward, evil forces had infected our relationship.

In Philadelphia, I picked up a pay phone and gave her a call, realizing that things would be worse—at least for me—if I walked into an empty apartment. We exchanged the typical surface talk that had come to characterize all our conversations, and at the end I said, "I'll see you in a couple of hours."

"Tonight?"

"Yes, I'm in Philly. I got out of San Francisco early."

"You're really coming home tonight!" She sounded legitimately excited, which took me aback for a moment. Actually, she cheered in a way that didn't seem remotely fake.

And what was better was what happened next: when she hung up, she missed the receiver, leaving the phone to sit on the shelf where we kept it, our connection inadvertently kept alive, which was maybe kind of ironic.

"Harry! Harry! Brian's coming home!" I heard her shouting. "Tonight! Harry! He's coming home tonight!"

She said it again and again as I stood at a bank of phones in a drab airport terminal amid announcements for final boardings and gate changes. My heart melted at the scene, this beautiful woman and handsome dog dancing around our apartment in Boston because I was coming off the road a day before the plan. And when I arrived, for that one night and for some nights after, it couldn't have been better. So we never had that talk. We never confronted what needed to be confronted. And that was a mistake.

Inevitably we sank back into what we had become, which was a shadow of what we should have been, and we kept sinking until a Saturday morning in June when there was no place lower to go. We had been in Caracas the week before, at the wedding of a college friend of mine and his Venezuelan fiancée, a biting contrast, watching two very demonstrative people tying the knot in a weeklong cavalcade of events and ceremonies as I was watching my own marriage come undone. Caitlin was harsh and moody. I was equal parts angry and aloof. We clashed and seethed until we got back to Logan airport.

The next day, when I asked if she wanted to drive to my sister Carole's with me to pick up Harry, she said she had other things she had to get done, which felt like a kick in the stomach. It was one thing for us not to get along, quite another if she didn't want to see Harry after a week away. When the two of us, Harry and I, got back to the apartment, she wasn't there, a fact he somberly figured out after trotting from room to room looking for her. "I'm sorry, pal," I told him. "She had to get some stuff done." In my gut, my heart, and my head, I knew it was over.

So we waited, Harry and I. We waited for the confrontation, for everything to be out in the open, to decide the path forward—and whether we would walk it together. Through tone and action, there was little question in my mind, whether she intended to or not, that she was pushing us to the brink.

I looked at a book I pulled off the shelf, a book about Vietnam, though to say I was reading it would be inaccurate. I was simply gazing at words on a page, biding time, anxious. Harry fed off my anxiety and paced the apartment for a while, from the front to the back, as if he was still looking for her, wanting her to be there, for everything to be all right.

Maybe it was an hour later, maybe it was two. At that point I had no idea. We finally heard a key in the lock, the familiar sound of the latch turning, her cowboy boots on the hardwood floors. I was in the living room and didn't get up. She crouched down in the doorway as Harry slowly but earnestly approached her. She kissed his muzzle as he licked her nose. Surprisingly, he then turned around, paced back to me, and sprawled at my feet.

"You boys have a nice reunion?" Caitlin asked.

"We did," I replied, startled at how thick my voice was, the words almost getting stuck in my throat. I didn't say anything else.

She gave me an odd glance and walked into the kitchen, to the refrigerator, to casually grab a Diet Coke. Still sitting, I said, "We need to talk."

And we did, briefly, intensely, with finality. It was the hardest and the worst conversation of my life. Toward the end, the tears dried, the anger softened, and there was only miserable silence, silence in which I thought back to how we had met, in the Washington bureau of a small news service, our wedding day and all that rain, the highs and the lows and the hopes and the fears and the ways a marriage should unfold, which certainly wasn't like this. Harry lay still on the floor, his head erect, fully aware that something, or many things, were about to change.

Marriages stay intact for one basic reason, because the people involved want them to, and in that desire, that determination, there are all the concessions and the acts of discipline and the private expressions of affection that make it work. Marriages fall apart for a million reasons, mine for one of the most clichéd, something not worth getting into. Even in the pain, I came to terms with some essential truths: we both shared the blame.

I got up. I patted my thigh for Harry to follow. We went to the door, and I opened it. I turned around and looked at Caitlin, hunched down in a chair set in our bay window, her elbows on her knees, her palms mopping up the moisture on her face. And we left.

We walked the five blocks to the Public Garden, Harry and I, both of our heads down, Harry sticking unusually close to my side. In the park I found an empty bench which, as it worked out, was not far from where Caitlin and I had gotten engaged. The weather was beautiful on that early-summer afternoon, meaning couples strode by hand-in-hand, toddlers trundled across the grassy fields, and the iconic swan boats glided over the smooth waters of the duck pond with happy families on board—pretty much a collage of everything I didn't have. And just to make the whole thing complete, a young couple were taking their wedding vows a few dozen yards away.

I tossed a ball for Harry, and he fetched it, brought it back, and placed it beside me on the bench. We did it time and again until he sprawled in the shade with a thick stick and gnawed on it until there was nothing left. I sat and thought again about how it had begun and how it had ended and so much of what happened in between. I thought of what I had done wrong, what she had done wrong. We sat until the sun faded and night approached and I worried that Harry needed something to eat. At that point, tired and confused, we headed home. She was mercifully gone, and so, I saw, were many of her clothes. I had probably never been more alone in my entire life than I was that night, sitting in an empty apartment, contemplating how endless possibility had crashed into failure. Yet I didn't quite feel it, for one simple reason.

"It's you and me, Har," I said. And it was.

> 4 <

Packages like this don't arrive in the U.S. mail every day.

It was a plain manila envelope with my name and address on a sticker, giving the impression that it had been shipped from a company rather than a person. It was sitting on the ancient tile floor of the foyer of my condominium building in the Back Bay when Harry and I returned from an afternoon walk. I carried it inside with the rest of the day's mail, placed it on a table by the door, and basically ignored it. I mean, who gets important mail? Or more to the point, who gets unexpectedly important mail? That was back in 2004, which, by the way, was nine years after the breakup of my marriage. Mailmen were groaning under the extraordinary weight of so many credit card offers, home equity line deals, free this, free that, just sign here and take our money. The U.S. Postal Service was basically delivering the downfall of the national economy, courtesy of the big banks.

But as I dumped two cups of Harry's food into his bowl in the kitchen and gave him fresh water and ice, my mind inexplicably darted back to the envelope that sat with the bills on the living room console table. Maybe it was the fact there was no return address or that the package had some volume to it, holding some indiscernible object, or that it had been funded with actual stamps rather than an imprint from a postal meter somewhere in North Carolina or South Dakota. So I strode back over to the table, fingered through the other envelopes until I got to it again, and tore open the top.

The crack security team at the *Globe* would probably have had a conniption about the fact that I had opened an unidentified envelope like this at home. It was post–September 11, post-anthrax, the era of American vulnerability, a period when precaution was the new normal. But I had never really signed up or on for any of that, so I plunged my hand into the package and felt around for what was inside, which hopefully wasn't white and powdery.

I found a long, thin, hard object, which my investigative reporter's sharp mind told me was a box. Well, my eyes and my mind. It was orange in color and carried the store name "Hermès," which, from my limited experience in the language arts, was French for "Very expensive."

It would have been impossible not to admire the box for a long moment, light and elegant and unexpected as it was. I couldn't imagine who it was from or what it held or what the occasion might have been. I pulled the top off, pushed back the tissue paper, and found an impossibly smooth, recklessly silky necktie with a pattern of dozens of small fish swimming in unison across a light blue background. None of it made a drop's worth of sense.

I fished—sorry—through the tie box looking for some explanation of the tie, which, for the moment, I had to assume was a mistake, or at least sent to the wrong place. Nothing. So I thrust my hand back into the envelope, where I found a smaller envelope that, in turn, held a card that said simply, "Thank you" on the cover. How typical of me is that? I thought to myself. I did something nice for someone that I couldn't even remember. But when I flipped opened the card, it was blank inside—not a single sappy word from the manufacturer, nothing scribbled by the sender.

There was, however, a small piece of white paper, no more than a couple of inches wide and an inch or so high, that fluttered absently toward the floor like a piece of confetti landing on pavement after a grand victory celebration. I picked it up and read the message, a lone declarative sentence in typewritten words, that said, "Thank you for making me smile."

That was it. No identification, explanation, or elaboration.

Now, I'd like to use this time to report that that was not a big deal, getting an expensive, anonymous gift from a secret admirer. I'd like to report that I'm far above that sort of thing and that the only emotion I felt, if it was even an emotion at all, was annoyance over this nuisance, because sooner or later, some person, presumably a woman, would emerge expecting a grand expression of my gratitude.

But the truth is, stop the presses. Let the world know: I, Brian McGrory, had a secret admirer. For the moment, rereading the card, running my hands over the smooth silk of the Hermès tie, I was a teenager again, with a big, stupid smile spilling across my ridiculous face. Harry emerged from the kitchen to give me a probing, squinting, analytical look that basically said, "Why are you standing there with that absurd expression?" It was one of those warm early-spring afternoons that provided a punctuation point to the run-on drudgery of another Boston winter, a day scented with possibility and now, perhaps, probability. The sun was pouring through my tall bay window. My mind rippled through every woman I knew, like a slide show snapping from one becoming image to the next, every one of them not just a possible candidate but a plausible one. Not to make too big a deal of it, but a world in which you get an expensive gift from a secret admirer is suddenly a very kind and fertile world indeed.

Not that it had been a bad world up until that moment. Quite the opposite. For lack of any better way to put it, not too long after I became single again, I gradually came to realize that singlehood became me. I reveled in the relative tranquillity of it all. I basked in the independence. I took advantage of the many offerings.

Admittedly, the first year or so after my marriage dissolved was brutal. Divorce, for me, and I presume for many others, marked the first significant failure of adulthood, a sharp turn from the storybook life of marriage, kids, and professional success until one day you're in a favorite cotton sweater walking along a sandy beach near your summer home chatting amiably with your impossibly well-preserved wife about the various trusts you've established for all your grandchildren. Instead, there's a sense of Hester Prynne, a giant scarlet D, whispers everywhere, *"He's divorced. Stay away. Damaged goods."* I spent those years in a dense fog, trying to find my way and figure out who I was again.

Then one night I was sitting at a bar with a woman I'd been casually seeing, a few glasses of wine into a very good time. We got to talking about life, hers and mine, our dreams and failures, when I mentioned the fact that, being divorced, I had huge obstacles to overcome if I ever wanted to go the marriage route again.

"Are you crazy?" she said, her forehead furrowing, her red hair that I liked so much seeming to flare even brighter. "What are you talking about?"

"You know, I already blew it once," I said. "Women are going to be wary."

She looked at me sympathetically now rather than incredulously, and not a good you-poor-guy-I'll-make-it-better sympathy but more of a you-absolute-moron-you-don't-know-the-first-thing-about-life kind of look.

"You're an idiot," she finally said, putting words to her expression. "You've got the best of all worlds. The fact that you're divorced shows you're willing to make a commitment, that you're not one of those losers who won't ever walk down the aisle because they feel like they're letting down their mommy. And you have no kids that can cause havoc in a relationship."

So the new life quickly began to suit me. I could work as hard and as long as I wanted. I had dinners all over Boston at the newest and best restaurants. I could write novels in the quiet of my study with the only interruption being my walks with Harry, which were always welcome. Some days, I'd go into my study in the middle of the afternoon, and by the time I emerged, the rest of the condominium would be pitch black from nightfall, Harry snoring from his favorite spot in the hallway.

Work, as in the *Globe,* was very good to me. Just a year after I split from Caitlin, the paper sent me to Washington to cover the White House, and I bought my first piece of property, a sweet little bungalow in the heart of George-town with a back wall of small-paned windows overlooking my own high-walled patio. It was heaven. I traveled the country and the world covering President Bill Clinton, breaking stories, meeting interesting people, remaining a staple on the front page. Newspapers were all but printing money in that era, the Internet being but a hazy concept, and I was anything but hesitant about spending the *Globe*'s profits—on business-class flights abroad, on some of the world's best hotels, at restaurants that could bring a gour-mand to tears.

Then the *Globe* brought me back to Boston to take the best position at the paper, that of a metro columnist, a job that gave me license to write about pretty much anything

I wanted, opinions encouraged. It was unshackling to be able to offer your thoughts, to never again have to hear mealy-mouthed politicians or their sycophantic aides provide heaping piles of bullshit and not be able to make them look like fools in print. It was also heaven on Earth to be back home in Boston, both for me and for Harry, on the streets of the one city that we truly loved. I sold my first novel to a major publishing house. I bought a condominium with twelve-foot ceilings and a marble fireplace in the heart of Back Bay, the nicest neighborhood in town. I acquired Red Sox season tickets the year the Sox won their first modern World Series, in 2004, my seats being a ten-minute walk from my couch.

I golfed when I wanted to golf. I wrote when I needed to write. My column seemed to be meeting with some success. I dined around the city so often that my paper asked me to fill in as the restaurant critic a couple of different times when the reviewers were on leave. I bought a small getaway house near my favorite beach in Maine. I was rolling sevens at every turn.

The same applied on the women front. I'm not exactly the smoothest operator in the world and miles away from the best-looking, yet I had inexplicable good fortune. There was the aforementioned redhead who I came to the difficult conclusion was too young for me. There was the ridiculously stunning woman whom Harry introduced me to. We were sitting on our front stoop together, Harry and I. He lay on a towel because he was fighting off a bout of arthritis. She came strutting by with her old black Labrador, Riggs, who promptly climbed the stairs in excitement as Harry growled quietly.

"What a handsome lab," I pronounced as she stood on the street below us, exquisite in a winter parka and jeans, her nose adorably red from the cold. I tried to inconspicuously grab Harry's collar so he didn't bite poor Riggs in the face, balancing opportunity and fear at the same time.

"Oh your poor, poor dog," she said, climbing the stairs to pet him. Oh my word, she was beautiful. Harry was growling. Riggs was squeaking. The woman was stroking away. And I just about needed to breathe into a brown paper bag. Within a couple of weeks, we were dating. A month after that, we were living together. We went our separate ways after probably a year, not in anguish but because it was time.

There was the attractive British business executive who always seemed to be taking ill. There was the brainy and beautiful heiress in Washington. The only way I can explain my luck in this regard—and truth is, it probably is simply inexplicable—is a virtually catastrophic shortage of even reasonably normal single men.

It was good, almost all of it. It was fun. It was a sharp contrast to the lives of my friends, who were dealing with demanding wives, stressful kids, and schedules that kept them busy to within a second of their rigid lives. It wasn't that I was actively avoiding any of that; it's more that I wasn't striving for it. It already felt as though I had more than I wanted or needed. There were World Series games, book-publishing parties, member-guest golf tournaments, weekends in Maine. Through it all, every up, every down, and all the flatlined days in between, Harry remained my one true thing, my constant companion, my ever-ready sidekick, no leash required.

He was coming up on ten years old then. His muzzle was gray, and he had lost a step in pursuit of the tennis ball, though it didn't particularly matter, not to him, not to me, because all it meant were leisurely rests in the grass between virtually every throw, time in which he seemed to happily contemplate his very good life and insist that I do the same. Our walks were every bit as long or even longer. The only thing the years had changed was the pace. Back in the day, Harry would typically trot a dozen or so steps in front, forced to wait patiently for me at curbs. As he hit midlife, he padded beside me, the two of us exactly in sync. And as he started to age, he lagged behind, taking his time, snout in the breeze, tail swishing from side to side, he and I making playful eye contact as I urged him onward.

We had become less a man and his dog, more a couple of old friends so comfortable in each other's presence that it seemed unimaginable to spend long stretches apart. So we didn't, at least whenever I could help it. We spent summer vacations together in Maine every year of his life. We moved to Washington and back again. During my regular travels from one city to the other, I often drove, Harry riding shotgun, my canine navigator. He would stay behind when I traveled the country and the world for the *Globe*, with my sister Carole or with a friend, serving, especially early on, as my reason to return from the road, my every reason, actually.

We were forced to live ápart just once, and it didn't go well. I had just returned to Boston to write the column for the *Globe,* relegated for a month to a dark and depressing corporate apartment that didn't allow dogs. Harry went to my sister Carole's, which was going to be fine because they had, for years, openly adored each other, offering no indication that their bond would fray with extended proximity. But fray it did.

At first, my very regular check-in calls with Carole were uncharacteristically short and muted. "He's, um, he's good," she'd say, with no elaboration or much inflection. "He's eating. He's getting exercise." No "He's wonderful." No "This dog is hilarious." No "I'm going to miss him so much I'll need to get my own when he's gone."

Finally, a week or so in, I probed deeper, hesitantly—is he sleeping, is he having fun, are you? There was a long, somewhat agonizing, only partially unexpected silence. "I didn't want to tell you this," Carole finally said, "and I don't want you to feel bad"—and there her voice lowered—"but every time we go out, he scratches so hard at the front door that I'm afraid he's going to hurt himself."

"You can't be serious," I replied, unable for the life of me to picture that calm and dignified creature panicked or destructive. "Harry?"

"Harry," she said, more firmly now that she had finally shared the news. I could tell her patience was wearing thin—and she's a famously patient person.

"Is your door okay?" I asked, expecting her to say that it was nothing.

Again, another pause, before she finally said, "I'm sure it'll be fine when we sand it down." She didn't sound so sure.

As I took it all in, she added, tellingly, "He's constantly moping around." Another pause, and then "Brian, I think he really misses you."

That immediately ended that. Within an hour, I had picked him up to begin his illicit stay in my temporary housing. I don't think he ever scratched at anything again in his life, save for the occasional tick he picked up from walks in the woods in Maine. Not that I'm casting judgment on his behavior. The truth was, I was out of sorts in his absence as well. I'd get up in the morning for those couple of weeks that he was gone, shower, and drive silently to work, realizing, as others filtered into the newsroom, that it could be 9 or 9:30 and I hadn't spoken a word yet that day. After spending more time at work than usual, I'd have dinner out, return to the grimness of the corporate apartment, and silently go to bed. I had become the working drone that I had so adamantly, fastidiously avoided being. There were no early-morning walks through an uncrowded city, random encounters with friendly strangers, late-night trips to the ice cream shop where every customer doted on the absurdly well-trained dog who held court at the door.

It probably makes sense how close we had become, given how the relationship had been forged in the fiery collapse of my marriage. Harry, not to overstate it, had served as my ballast when things came apart, the receptacle for so much emotion during what was an uncommonly emotional time in my otherwise straightforward life. God knows what might have happened, where I might have gone, what I might have done, if I hadn't needed to be home every evening for a long walk, a slice of pizza at the local shop, an hour on the stoop, me with a magazine, him with his paws dangling over the top step contentedly watching the world go by. But *needed* is the wrong word. No, I wanted to be there.

There was something enlivening about being with Harry, something lightening about it as well, the mutual dependence, the channeling of each other's emotions, the unimpeachable confidence that he would always be there when I needed or wanted him, qualities that undoubtedly took on outsized importance because of the way my marriage dissolved.

Episodic celebrity did nothing to change him. My late cousin, the great *Washington Post* writer Mary McGrory, featured Harry in a couple of columns, describing him as "an elegant and amiable creature, with just a dash of con man and pol." She first wrote about how he'd climb into holes in her garden that we had just dug for impatiens, later about how he had people gushing over him on our Sunday-afternoon walks through Cleveland Park, and finally on the time I asked her to wait with Harry in the vestibule of Lord & Taylor in Boston on a particularly frigid Christmas Eve afternoon while I furiously grabbed last-minute gifts. Frazzled shoppers at the very end of their holiday-season rope turned to him for a moment of calm.

"Harry," Mary wrote, "had a miraculous effect on them. Everyone spoke to him. The most clouded countenance lifted and broke into a smile at the sight of him. People who obviously did not have time to breathe stopped to scratch his ears and whisper endearments. They wished him a Merry Christmas, often graciously including me in the greeting."

His fame was not limited to print. Harry appeared on the popular Boston evening television magazine show *Chronicle*, slowly padding down the sidewalk of our street, an agile—and beguiled—cameraman backpedaling in a crouched position in front of him, the camera hanging just a few inches from the ground. The segment was supposed to be about me and one of my novels, but every call I got on it was about my dog.

And his fame was not limited to the media. When I was the *Globe*'s White House reporter, I covered Bill Clinton's vacations to Martha's Vineyard, including the summer in which the Monica Lewinsky story broke. Harry was where he often was on those trips, which was lying at my feet in the press center in the old-fashioned gym of a local school, occasionally sighing in abject, you-really-owe-me-a-long-fetching-session-at-the-beach boredom, as I typed a say-nothing story on another uneventful day with a Clinton family whose members weren't really speaking to one another. Suddenly, in a whir of commotion, White House

Press Secretary Mike McCurry came striding to the podium, tapped the microphone to see if it was on, and said he had an announcement. The president, the grim-faced McCurry declared, had ordered bombing runs against Afghanistan and Sudan in retaliation for the attacks on two U.S. embassies in Africa earlier that month.

The room surged with sudden energy. Reporters who had been napping or playing computer games a few minutes before were now shouting urgent questions. Cameramen were cuing up shots. Young producers were barking into cell phones. National security advisers gathered just out of range to brief small groups.

All Harry saw was a guy he genuinely liked—McCurry—standing but a few feet away in a pretty good position for a game of indoor fetch. *Finally, someone to play with.* So he struggled to his feet, sashayed toward the podium, and dropped his tennis ball at McCurry's feet. The spokesman ignored him as he ticked off a litany of facts on the bombing runs, the planes used, the number of troops employed, the munitions dropped. Harry would have none of it. He announced himself with a low, guttural, playful growl, picked the ball up, and dropped it on McCurry's shoes.

"Not now, Harry, not now," McCurry said, squelching a laugh as I tried to collect my dog outside of camera view. Harry looked at me as though I had completely lost my mind while I tugged him back to my desk. Years from now, as historians struggle to define the Clinton Doctrine, they'll undoubtedly listen to the tapes and read the presidential transcripts and look at this mysterious aide, Harry, as holding the answers that are so elusive.

But back to the package in my foyer in Boston. There was no limit to the number of suspects—at least in my own mind. Who had I made smile? Could it be the woman I was currently seeing? That wouldn't be much fun. Could it be any number of the aforementioned ex-girlfriends making a dramatic bid to get back into the picture? Hey, why not? Could it have been someone I casually knew from the neighborhood, someone from the coffee shop, the gym? Yes, yes, and yes.

I didn't share this grand development with everyone, though I might have let on to a few people that I'd gotten a little something in the U.S. mail, enveloped in mystery, and wasn't it insane—as I waited for them, always in vain, to tell me it wasn't. The larger problem, even for an experienced truth seeker like myself, albeit one who was seriously and somewhat suddenly full of himself, was that flushing out information on such a delicate topic did not prove entirely easy. There was the direct method, involving the straightforward question "Hey, did you by any chance send me the nicest tie with the most touching note?" The one and only time I tried it, I was told, "You cannot possibly be serious!" followed by gales of laughter. Let's just say I crossed that person off my list of suspects.

So I summoned some diplomatic skills that were as uncommon as they were uncharacteristic, rang up a few other women I knew, and, in a casual conversation about nothing in particular, innocently dropped word of my secret admirer. *Oddest thing came in the mail the other day. I mean, c'mon, who has time for any of this nonsense?* They certainly didn't, at least from the responses I got, which ranged from "What case of arrested development would pull that stunt?" to "Are you sure it was your name on the envelope?" Everyone, everywhere became my suspect, but they all did a wonderful job of not acting even remotely suspicious. What had begun as an ego boost was quickly turning into a shot at my ego, yet it still gnawed at me just the same—who, why, what?

It gnawed until the evening I walked through my condominium door and found something I didn't want to see, and that, in every way, changed everything.

> 5 <

It's funny, though not in a humorous way, how life can assault you when you're expecting nothing more than its usual passive-aggressive indifference. In this case, it was a toss-away Tuesday in the beginning of January, that painful month in Boston when the beauty of a New England autumn is too distant to remember and the relief of spring is too far away to see.

That particular day defined nothingness—an average column in the paper, lunch with a boring politician, a lethargic workout at my gym, a night with no sports on television. My only salvation was a walk with my dog, followed by a pressed turkey sandwich at the local sub shop, which in my neighborhood they referred to as a "panini shop." Such days happen. Life is better when they don't happen all that much.

In terms of context, Harry was always waiting at the

door when I came through it. I've never been sure if he could sense me coming down the street, knew the unique noises I made in the building foyer, or simply lunged to his feet from a deep slumber when he heard the key in the apartment lock. Once I came in, he would quietly squeal, squirm repeatedly through my legs, and sit directly in front of me, making penetrating eye contact until I kissed his forehead. To miss the greeting was like Donald Trump missing the chance to use the word *I*. It simply never happened—until that night.

There was no Harry, no squeals, no nothing. It was bizarre, this open expanse of absolute quiet. "Har?" I called out nervously. The thought struck me that maybe he was at Carole's house and I had simply forgotten about it in a haze of boredom, but that wasn't likely. Maybe he was just getting old and was zonked out on my bed, but I doubted that, too. "Har!" I yelled again, my voice dissolving into the dimly lit expanse of the living room like milk into black coffee.

With my gut in a tight knot, I finally saw him. He was lying beneath the table inside the bay window, his favorite spot, his head up, his tail down, none of the thumping I usually got just by looking his way. His eyes bored into mine, filled with fright.

"Har? What's the matter, handsome?" I asked gently.

He lifted his snout up a little higher and blinked rapidly. I assumed he had done something that he thought was wrong, had maybe knocked down a picture by mistake or had had a sour stomach and left some unpleasant deposit on the bedroom rug. But I couldn't see or smell anything amiss.

"Har, what's going on?" I approached him, slowly, still expecting him to get up and greet me, everything all right, as if I had woken him up and he only needed to shake the cobwebs out of his regal head. Instead he kept staring, his eyes locked on mine, searching me for answers to questions that hadn't yet been asked. As I pulled to within a step of him and crouched down, he did something utterly amazing, though not really surprising. He rolled over on his back and splayed his hind legs. In that motion, he revealed a raw patch of blood on his lower stomach, bright and oozing. Harry wanted me to see the problem, the reason he hadn't gotten up. My dog, I must say for roughly the billionth time in his life, was brilliant.

I pressed my face against his snout, still not wanting to seem panicked, and told him everything would be all right. I rubbed his head, his ears, his neck, and gently worked my way down to his injury, which I could see was some sort of puncture that he had probably been gnawing at all afternoon, something very un-Harry-like. He wasn't a dog that needed one of those ridiculous Elizabethan collars whenever he got stitches at the vet. If I asked him not to chew on himself, he didn't, plain and simple. To act any other way would have been deeply beneath him.

I told him to stay put while I got a cloth with warm water and returned to wash his wound, which seemed to be excruciatingly sensitive to the touch, though still he let me do it. I don't believe I'd ever seen this innately confident creature this frightened, which told me that the situation was somehow even more severe than it looked—and it didn't look good to begin with. When I coaxed him to his feet, he toddled uncertainly, then slammed himself back onto the floor. He did that again and again, leaving me no doubt that we had no choice but to get him to a doctor. I swooped him up in my arms, felt his head come to rest on my shoulder, and lurched uncertainly—he was about seventy-five pounds of pure muscle—out the door and down the block toward my car.

Harry's vet was closed at that hour, so we drove straight to Angell Memorial Hospital about fifteen minutes away, fifteen minutes of hell as I tried to mask my own anxiety with constantly soothing talk to my best friend in the backseat. "Everything's going to be okay, Har-Bear. You're going to be fine. Nothing's going to go wrong here, you good boy." I only wished I believed it myself. He didn't exactly look as if he was on board with it, either, staring down or straight ahead rather than watching the passing scenery as he usually did. At Angell, we registered at the front desk with a receptionist who couldn't have seemed any less impressed with the situation, then were directed to a vast waiting room filled with a cacophony of mewing, chirping, barking, and various forms of grumbling. The animal kingdom on its best day is a chaotic place. The animal kingdom in distress, in the charmless environs of a hospital anteroom, is another matter entirely. Harry wanted no part of it. He squeezed between my legs, hid partly under the worn bench, and morbidly waited, wide-eyed over his situation and aghast over our location. I kept a hand on his head, caressing his ears, quietly telling him that he was going to be okay.

An hour or so later, we were taken into an extraordinarily plain exam room where an overtired resident who must have been about a day out of college absently said, "Everything good?" as she flipped through our registration sheets.

Yeah, things are great. I just wanted to get some home decorating ideas and I really like these lamps bolted to the wall. That's not what I said. I didn't actually say anything until she looked up from the clipboard a few minutes later, and I explained, "This is Harry. He's a pretty remarkable dog." As I said it, I realized that pretty much every dog owner who comes through the doors of this hospital must say—or at least think—that exact thing. "When I came home tonight, he wasn't right. He didn't meet me at the door. And he showed me this wound on his lower stomach."

Harry, by the way, wanted exactly no part of her. He was well aware of where we were, what she was there to do, and what might lie immediately ahead, so he had positioned himself very firmly on the floor between my legs. As I finished my synopsis of the situation, I crouched down, placed my hand against his shoulder, and rolled him over. His eyes got a little wild, but he knew why I did it.

She took a long look, running her fingers around the

outside of the small, bloody area. As I continued to hold Harry down, she grabbed some sort of instrument and extracted a small piece of the wound, causing Harry's legs to cycle furiously until I let him go.

"He's okay now," she said, but she wasn't referring to his health. She pressed a stethoscope against various parts of his sides and chest, peered into his big brown eyes, and opened his mouth to look inside.

"I'll be back in a few minutes," she said.

It was more like thirty, each of them a little more anxious than the one before. When she stepped back into the room, I sat on a metal stool. Harry cemented himself to the floor between my legs. The doctor leaned against an exam table and said in a startlingly casual way, "We should get this tested, but I can almost guarantee you that it's mast cell cancer."

I could feel the blood drain out of my face. Cancer. I looked down at Harry to catch his reaction, forgetting that *cancer* wasn't part of his sprawling vocabulary. He just kept looking straight ahead, all but willing himself to be back home, resting on the rugs or the hardwood floors that were so familiar, all his sounds, around his stuffed toys. As I tried to get my bearings, she continued to talk, either indifferent to my emotions or lacking the time to deal with them. Either way was okay.

"—most common type in a large dog like this, and with a very high cure rate," I heard her say. "But we should do surgery almost immediately, sometime this week."

* * *

Two surgeries (they found a second tumor) and a few days later, Harry was milking his recuperation in full Harry fashion, accepting visitors at our condo and delicately nosing through the bowls of chicken and rice I made for him each morning and night in search of the most overdone pieces of meat. There was good news in that; just five or so years into owning the condo, I was already using my stove.

What neither of us could have known in that winter of recovery was that the worst was yet to come—and soon. Harry, unbeknownst to me, had actually begun a downward spiral, the mast cell cancer being as much a harbinger as a disease. By March, he couldn't keep food inside him, and his once proud frame began slowly melting away, almost imperceptibly at first but before too long at a much more rapid, noticeable clip. When I couldn't ignore it any longer, we found ourselves in the exam room of his lifelong vet, Dr. Pam Bendock, where we were regulars because of Harry's famously sensitive stomach and his chronic arthritis.

A word about Pam: beautiful. Another: soothing. There are also charming and, breaking the bonds of free-standing adjectives, one of those rare people you like the absolute moment you meet them. Her clinic was situated on the second floor of an old town house on Newbury Street, the most fashionable shopping boulevard in Boston. Her clientele was high end and filled with questions and demands. The latter description included me. This was not some operation in the distant suburbs where the doctors ruled and obliging clients did whatever they were told. For those reasons and more, Pam was a master of diplomacy. She pushed open the far door and walked softly into the exam room, her blond hair pulled back in a ponytail and a white lab coat covering her long, lean frame. All that was exposed was the calves of her jeans and a pair of clogs. James Herriot she was not, and I mean that in the best of ways.

"How are you guys doing?" she asked, looking from one of our faces to the other, smiling.

Harry did nothing to mask his lifelong crush on her, and I'll confess, I didn't do much more. He sauntered up to her, and she crouched down and pressed the smooth skin of her cheek against his face and said, "You don't feel well, Harry? Well, we're going to make you better." And in one fell swoop, she lifted Harry up onto the examination table before he or I even knew it was happening. That was just like her, a study in contrasts—thin but surprisingly strong, schooled in the unyielding realities of science yet always humane in presenting her diagnoses, a woman who would think nothing of expressing a patient's anal sacs with the same bare hands that an expensive Newbury Street manicurist had touched up the day before.

When she pressed her stethoscope against Harry's chest, it was as if she wasn't listening just to his heart but to the secrets of his soul. The room was still. Harry lifted his head to accommodate her.

"Any good vacations lately?" she asked me.

Huh? Me? I snapped myself back into the moment from, well, the moment.

"Nah," I said. "I've been in writing mode. Too much work."

Don't get the wrong impression, by the way. Pam was married. She had kids. I was not interested, in terms of being really interested. What I was could be best described as enchanted, and in that I was anything but alone; to be in her presence was to fall within this soothing spell of hers, such that you really and truly believed, as she said to Harry, that she could and would make things better. Men felt it. Women felt it, too. Pam Bendock had that way about her.

She had met Harry nearly a decade before, back when he had been a blocky fifteen- or sixteen-week-old puppy and she'd been a new, young veterinarian working in a frenetic pet shop on Newbury Street where she seemed markedly out of place. She was too good for it, all the cackling birds and the smells from the aquarium and the young, tattooed shoppers who came in to look at the lizards just for kicks. Over the years she got to know Harry well through bouts of arthritis so vicious that he would hobble along the city streets on three legs. She learned the ins and outs of his fragile constitution, which seemed to be always in need of care. She knew that his owner would never just, as the receptionist always recommended, "leave him for the day," that I needed to be called the moment he came out of any procedure, and that I preferred to be—no, insisted on being—in the waiting room as soon as he came to from his anesthesia.

As Harry grew to be a calm and confident dog, a fixture in the Back Bay where he always sat untethered on the top step of our stoop gazing at the world around him, Pam, too, became a fixture. She graduated from the pet store, which shut down, to her very own clinic on Newbury Street. She took it from a tiny practice with just her and a couple of technicians/receptionists to a staff of doctors tending to a sprawling roll of clients. She was also one of those people, those women, who got more attractive as they aged. Experience suited her well in just about every way.

"The Caribbean with kids is a new one," she said, smiling, her eyes widening to show that it wasn't the tropical bliss she had grown accustomed to. As she spoke, she ran her hands calmly over, under, and across my contented dog, checking, feeling, softly probing in a way meant to relax rather than alarm. She peered into his ears. She drew blood without his even flinching. She could have amputated an eye, and he would have just given me a (one-eyed) look saying *Sure, no problem, I trust her.*

She looked at his chart for a moment, then said to him, her face just a few inches from his, "You've lost some weight, Harry. I'm not sure I like that."

She asked us to come back the next day for an ultrasound. I told her I couldn't be there because I was traveling, but I'd have Carole bring him in.

"He's going to be fine," she told me, making long eye contact in the way she always did. "We'll figure this out and take care of it." She gave Harry a kiss on the snout— lucky dog—and bid us both farewell.

*   *   *

By that night I was in Washington, visiting my ill cousin Mary McGrory. Mary was, to newspaper readers in Washington and around the country, to national politicians of a certain era, to people who bent left in the political breeze, a living legend. She'd broken into political reporting when her editor at the *Washington Star* had sent her to cover the Army-McCarthy hearings on Capitol Hill in the 1950s with the advice "Write it like a letter to your aunt." She never looked back. She penned the famous line "The world will never laugh again," after President John F. Kennedy was assassinated. She won a Pulitzer Prize for her columns about Watergate in 1974. She made Richard Nixon's enemies list, perhaps her proudest accomplishment. She wrote an unapologetically liberal, widely syndicated political column for the *Washington Post* right up until the afternoon in 2003 when she couldn't write anymore.

I met Mary, my father's first cousin, when I was a junior in college on a Washington semester working my first ever newspaper internship—maybe the most exciting couple of months of my young life.

I'd heard a little bit about her from my parents, but they didn't know her all that well. Both of my parents' families lived in the Boston area, and Mary had left for Washington by the late 1950s and never looked back, except for holidays and weddings and the like.

One day I plugged a quarter into the pay phone in the hallway of my dormitory at American University and called the *Washington Post*, which was basically like some high school baseball player calling Yankee Stadium and asking to speak to Derek Jeter. Her assistant answered and transferred me to her, and I said simply, "Hi, Mary. My name is Brian McGrory, and I think we're related."

"Excellent," she responded. "I'm having a party this Saturday. Can you come by the house around six?"

It was less a question than an order. Before I could pull a response out of my throat, she gave me her address and said, "I'm looking forward to seeing you. I've got to run now. On deadline." And that was it.

I was about as nervous as I'd ever been. Mary's Macomb Street apartment was a fixture on the society pages for the salon dinners she held, with Tip O'Neill and Ted Kennedy singing Irish ballads as other House members, senators, White House advisers, cabinet secretaries, and high-profile journalists hashed over the most critical issues of the day. And that Saturday there would also be me—me trying to hold my own in conversations about the double-digit unemployment rate at the time, about David Stockman and supply-side economics, about the impact of a missile defense shield in the Cold War. Good God, I was a wreck. At the appointed hour, I got buzzed into the outside door of her condominium building, took the elevator down one flight as instructed, and walked slowly down the long, dark hallway, past the trash room and an emergency exit, to her corner apartment. I stood outside the door for a long moment, collecting myself, probably feeling a bit like the scarecrow the moment before he met Oz. I was about to walk into the home of the most famous journalist I'd ever met, who also happened to share my last name. I was also entering a world in which I was entirely unsuited to be. My mind was crammed with every possible fact from the day's *Wall Street Journal, Washington Post,* and *New York Times,* to the point that I could have passed a final exam at the Fletcher School of Law and Diplomacy on the conflicts in the Middle East. But the minute the first guest asked how I was doing, my eyes would probably roll back inside of my head and I'd faint. You can see the *Post* gossip page headline: "Mystery Guest Arrives by Metro, Leaves by Ambulance."

I knocked. I heard nothing, then shuffling, then some clatter, and the door opened slowly. A very pleasant-looking sixty-something woman with a soft expression on her face eyed me up and down, from the brown plaid pants my mother had bought me for this kind of occasion to the corduroy sports jacket that didn't fit. I broke the reverie by thrusting out my hand and saying "I'm Brian McGrory. It's a real honor to meet you."

She took it softly, not to shake but to hold, and in that moment, I couldn't possibly predict the hundreds of dinners we'd have together over the years, the thousands of telephone calls, the Sunday night meat loaf, the annual Christmas Eve lunches, the column critiques, presidential campaign trips, crazy voice mails in which she thought she was actually on hold ("Hello? Brian? Hello!"). What I did know, instantly, was that I was suddenly very happy to be there—and relieved.

"Yes, yes," she said, her voice melodic, a look of bemusement on her face. She led me into a sitting room, where she pulled an old, yellowed family photo off the wall and said, "Here. Look. Do you know this man? You look exactly like your grandfather." She was right.

She was dressed—how else to put this?—flamboyantly, though that shouldn't be confused with revealingly. I mean, lots of satins and silks, and I specifically recall some feathers, all part of a palette of colors that may or may not have matched. Mary was not into earth tones. She had a wry way about everything she did and, clichéd as it sounds, a certain twinkle in her eye as she regarded the world around her. Nothing was too serious, but nothing was an overt joke.

I asked, "Where is everyone?"

"The guests," she said, "arrive at seven." *Guests.* "Come on," she said and led me into another, bigger, brighter room, where she showed me to the bar, instructed me where I could find the ice, and advised me how to get drink orders as soon as the *guests* came through the door and to fill them quickly. I needn't have been worried about fitting in. I was the help, and unhired at that. I should've been reading up on gimlets instead of the turmoil in Beirut.

I came to learn that I was in good company. George Stephanopoulos later confided to me that he, too, had begun in the Washington social circuit as Mary McGrory's bartender, as had many others. Some months later, I graduated to become her gardener. It wasn't until I returned to Washington a couple of years after that as a young reporter for the *New Haven Register* that I became an actual guest, though even then my designation might have been in some dispute. By my third tour of Washington, as the *Boston Globe*'s White House reporter in the 1990s, Mary and I had become fast friends, dining with each other almost every Sunday night, taking long walks with Harry through Cleveland Park, talking during the week about her columns or my stories or the various goings-on on Capitol Hill.

We had our rituals. She met my friends. She hosted book-publishing parties for me with A-listers from politics and journalism. She once delivered the single nicest compliment I've ever received; she had just been rushed to the hospital after suffering a minor heart attack. I was living in Boston at the time but happened to be in D.C. on a column. Mary's assistant called me with the news, having no idea I was in town, and I raced to her room and found her sitting up in her hospital bed, all alone, snacking on a plastic container of fruit Jell-O while watching CNN. She looked at me, surprised, a big smile spreading over her pale face, and said, "You always have a knack for showing up at the exact right time."

About a year later, Mary, a proud neo-Luddite who used to write her columns longhand on a yellow legal pad from the road, watched as her computer seized up on deadline and devoured her words. Moments later, she fell to the floor with what would later be diagnosed as a stroke. It was devastating. When she gained cognizance many days later, she suffered from aphasia, meaning that words tumbled out of her mouth in a jumble of incomprehensible syllables.

A woman who had made a career out of her incomparable ability to write elegant prose could no longer speak a simple declarative sentence. She couldn't read or write. Her brain knew what she wanted to say, but her words came out garbled, frustrating nonsense that made her a prisoner of her own mind.

Mary never married and never had children, and she expressed occasional regret about that, even as she rose to the pinnacle of her high-profile field. Maybe for that reason, she always took unabashed interest in who I might have been involved with, what they were like, would I bring them over. Happiness, she knew, extended far beyond the newsroom, and she wanted me to be well aware of that as well.

When she fell ill, her colleagues at the *Post* were terrific with her, constantly paying visits, bringing her food, taking her on rides, guiding her back into the newsroom for occasional visits. I headed down every few weeks, alternating visits with Mary's nephew and niece from Boston. A few hours after Harry's appointment with Dr. Bendock, I flew to D.C. because Mary had had an emergency appendectomy a couple of days before and I wanted to pay a surprise call on her at the hospital. It was why I'd asked Carole to take Harry to Dr. Bendock's clinic the following day.

I arrived at the Madison Hotel in Washington around 9:30 P.M., figuring it was too late to see Mary that night and I'd catch her first thing in the morning. As I walked into my room, fumbling for the lights, my cell phone rang with a 202 number that didn't look familiar. When I answered, it was Mary's home nurse on the other end of the line. "Mr. Brian," she used to call me, kind of half jokingly, even when I told her all the time to knock it off. This time there was no joking tone. "I'm sorry," she said, "but your cousin died unexpectedly a few minutes ago."

There I was, ten minutes away, and Mary McGrory had died pretty much alone. Some knack, I thought to myself.

I'd still be in Washington the following day when the call came in about Harry.

* * *

I had been dealing with funeral home directors, lawyers, and priests the entire next morning and didn't think it could get much worse, but when I picked up my ringing cell phone and heard the way Dr. Bendock said hello, I knew it was about to. Her voice actually cracked as she talked in uncharacteristically formal fashion. The ultrasound, she said, showed that Harry had lymphoma, a very deadly disease. Of the two kinds of lymphoma that a dog could have, his was the worst, difficult—though not completely impossible—to treat.

My legs began to buckle, so I sat abruptly on the end of the bed in a hotel room that seemed to be getting smaller by the moment. It was as if a cold gush of air was coming through the phone. Dr. Bendock was talking, but I couldn't really hear what she was saying. Stay calm, I kept telling myself. Listen to her. Take in the information.

"How long do dogs generally live with this?" I finally asked.

There was a long pause, as if she didn't want to answer but knew she had to because I wouldn't accept any sort of evasion. "It could be just a few months," she said.

Mary was gone. Harry was next. I'm by no means equating the terminal illness of a dog to the death of a wonderful human being—or any human being—but the combination was devastating—two of the most vivid and vital presences in my life taken away just a few months apart. On the phone, Dr. Bendock continued talking, about chemotherapy that could possibly pound the disease into remission, about steroid treatments that could possibly halt the spread, about the fact that dogs can be resilient and Harry especially had a knack for not letting things get him down. If I'd believed it, any of it, that would have been nice, but as she spoke, Dr. Bendock was crying, and the tears said much more than the words.

> 6 <

We sat on the front stoop trying to hold on to the moment: me wishing for the world that I could push back time, Harry sprawled in his usual spot next to the faded pot of impatiens, his front paws dangling over the top step. I was leaning against him, absently rubbing his furry ears.

When Dr. Bendock arrived, clutching a brown paper bag, Harry thumped his tail and struggled to rise, then remembered that his bones were too weak and his muscles too sore. She began to speak but realized there was nothing good to say. So she leaned down and kissed his forehead, and I said, "If you'd like to head in, we'll be there in a moment."

In those few moments, Harry gazed forlornly at the world before him—the century-and-a-half-old side street where we lived, the brick town houses that lined it, the sidewalk from which his friends and admirers so often approached, schoolchildren and neighbors and workmen who always had time to talk. It was a nice world, a soft world, a generous world—Harry's world.

"Come on, pal," I finally said, standing up, my voice starting to crack. He pulled himself obediently to his feet, heartbreakingly so, his gaze falling downward as I held open the heavy door and gently guided him inside.

Harry was a month shy of his tenth birthday then, the most intuitive and wonderful creature that I have ever known. He was, to the end, as smart as ever, as kind as he had always been, as knowing as any living being I had ever met, my constant companion on foot, in the car, at home, in stores, in parks, never on a leash, always getting my jokes and playing more than a few himself. We had battled his lymphoma hard these last five months, battled it with steroids, chemotherapy, a new diet; any straw of hope, glimpse of a prayer that we could find, we tried. He hated it, every bit. He'd flop under my legs in the waiting room of the oncologist's office in suburban Boston and force me to carry him into the treatment area when his name was called. There he would lie on the dog bed as the technicians poked and prodded his veins for yet another round of drugs, always staring straight ahead, more beleaguered than dejected. Finally, the stern oncologist named Kim who never seemed to like animals all that much, or at least Harry, told me there was nothing more she could do.

We spent most of that August at a rented house in Maine a mile or so from the beach he loved, and Harry made the most of every minute. He padded slowly along the sand, waded gloriously through the cold surf, and slept soundly in the shade of the wooden back deck as I pecked on a laptop beside him. As inseparable as we were in the rest of his life, we were Krazy Glued together that summer. When I picked up my keys, he didn't even look at me with a question about whether he was coming, he just sashayed over to the car.

By then his fur had grown long and even more tousled. His face was completely gray. He had aged about twenty years in the past four months, but somehow he looked more appealing, more dignified, more Harry-like than ever. When we got back to Boston on Labor Day, I feared the lack of beach and constant fresh air would depress him, but no. He still loved his morning walks, his evenings on the stoop, his time under the coffee table as I watched the Red Sox make an epic run toward their first World Series victory in eighty-six years. All the while, he was fighting intense bouts of stomach pain, but he refused to surrender, to give me a sign that it was time to go.

"Harry, it's okay if you want to give up," I would tell him softly as he moaned in the dark of the night. But no, he didn't, or wouldn't, not until the Sunday in the middle of September when he refused to go out for his last walk of the night and hung his head so low that his nose just about scraped the floor. He slipped into my study and slept alone under my desk, his breathing labored when I got up in the night to sit silently with him.

He appeared even weaker and more dejected the next morning, so I called Dr. Bendock to let her know it was time. I had vowed not to keep him going on my account, and another day would have been cruel.

Dogs don't fear death, I convinced myself. They don't even think of it. It's just what comes at the end. I was adamant that his last hours would be as natural, as dignified, as the life that had led up to them, meaning there would be no morose music, no storm of tears, no darkened rooms, just Harry, living as he always had until he couldn't live anymore.

Inside, Dr. Bendock had unpacked the blue solution and needle and waited. Harry stunned me by picking up a stuffed toy and tossing it around for the briefest moment, showing off for the vet on whom he had always had an obvious crush, until he collapsed on the floor in his favorite spot beneath the bay window with a raspy sigh. He lacked the strength or the will ever to lift his head again.

After some long, silent moments, I nodded, and Pam brought over the syringe. I placed my face next to Harry's as she rubbed fluid on his leg. "Not yet," I said softly, and I told him I loved him, familiar words for him, that he was the best friend I would ever have, which was also old news, and that I wouldn't trade one minute of one day with him for anything in the world. All of the thoughts fit together into an irrevocable truth.

Harry had taught me patience. He had instilled empathy in me. He had made me slow down, to take my time, to collect my bearings along life's winding path. He had gotten me up on quiet, beautiful mornings that I would never have seen and taken me out in invigorating night air that I would never have felt. He had introduced me to dozens of people, very good people, I would never have met.

Tears rolled from my face onto his, despite my best effort, and he looked up at me from the corner of his eye, knowingly, it seemed, though that might just have been me. I nodded to Dr. Bendock, and soon I could see the fluid flow slowly through a tube and into his leg. Harry closed his eyes. I stroked his face. Pam cried softly. A moment later, he was gone.

We didn't talk much in the moments after, Dr. Bendock and I. Hours of consultations and conversations in the weeks and months before, and now there was nothing left to say. Her cheeks were glistening as she collected her things. I told her I'd bring Harry to her clinic, a few blocks away, as soon as I got myself together.

Alone, I sat on the floor next to him and thought about the December evening ten years before when he had arrived in the cargo terminal of Logan airport, the absurdly cute puppy so frightened that he hadn't wanted to come out of his crate. I thought about the look on my then wife's face when I had given him to her for Christmas, the kind of moment it would be impossible to ever forget.

I thought about his paws slapping the water the first time he swam. I thought about playing in the Boston Public Garden all alone in a late-night blizzard, until Harry got so tired he stood by the gate and insisted on heading home. I thought about our first nights alone when my marriage had ended, the drive to Washington to work at the White House. I thought about the thousands of miles we had walked together, the tens of thousands of throws he had fetched. I wished I could remember every minute, every step, every toss. As Frank Skeffington asked in the classic Boston novel *The Last Hurrah,* how in the world do you thank someone for a million laughs?

As I sat on the floor with him that day, I thought only of what had been, not of what might come. I didn't realize, couldn't realize, that Harry, even in death, would lead me to a wife, and that wife would come with a family, and that family would include—there's no subtle transition to this, in print as in life—a rooster named Buddy.

> 7 <

It was like nothing I had predicted or expected or ever experienced, the pain of losing a wonderful dog. There was that awkward touch of relief that Harry was no longer in pain. I no longer spent just about every cognizant moment on edge, feeling awful for him, imagining the piercing feeling in his gut, the helplessness of it all, the confusion that he must have felt over the fact that his very own body had turned on him.

But that relief was swallowed up by acres of emptiness like I had never imagined—an emotion that non–animal people could never possibly understand. As heretical as this may sound, losing a cherished dog may be worse than losing a parent. As much as you appreciate your mother and father and are hopefully close to them and you owe them for all they've done, they are not a daily, moment-by-moment presence in your everyday life after you enter the world of adulthood.

But a dog? The best ones are confidants. They are trusted advisers. They are occasional excuses ("Oh, I'd love to, but I've got no one to care for Sammy"). They keep you honest. They keep you in shape. They introduce you to a larger world while giving you an odd comfort within the smaller environment of your home.

When I lost Harry, part of me was just no longer there—the part that didn't allow bad moods or sedentary habits, the part that never felt alone. Harry was a fixture, an unflappably vibrant presence, riding shotgun in the car, always nearby as I walked along city streets, beside me on the stoop, sprawled by the entrance of a store patiently waiting while I got whatever it was I needed or wanted. He was serious and comic, wry and earnest, accommodating and headstrong. He was the one who constantly urged us outside, always introduced me to new people, and forever seemed to get my jokes. And then, one long-feared day, he just wasn't there. I felt like Nixon in his final days at the White House as I wandered our home in the middle of the night talking to the large photograph of Harry on the mantle, stroking his face, telling him he was the best thing that had ever happened to me. Maybe some people would have seen the newfound freedom in the morning as a luxury, no long walk dominating the start of every day. It felt more like a punch to the gut. I was quickly turning into the exact kind of working drone I'd never wanted to be: rise, shower, commute. Rise, shower, commute. Sometimes, I'd get in to work at eight o'clock and realize I had yet to actually open my mouth and speak a word aloud. By contrast, every morning with Harry was a subtle adventure born in a welcome routine. He splashed in the Charles River. We saw the seasons change in the Public Garden. We were the first to know of store closings and openings on Newbury Street. We walked down the middle of unplowed boulevards after overnight snowstorms.

And now I had exactly none of that.

It was an eventful autumn in Boston that year. The Red Sox, down 0–3 to the New York Yankees, staged the greatest playoff comeback in the history of professional sports and brought the first World Series title to their appreciative city in eighty-six years. Massachusetts' own John Kerry was striving to become the president of the United States—and it was looking as though he might succeed. In a city famous for both sports and politics, we had it going both ways that October 2004. I went to Fenway for every playoff game, traveled to Yankee Stadium for two games, and ran around the nation reporting on the Kerry campaign. I didn't have to worry about finding care for Harry. I didn't have to feel guilty about leaving him behind. It should have felt liberating, but with nothing or nobody to pull me back home at the end of a night or a trip, specifically not a grand animal, a wonderful friend, whom I had raised since he was a shy eleven-week-old pup, I felt untethered. Total freedom sounds great until you have it, and then you realize the extremely fine line between independence and hollowness.

My girlfriend at the time, that very attractive British

woman with an enticing accent, meant as well as any non–
dog lover could mean. But she didn't get what I was going
through, and I didn't have the energy or the desire to explain. It wasn't her fault. It was probably mine. I knew
when I didn't call her within a few hours of Harry's death
that our relationship had died as well.

All of which is a long way of explaining how I happened
to be sitting in my apartment in the middle of a Tuesday afternoon, absently flipping through old photographs
of Harry instead of writing my column, when my phone
buzzed with a call from the foyer. Since I was on the first
floor, next to the entry, I just opened my door to see who
was there. That's when I came face-to-face with Dr. Bendock, whom I don't believe I'd seen since that day with
Harry a few weeks before.

She was, as always, relentlessly attractive, though with
her it's tough to separate the warmth from the looks to figure out which carried the most appeal. She was laden with
shopping bags and smiling through the glass door.

"Sorry to barge in," she said, and I gave her a moment
to finish the thought, to explain what she was doing there.
There was a brief silence, until she added, "Just checking
up on you to make sure you're okay."

"Come on in," I said, sort of awkwardly, letting her slip
by me as I held the door.

She walked into my apartment and sat in the exact place
on the couch where she had been the morning of Harry's
death. I quickly gathered up the photographs and placed

them in a cabinet, but I'm pretty sure she'd seen them. I offered her a bottle of water from my sad, empty refrigerator, which she accepted.

The way she was sitting, kind of closed off to the world, the look on her face uncharacteristically dark, her voice unusually soft, told me that something was wrong. It was strange to be in the presence of Harry's vet, even a vet whom I had known for a decade, without Harry around. He had been our only bond, aside from the vacations we used to talk about or the restaurant tips we traded, all of it just idle chitchat, interesting as it might or might not have been.

I took a seat in a chair in the corner of the room. "Everything all right?"

"Things are fine," she said. She talked some about her kids, about her clinic, about business, all of it light, no real substance, as if you could wave your hand right through the conversation and hit nothing that really mattered. Still, there was an edge to her, a sense of restlessness that belied the calm presence I was so accustomed to in her exam rooms. She asked me how I was in a tone of voice that suggested she knew exactly how I'd be—sad, a little uncertain, but fully realizing that when a dog dies, as big a hit as it is to the head and the heart, you dust yourself off and move on. It's just how the world works.

"It's a little harder than I thought it would be," I said. "But you can't get too caught up in it, or it defeats everything you learned about life when you were with him."

"Have you thought about getting another?" She paused

for a second, realizing it might have been too soon, then added, "You're too good a dog owner not to have one."

Truth is, in Harry's final weeks, I had sworn off any future dogs for a variety of reasons: I didn't want to have my heart broken like that again; I needed freedom going forward; and I was at a much different stage in my life than I had been when Harry arrived. Those were all true, but the vivid fear that any new dog wouldn't be anywhere near the dog that I'd already had overlay them. How do you follow perfection?

But I missed Harry dearly, and I missed the routines that formed the foundation of our very good life. I needed the constant companionship, the morning walks and long tours of the city. I realized that with him had come purpose and passions. Not to have this was not to have the life I knew and very much liked, not to be the person that, with Harry's friendship, I had become.

"I don't know yet," I told Pam, but the way she looked at me, she knew I was lying.

"You'll be getting one very soon," she said, and not for the first time or for the last, she was right.

Then the thought struck me, maybe suddenly, maybe gradually, maybe out of nowhere, or maybe out of somewhere where it had been growing in silence for a while. My mind flashed to the tie, the Hermès necktie, which had been sitting on a shelf in the living room all these months in its original orange box, the great mystery of the sender unsolved, the minidrama or melodrama overtaken by the realities of everyday life. I caught a glimpse of the tie sitting on its perch, then said, innocently, "You're not going to believe what I got in the mail a few months ago."

She flashed me a strange look and took a self-conscious pull from her bottle of water. "What?"

"A tie," I said. "An Hermès necktie." Pause.

"With a card that had no signature," I added. "A secret admirer, basically." I paused again. "Have you ever shopped at Hermès?"

She hesitated. Pam Bendock didn't lie, so she didn't lie well, which says precisely everything about her. "Not really," she said, "a little too rich for my blood. And too formal."

Note, she didn't add anything about the absurdity of an anonymous gift. She didn't wonder aloud about the giver. I caught her looking down at her lap for a long moment, which is when I leaped up a little too fast, retrieved the tie from the shelf, and laid it in front of her.

"This is it," I said, and sat back down.

Her head remained down. Her eyes stayed on the tie. No *"Nice tie"* or *"Lovely gift"* or *"What the hell were they thinking?"* Just an odd silence, unlike any other reaction I'd gotten from the roughly two hundred women I had interrogated before.

As I improvised, it started making sense, and in fact, given how I was pressing the point, this possibility had undoubtedly been in the back of my mind all along. We had known each other forever. She'd never seemed to regard me as a garden-variety veterinary client, and she'd taken extraordinary care with Harry. Sitting there, watching her squirm in the middle of the afternoon on this surprise visit to my house, it emerged with the full force of truth: it was Pam.

"It was you."

She didn't even look up at me when I said it. Her head stayed down, her eyes staring vacantly in the general direction of the tie. "I'm really sorry. It was an obnoxious thing to do."

*　*　*

Ten years I had known Pam Bendock. For every one of them, I felt a nice, casual connection. We'd talked about vacations, restaurants, Back Bay, my dog. She exuded unflappability and quiet confidence, jeans and a T-shirt under a sharp white lab coat, a woman who had a world-view that seemed similar to my own. But a relationship? A connection outside of the exam room? No. No. And more no. In retrospect, I should have thought of Pam earlier, and in some distant part of my brain, I probably had, but she'd never come close to making my obvious list of suspects.

For one, she was spoken for, loudly, by a husband and two young girls, and, unlike some people, she didn't seem like the type to head off in another direction on an inexplicable whim. Quite the opposite, actually. That was part of her appeal.

Beyond that, we came from different worlds, albeit worlds just a few miles apart. I lived in the city, remained uncommitted, ate late dinners on just about every given night, and remained embarrassingly void of any meaningful responsibilities. She came from the land of lawn services, anxiety over perfect end-of-year gifts for grade school teachers, neighborhood Christmas cookie swaps, and tables for four at safe restaurants on Saturday nights with like-minded couples that you don't actually know all that well.

Sitting in my living room that weekday afternoon, watching the top of her head because she kept gazing down at the tie on the coffee table, I couldn't have been more floored or, oddly enough, annoyed. The thought flashing through my simple head was that she was basically trying to use me, intentionally or not, as a little distraction from what I could only assume to be her mundane suburban life.

"You're married," I said.

"I'm not," she replied. She looked up for the first time since the Great Discovery, revealing teardrops on her smooth cheeks.

"We're all done, unfortunately," she said. "We made each other miserable."

I let that hang in the air and in our heads for a long while. There was nothing obvious to say here, no dog filling the void between us.

Finally, she gave in. "I'm really sorry about this. This was stupid. I have no business being here."

Neither of us said a word until she asked, "Do you want to know why?"

"I do."

She didn't reply immediately. There was a long pause in which I heard the passersby outside.

"I was sitting at Stephanie's having lunch with a friend one day," she finally began. Stephanie's is a restaurant on Newbury Street a few blocks from my place.

"It felt like my whole life was falling apart. My marriage was a wreck. Things weren't going right at the clinic. Everything was just coming down on me, you know?"

She paused, still staring down.

"We were on the outdoor patio. It was a warm spring day, and you came walking toward us. You were on the other side of the street, and you and Harry stopped and waited for the light to change. You were standing there not really paying attention to anything, and Harry sat right beside you."

Another pause. She seemed more collected now, and she looked across at me with wet, red eyes.

"And you did this thing without even really realizing it. You reached your hand down and pulled Harry's muzzle against your leg. You just kind of rubbed him for a moment, not even thinking about it. The light turned and he gazed up at you, and then the two of you just started walking together."

She was gaining momentum here, more the Dr. Bendock I knew than this woman Pam who had just broken down crying in the middle of the afternoon in my house. Her gaze was fixed on me now.

"And it just kind of hit me at that moment, randomly

but not really, that, yeah, this is why I do what I do, not to argue with some know-it-all about a five-dollar hike in our grooming charge, but because of that exact scene—you and Harry and what the two of you had together."

By now I'll confess that I went from annoyed to interested, which is not as long a journey as I might have thought. You think you know someone, standing with them in the confines of a small veterinary exam room over the course of ten years, across all the many seasons of a wonderful dog's life. But all you really know is his or her silhouette, the vaguest outline. The vividness of what burns just beneath, you have no idea.

"Then I don't know what came over me," Pam continued. "That afternoon, I walked down to Hermès and got the tie."

She pronounced it differently than the way I had, more French, accenting the second syllable, which I assumed was more correct.

"I bought the card at the stationer on Boylston Street right afterward. You made me smile at Stephanie's on a day I didn't think I could smile, so that's what I wrote. I sent it the next day, April 15, tax day. There was a long line at the post office, and I almost walked away and stopped the whole thing. I've never done anything like it. Never even thought about anything like it."

What I was quickly learning about the Pam I didn't know, as opposed to the Dr. Bendock I did, was that if I didn't speak, she filled the void. I kept my mouth shut.

"You did something nice for me, so I wanted to do

something nice for you," she said. "Then, right after I did it, Harry got really sick and I'm thinking 'Oh no.' The timing couldn't have been worse for anybody. I just had to put the whole thing away and not let you know."

Then she added, "I hope it wasn't a big deal to you."

Nah, no big deal. It had barely registered. All I'd done was turn every single relationship I had with every woman I knew completely upside down in the search for a secret admirer. I'd made a total fool of myself in front of countless numbers of people. I had obsessed over it for weeks. Not a big deal at all.

We talked for a while about the vagaries of life and the unfairness of fate. We talked about how nice it would be if differences could be bridged, but too often they only divide. We talked about where we each had been, where we were now, and where we might be headed. We talked as the light from the tall windows grew pale and the room grew cool.

The contrasts kept flashing in my brain, vividly so, as if on a giant LED sign—my city life and her suburbia, my independence and her massive family responsibilities, my relative lack of any relationship baggage and her soon-to-be ex-husband. In the end, as she headed reluctantly for the door, I'm not exactly sure what was on her mind, but I'm positive what was on mine: alluring as she was, Pam and I would never be.

> 8 <

Pam and I had just wrapped up an afternoon of house hunting with dinner at a small Mexican restaurant in the far-flung suburb where we were looking. I may be the most self-involved person I've ever met, but even I drew the line at asking her kids to leave their school and everything familiar so we could move closer to Boston.

It was there, in a booth in Sierra's with a pretty damned good basket of nacho chips between us, that Pam first mentioned Abigail's second-grade science fair project, which involved the incubating and hatching of chicken eggs. Roughly four years had passed since that afternoon in my Boston apartment when I'd learned she was the secret admirer who had mailed me the tie, four occasionally trying years, sometimes joyous years, always eventful years, each of them leading, even when they weren't, to the immovable fact that one day we would combine our lives and see where it all went from there.

"That sounds fun," I said absently, not really paying attention—and believe me, I had my reasons for being distracted.

First off, I worked for a newspaper, and this was the late winter of 2009, the doomsday period for just about every major American daily, most especially mine, the *Boston Globe*. Specifically, I worked as the metro editor, running the vast bulk of the news operation, managing the 120 or so reporters and editors who provided the backbone of our daily report. In my job, I knew something that most others didn't, which is that the *Globe* was hemorrhaging money, that advertising had plummeted because of the miserable economy, that circulation was continuing to plunge because the technology-savvy residents of greater Boston could read us online for free. I was only too aware that the consequences for the newspaper to which I had devoted pretty much my entire adult life were going to be deep and they were going to be dire.

There would be layoffs, severe cuts in the news hole, harsh decisions about what we continued to cover and what we left alone. In early April, the paper would publish a story that exceeded every worst fear: the *New York Times,* owner of the *Globe* since 1993, was preparing to shut us down if it couldn't wring major givebacks from the unions and tens of millions of dollars in cuts elsewhere in the enterprise. Boston without the *Globe*—it would have been ludicrous if it wasn't so frightening, and suddenly possible.

Even a few years out from the stock market crash of autumn 2008, it's easy to forget how bad things had become during that miserable stretch of total uncertainty. Major companies were cutting staff by the thousands. Small businesses were letting longtime workers go. Big banks were teetering on the precipice. If you hadn't already lost your job, you worried that you were about to. Couples sat at kitchen tables slashing through the small luxuries before taking the ax to basic necessities. 401(k) accounts had shriveled in half. Foreclosures soared. Pension plans were going under. Even big, beefy stalwarts such as General Motors were heading into bankruptcy. One late night, I sat in side-by-side leather chairs in the hunter green study of a wealthy Beacon Hill resident whom I was trying to convince to buy the *Globe*. He told me he had literally cashed money out of the stock market at desperate lows because he thought it possible his family could end up sleeping on Boston Common. You knew the economy was in free fall when an absurdly successful guy who lived in a six-story mansion is scared.

And in that environment of loss, Pam and I were trying to build something new, which was a future together. It hadn't been a particularly smooth ride from my living room in Boston on that day of the discovery to this late-night dinner in her suburban town west of the city, but it was by every measure an eventful one. We hesitated for a good year or more at first. Pam was going through a divorce, feeling every bump, every pull, every moment of strain along the way. I was wandering from steak house to steak house, living life one day, one night, one meal at a time, with no grand plan.

Pam and I made a good solid run at things, and they were great until the day they weren't, which is when we gave it a rest, perhaps for good. Pam was feeling guilty about her failed marriage and its impact on her two daughters. I was scared out of my mind about pretty much everything that Pam represented: the responsibility, the house in a distant suburban town, the two young girls who were smart, expressive, and lacking even the slightest sign of interest in me.

Actually, the girls, they terrified me. On a child familiarity scale of 1 to 10, one being, say, Jake Barnes in *The Sun Also Rises,* 10 being Julie Andrews as Mary Poppins, I was hovering in the 1s and 2s. It probably didn't help that the girls weren't exactly demure. They were outspoken on just about everything. They were emotional. They liked nothing about baseball or golf or basketball, meaning the things I liked. They didn't ever want to go to Friendly's for ice cream. (I'd thought that part would be easy.) They couldn't be bribed with pasta twirling in the North End or the popcorn guy at Fenway Park. They were avid horse riders, American Girl doll fanatics, and basically fussed over names for hundreds, even thousands of animals, real and imagined. They loved little more in life than their mother's home cooking. When they paid attention to me, it was mostly to repeat that their mother was, in their stern words, "Ours, not yours." I had a lot to learn.

Still, Pam and I kept finding our way back to each other. For me, clarity arrived in the midst of a classic September pennant race. I was sitting in my regular box seats at

Fenway when a casual friend, a reasonably well-known guy-about-town, stopped by to say hello. I knew him enough to enthusiastically talk over golf plans but not so well that we'd ever consummate them. Anyway, on that night, I asked the whereabouts of his fiancée, a woman, in truth, with much more to offer than him. The guy was in his early fifties, never married, and had been engaged to this extremely nice teacher for the past four or five years.

"Yeah, that didn't work out," he said, grimacing.

And finally I saw it. Of course it didn't, and the next one wouldn't either, nor would the one after that. He was that type—the guy who couldn't commit—and that type was everywhere. There was an editor at the *Globe* just like him, a few squash players at my gym, and another guy with whom I actually did regularly golf. In your thirties, it's something to be admired, the guy in no rush, confidently waiting for someone special. In your forties, there are suddenly suspicious character traits—narcissism, chronic indecision, or harmful perfectionism. In your fifties, if there's still even lip service to wanting family, partner, commitment, you're bordering on the pathetic and well on your way to being the eighty-five-year-old in the nursing home just hoping that someone else's visitors give you a few minutes of their time to break up the loneliness of your day.

As I sat in judgment of this acquaintance, shaking my head that he couldn't pull the trigger, something very familiar nagged at my core: me. Pam and I had been doing this absurd shuffle for too many years, but we had excuses. Melding two mature lives, I told her (and myself), was never an easy undertaking. She didn't have the freedom to move towns. I didn't have what it took to live amid lawns and laundry rooms that were forty minutes from the nearest bistro.

But my commute to see her and her kids on a virtually nightly basis was getting old, as were her attempts to shoot into Boston whenever she dropped off the kids at their father's. The whole thing was exhausting and in too many ways lacking. Something had to change, and that something, it ended up, had to be me.

So there we were at Sierra's, having just toured several more uninspiring houses.

"Yeah, evidently, their father got them this prepackaged hatching set," Pam said. "It comes with an incubator that slowly heats and turns the eggs, as if there was a mother hen sitting on top of them." She always sounded enthusiastic when she talked about any kind of animal, even more when the topic turned to the unusual things they do in the name of their young, in this case rotate the eggs at least three times a day.

The nice waitress dropped sizzling chicken fajitas on our table for me and a burrito for Pam, and I signaled for another glass of wine that wasn't half bad. Actually, it was pretty bad, but it was also really cheap.

"That'll be fun for them," I said, offering it little thought. And that was it for the egg-hatching talk for the night. Looking back, I can summon up no good excuse for how it slipped through my defenses, how red flags weren't furiously flapping in the breeze of fear that guides so much of my life with the opposite sex. There are member nations of the NATO alliance that lack the sophistication I have in sensing mounting threats, or at least overt changes, from miles and weeks away. I once noticed Pam in the condiments aisle of a supermarket in Maine briefly touch a small Heinz ketchup bottle before putting it back and casually picking up the larger one, even though it was April. I knew then and there that she planned to have her kids up to my house for a two-week vacation later that summer. Sure enough, come August, I would be sitting on the deck with the girls eating hot dogs and pasta watching Caroline, the younger, liberally squirt the ketchup from that same large bottle in the midst of a long visit.

I once knew the moment a former girlfriend asked me my favorite month—October, by the way—that within weeks, she would begin talking about how nice it would be to get married in the fall. And she did, remarking one night after a couple of glasses of wine, "Wouldn't it be great to have a wedding in a field in the middle of the autumn with every single tree burning bright red and orange?" It would have been, just not with her.

I could go on about this talent that I'm not necessarily proud of but that's served me well over many years. But in the case of Pam and her kids and the chicken eggs, it's a talent that completely failed me, making me reassess whether I actually had that kind of talent at all. I mean, it should have been obvious. Pam's a veterinarian, an excellent and compassionate one. Her daughters seemed to inherit every bit of her love of animals. Neither she nor they have ever in their lives given an animal of any sort away. This thing should have played out with the obviousness of a fast-moving PowerPoint presentation, the slides flipping from an incubator to an egg with a crack to a little chick to a big chicken to a big ornery chicken chasing an innocent Brian across the dewy grass of their front yard.

But I don't care how sophisticated my radar for trouble may or may not be. I don't care how prescient I am or I'm not about the twists and turns of the future. There was precisely no way that I could have predicted the hell that was going to come out of Abigail's science fair project at the General John Nixon Elementary School. No way whatsoever.

*　　*　　*

Typically I didn't spend the night at Pam's place on weekdays, under the guise of it not sending a good message to the kids but more secretly because the thought of starting my weekday in the chaotic environs of a house filled with three females furiously and simultaneously getting ready for school and work, all of it unfolding more than thirty minutes from Boston, made me nauseous with fear.

I would do it on weekends, happily, when my only morning obligation was to take the dog portion of the group to a pretty field for their morning run, then stop at a nice Dunkin' Donuts to pick up Munchkins for the girls. But otherwise I needed my weekday tranquillity and work proximity, so shortly after the kids went to bed each night at 8:30 or 9, I'd get back into my car, drive to my condo, and spend a pleasant stretch of time on my couch catching the end of the Red Sox game or a few more pages of a book, spooning Brigham's chocolate chip ice cream into my big mouth, savoring every second and bite, knowing that that part of my life was very much on the block.

On Saint Patrick's Day morning, though, I was in their house for reasons I can't remember. Let's assume it was fate. The phone rang, and I heard Pam shout out, "Abigail, it's your dad! Pick up and talk to him." I heard silence and then a shriek of joy and then her little voice shouting, "Mom, it cracked! The egg cracked! The brown one, it cracked!"

From downstairs I heard her frantically running around her bedroom one floor above, undoubtedly getting dressed in a rush. I heard water running, which was Abigail brushing her teeth. I heard feet pounding down the narrow front stairs. Then she was there, right in front of me, this little Mini-Me version of Pam with long blond hair and big knowing eyes and a brain that worked as fast and as hard as a turbocharged sports car.

"The chick is coming today," she said, trying to play it down a bit. I was leaning against the kitchen sink, reading the morning paper, trying to stay clear of the mayhem of their morning routine.

"How do you know?" I asked.

"Our dad called. He said there's a crack in the egg and he can almost see the chick getting ready to come through."

She paused and added, "Mom's going to take us by to see it for a minute on the way to school."

Even that didn't give me a moment of pause. But in defense of my lack of defenses, what sane person would ever look into the future and see a chicken—actually, a large snow-white rooster with the darkest of hearts—as his household pet? How, from my sheltered vantage of a brownstone condominium with a job that allowed me to call virtually all of my own shots, could I ever have fully anticipated the sense of powerlessness that was to come?

That said, I have to concede that there were plenty of signs that my life was changing all around me. Take the night that my cell phone rang on my drive from the *Globe* to Pam's house in suburbia.

"Hey, I hate to ask you this," Pam said, "but Caroline is begging me for these things called Silly Bandz. Abigail's got homework to do. I don't want to leave her home alone. Would you mind stopping on the way out and picking some up?"

"Sure," I said, already a little wary of all that could go wrong—the wrong store, the wrong bag, the wrong size, any or all of which would leave little Caroline in tears and Brian the clueless antagonist.

"Great," Pam said, sounding relieved. "These things are all the rage at school right now. Everyone's got them. She wants the tie-dyed bands, probably animal shapes. They should sell them at the Paper Store right in the plaza next to the supermarket."

I looked at my car clock—7:40 p.m.—and immediately

sensed trouble. I was about twenty minutes away from where I wanted to be, and my guess is that the Paper Store, sort of an all-purpose clearinghouse of stuff that no one actually needs but once you're around it, you inexplicably want, would shut down at 8 P.M. That did not feel right.

As I pulled into the parking lot, relief flowed through me at the sight of the brightly lit store. A couple of women were inside, one behind the cash register, another prettying up the displays and shelves. So far, so good.

But when I merrily pulled on the doors, they didn't budge. I looked into the store, and neither woman—one middle-aged, the other a teenager—even glanced in my direction. I tried the doors again in that pointless way that people do, thinking maybe they were just caught on something the first time. They weren't. I checked my phone and saw that it was 8:03.

Dread started pounding every cell of my very being. I pictured the scene. Brian: *Sorry, Caroline, I got there too late and the store was closed.* Caroline: utter silence, her head down as she skulks away, disappointed that this cretin named Brian had failed her yet again. The next day, Caroline would be the only member of her first-grade class not to be proudly sporting Silly Bandz, and a fight in the cafeteria would ensue. I knocked, probably a little too firmly, desperation getting the better of me. But neither the teenager nor the older woman would look up from what she was doing. I wanted to pound on the damned door at that point, but that wasn't going to get me anywhere. No worker is going to approach and say, "I'm sorry,

I didn't realize that you were crazy and aggressive. Let me unlock this door now and allow you inside." I moved a few feet away from the door, called 411, got the number for the store, and rang through.

I could hear their phone ringing in stereo—live and through my headset. I saw the younger woman pick up a portable phone as she was moving potpourri around a display table.

"The Paper Store," she said.

"Hi, I'm wondering if you carry Silly Bandz," I said.

I saw her glance toward another table and say, "Yeah, we've got a ton of them. Every kid has to have them."

"Great," I said. "What time do you close?"

"We already are. We're open tomorrow at nine."

Nervously, I went in for the kill: "Listen, I'm standing right outside. I've got a desperate six-year-old at home who all she wants is a pack of Silly Bandz tonight. Is there any possible way you would be willing to sell me a package? I guarantee you that I'll get in and out in less than a minute."

She hesitated. Hesitation is good. My entire career as a newspaper reporter, columnist, and editor taught me to work with hesitation, and I was no novice at turning the hesitant into the adamant. Through the window, I could see her turn to the older woman behind the counter, point in my direction, and say something. Suddenly they were both peering at me, so I gave an absurd little half wave, trying to look as genial and unobtrusive as possible, the kind of guy you'd let in your store after hours because you're fairly certain he's not going to bind and gag you and then ransack the place of all cookbooks, stationery, and figurines.

Her voice was in my phone again. "We don't have any change. The cash register is all locked up."

"I have change," I said, maybe too abruptly. As I said this, I was doing a mental inventory of my pocket and couldn't picture anything other than twenties, but that was a small price to pay for the ultimate prize.

Silence. She looked again at the older woman. "I'll be quick," I said pleadingly, a little bit pathetically.

I could see the two of them talking, the older woman looking above her reading glasses at the other, the younger woman saying something back, the older woman shrugging, the younger one nodding her head. There were some restaurants in Boston that would fire up a wood-burning oven after closing hours to feed me if I showed up late, and here I was at the total mercy of two shopkeepers who pretty much controlled the direction of the rest of my life.

Finally I watched the younger woman take a step in my direction. I ended the call and put the phone away as I watched her pull keys from a pocket in her long sweater. When she opened the door, I heard a chorus rain down from the heavens singing "Hallelujah." I stepped inside, thanked her profusely, and she said, "They're right back here." Her tone was one of sympathy more than empathy. Triumph.

It's kind of amazing how few Silly Bandz you get for $20, but no matter. When I got back into the car, I realized I was sweating, even though it was a cool autumn night. When I got to the house, it occurred to me that Caroline could have already lost interest in the way that kids often do.

But when I put them on the kitchen table, she furiously turned over the bag and shrieked at what she saw. "Abby, animal shapes!" she yelled.

Pam smiled that easy smile of hers, her blond hair pulled back into a lazy ponytail. "You're a big hit," she told me, adding "I hope it wasn't any trouble."

No, no trouble at all. Why would any of this be any trouble?

> 9 <

For the first few weeks of her fussed-over life, the chicken was known to me only through excitedly told stories about her unfailing cuteness and the photographs the kids were constantly shooting of her. The chick lived at the kids' father's house. Pam and her kids were still living in their rental house. I was still living in Boston. Everything was about to change.

There's no denying it, the chick did look cute in the way that chicks always look cute, which isn't much different than how bunnies or puppies or kittens have universal appeal. The pictures showed her as a tiny yellow fluffball, her little feathers constantly tousled on top of her miniature head, her beak almost taking on the appearance of little lips.

"She is soooooo cuuuuute," Abigail would constantly say, with Caroline chiming in her agreement.

Then, one otherwise uneventful evening, my very first

hackle rose—not high, mind you. Rather, it stood out a little bit, just barely sensitive to the fact that something might have just started to go ever so slightly wrong. It was a school night, and Abigail was on the phone with her father in their regular prebedtime call when I heard her ask, "How's Buddy?"

"Who's Buddy?" I asked unassumingly when she got off the phone.

"My chick," she said, plain as day.

The chick had a name.

"That's nice," I replied, kind of absently. The truth is, I had been somewhat absent, at least emotionally, of late. Most of my energy was still directed at the *Globe,* at the budget cuts that were hurtling down the pike, at the people I might be forced to lay off, at the fact that I could lose my job in all this as well, which was making me think of what else I could and maybe even should do. There were more than a few moments when I allowed myself to think how nice it would be to work in an industry that was growing rather than dying. The only problem with that was the only problem in my entire professional life: it was the only thing I'd ever wanted to do. When I was in the fifth grade at the Abigail Adams School in Weymouth, Massachusetts, we launched a student government. Some kids ran for president, other kids ran for the Senate. I opened up my own newspaper and criticized everyone seeking office. It was pure heaven. All through high school and college, all I wanted to do was get a job writing for a newspaper. When I got out of school, my most daring dream was to land a job at the *Boston Globe,* my hometown paper. When I got there at age twenty-six, it was better than I had ever imagined. I traveled the country and the world. I met senators, presidents, and prime ministers. I chased a congressman from office. We got prominent politicians indicted. I gained an appreciation for readers as smart, engaged, and filled with common sense. I had been doing this for more than twenty years, and all I wanted was more. And now someone was trying to shut it down, to take it all away.

Whatever little remaining attention I had was directed toward the inevitable move from Boston to suburbia and the house that Pam and I needed to spur it. Pam's rental was too small, and it was old, meaning that things were breaking down and I didn't have the slightest idea how to fix any of them. Beyond that, we were in the throes of the Great Recession. People's finances were generally a wreck, mine being no exception. Fear trumped hope. The housing market was in shambles. Standing in the kitchen that night, I was about to ask Abigail what the plan was for Buddy the Chick after she outgrew her little cage, but something stopped me and I'm not entirely sure what that was. Maybe deep down, I already knew Buddy's fate but was protecting myself from knowledge I couldn't handle. Or maybe I just didn't want to concede in any way at all that this seven-year-old blue-eyed blonde standing all of about four feet high had more say over my life than I was about to have. At that point, it was impossible to know what an ornery presence Buddy would grow up to be, at least toward me. But I feared what a bizarre addition she would be to the already unfamiliar environs of a suburban house and lawn.

What I said was "Well, I'm sure Buddy loves you very, very much."

Abigail smiled and replied, "She really does. She's the best chick ever."

Nice work, Bri-Guy. I was really helping the cause.

*　*　*

It was Abigail's eighth birthday party. I had just walked into their house carefully balancing a pair of oversized boxes holding an overpriced cake and many duplicate cupcakes and vaguely noticed something that hadn't been there before. I was too wrapped up in the magnitude and majesty of what a child's birthday party was in towns like this one: God help us all. This must have been what it was like in Rome in the days before the empire fell. Maybe it was what the United States was in the hours before the market crash of 1929. When I was growing up (a phrase I never thought I'd use), birthday parties basically involved a few cousins, a couple of neighbors, a Duncan Hines cake, and a rousing game of Pin the Tail on the Donkey. We never wanted more. We never needed more. We never knew there was more.

In this town, among this class of kids, there's always something more. My introduction to this culture came when Pam asked me to stop by a bakery in Newton, a town nearer to Boston, on my way out from work and pick up the birthday dessert. I'm thinking old-fashioned bakery with a guy named Ernie in a flour-covered apron, display cases filled with sugar cookies, hermits, and homemade breads, all of it tended to by matronly older women who looked as though they've sampled more than their share of the fare.

Not exactly. I walked into the place, and the first thing I noticed was that there was no display case. There were no cakes, no cookies, no nothing. It ended up you don't just whistle through the door, casually pick out a cake from the dozen or so that are waiting, and ask them to write "Happy Birthday Trevor" in blue frosting. Ended up, that would be like driving up to Augusta National because you feel like playing a round of golf. What I did notice was a conference room off what they call the "showroom." I quickly learned that if you want a cake from this particular bakery, you sit in that consultation room with the confectionary advisers at least a week ahead of time, plotting out exactly how you want everything to look and taste for little Jessica's birthday or Nathan's bar mitzvah. At the very least, you've probably sent an email with a PDF of a rough sketch of the masterpiece that's on your mind.

I gave Pam's name, and a nice man appeared from the back with two large boxes.

"I think we just had one cake," I said.

The woman laughed as if I had just cracked a very funny joke. "You have a cake and then some matching cupcakes," she said. Of course.

The cake was, by every possible measure, stunning, which perhaps is what the man and woman were waiting for me to say as they held the box open for me to inspect and admire it. The frosting portrayed young girls in sleeping bags watching a flat-screen TV, matching the theme of the party, which was a movie and a sleepover.

"Be kind of funny if you made the TV a big old clunky Magnavox and none of the kids knew what it was," I said.

No one laughed with me. They were too busy preparing the whopping $150 bill. For a birthday cake. For eight-year-olds.

When I would chide Pam about the lengths she traveled for her kids' parties, she would tick off the various portable petting zoos, limousine rides, expensive restaurants, magic acts, and traveling bands that were the focal points of other kids' soirees. The fact that she was also having manicurists and pedicurists straight from a Boston day spa, complete with all their various instruments and a rainbow of polishes, still meant she was doing it on the cheap, she said. I was just smart enough not to push the point.

I arrived at the house a couple of hours ahead of the starting time, and everything was all decked out with balloons and bowls of M&Ms and a hallway lined with the requisite swag bags that each attendee would take home. That's the other thing about modern birthday parties in gilded suburbs: gifts aren't just for the birthday boy or girl, they are for everyone, just as trophies aren't just for winners but for the kids who come in last. As I came through the door, I nervously balanced the two cake boxes in my arms. There was so much visual stimulation, so many jangled nerves over the possibility of dropping the precious cakes, that I missed Buddy's cage.

In fact, it didn't register until young Caroline grabbed my hand in the kitchen and said in her adorably squeaky voice, "Come meet Buddy." The next sound was my heart clanking on the floor. I swear, if anyone else was in the room, they'd have been scurrying around on their knees looking for whatever it was that just fell. *Come meet Buddy.* Everything that had been concealed for weeks was coming out into the open—every vague fear, every ounce of trepidation, every outspoken outcome that had been lurking in the furthest reaches of my mind.

As Caroline guided me toward the living room, Pam appeared with a smile and said, "Wait until you see how cute she is."

Oh, I'd like to wait. I'd like to wait until some nice country farmer in a pair of faded overalls sends us a picture of Buddy fitting in beautifully with an extended flock of happy chickens, and gosh be all, she certainly is the championship egg layer of his whole impeccably well-kept henhouse. But no, I didn't have to wait; I was about to meet Buddy exactly then.

As we approached, Buddy was sitting on a bed of shredded papers in what had probably been a small bunny or hamster cage, sitting still and softly chirping at nothing at all. She was a little ball of yellow fluff with a tiny bill and miniature stick legs. If I hadn't known any better, if I couldn't have heard the faint chirps, I would have assumed she was just a little stuffed bird, some nice girl's favorite bedtime toy. It'd be a lie of omission if I didn't confess that she really was adorable.

"Hold her," Caroline said as she expertly flipped the cage open, gently pulled Buddy out, and deposited her in my hands before I could object. Suddenly I felt the soft tickle of her scratchy little feet gently moving across my palms—a mild sensation until the adorable little creature opened her tiny bill and bit my thumb.

"Jesus!" I yelled in surprise.

Caroline laughed. At that exact moment, Abigail skipped into the room and exclaimed, "Buddy, my favorite little girl!"

She scooped her out of my hands. The two kids placed the creature back into the cage, Abigail giving her a kiss on the top of her yellow head in the process. As we headed back to the kitchen to admire $150 worth of cake, I asked the kids, "Um, how long is Buddy here for?"

After a frighteningly lengthy pause, Abigail said, "Mom said maybe for a while." After she said it, she flashed what I took to be a sinister and hopeful little smile.

*   *   *

It's tough to define "a while," but apparently, "a while" Chez Bendock means at least two weeks. A fortnight later, young Buddy was still every bit at home in Pam's house. Her circumstances had changed. Gone was the tiny cage with the shredded paper on the console table, replaced by what had been a dog crate situated smack in the middle of the living room floor that allowed her all sorts of room to roam. I wouldn't exactly have billed her as a free-range chicken at that point, but she was certainly aspiring to it.

Pam filled the crate with soft straw. She put in a log upon which Buddy perched. She placed a fuzzy stuffed chick up against the log, and Buddy spent inordinate amounts of time pressed up against the toy. Maybe she thought it was real. Maybe Buddy wasn't that bright. Maybe it doesn't matter. There were little food bowls and a water bottle and constant activity. Buddy flitted around. She chirped. She slept soundly. She seemed to love every moment of her young life.

She especially loved the attention lavished on her by the two kids, who would constantly pull her out of the crate, cradle her in their arms, and place her in between them on a towel on the couch as they watched *iCarly* and *Wizards of Waverly Place* on TV. They cooed at her, fed her little bits of oatmeal, and gently stroked her soft, fuzzy feathers. Buddy cooed her constant approval in return.

Her comfort began coming at my expense, most noticeably on a May weekend when Pam's kids were off to their father's house. I had visions of a quick getaway trip to Maine, dinner at our favorite Portland restaurant, running the dogs along a beautiful stretch of Goose Rocks Beach. At the very least, Pam would come into Boston, as she almost always did, and we'd walk the dogs in the city for hours at a time and stop for something to eat in any number of great places in the South End.

"I can't," she said on the phone Thursday afternoon.

"Huh?" Literally, I was shocked.

"Buddy," she said.

Buddy.

"Is there any such thing as a chicken sitter?" I asked. I'd later come to learn that in fact there is, and they are expensive.

But for now Pam said, "I wouldn't feel right leaving her. She's just getting used to the new crate and all that. Why don't you come out here? We'll grab a pizza and watch the baseball game."

So I did, and we did, and when I woke up on Saturday morning at dawn's early light, it was to the sound of a surprisingly virulent chirping emanating from the living room of Pam's house. "What the hell is that?" I asked, groggy.

Pam, smiling in bed at this unholy hour, simply said, "Buddy." Then she added, "Isn't she hilarious? She's so happy."

Later that morning, after I returned from the field with the dogs, I found Pam sitting at the kitchen table reading the newspaper with Buddy curled up on her lap, sound asleep. I fed the dogs—quietly, at Pam's request, so as not to wake the bird—and sat down with her. I finally summoned the courage to ask the question that had been in the forefront of my thoughts for the last several weeks. "What are you going to do about Buddy?"

I remained fairly confident—or maybe extremely hopeful—that she had to do something. I mean, people don't keep chickens as pets—or at least that's what I thought at the time, until I read up on the topic and realized that, actually, many people do keep chickens as pets. But at the time I could make the effective argument that to keep a chicken in a suburban home was unfair to none other than the chicken, who wouldn't be allowed to explore her full chickenness living in a cage in a living room and waiting every night for another episode of *SpongeBob SquarePants* with her two little girls.

Plus I didn't think I'd have to make the argument for a busy mother with a demanding job owning a veterinary clinic at a point in her life when she was preparing to move into a new house with a somewhat pain in the ass but relentlessly charming guy that a chicken just didn't fit. It was obvious.

But I knew Pam. I knew her kids. I knew their bottomless capacity for animals and that it transcended species. They loved bunnies and had two, which I didn't quite understand. They loved horses, which I definitely didn't understand. They loved cats and guinea pigs and hamsters and rats. If it could walk or crawl, they basically loved it. They loved this chick, and their love scared the living bejesus out of me.

Pam didn't really look up at me while she answered, which was never a good sign. Staring straight at her newspaper, she replied, "I'm going to find her a home. I'll get her on a farm around here, hopefully close enough where the kids can go visit her."

That washed over me like warm water in a whirlpool tub, that dose of common sense. She had thought about it, even calculated it, and agreed that the chicken would be better off living among her own breed. Not knowing when to let good things lie, I added, "You really need to let her be a chicken."

Pam didn't really need to hear that and shot back, "She is being a chicken. I've been reading up on it"—okay, very bad sign—"and there are a lot of ways to be a chicken, all of them better than being crammed in some tiny henhouse forced to lay eggs for an unappreciative dairy farmer. I just need to find the right place for her."

I said, "What about your ex? It was his idea. His experiment. His chicken. What does he propose doing?"

"He called Barn Babies. It's that traveling petting zoo he hires for all the kids' birthday parties. They said they'd take her. But I called the owner and asked what happens when Buddy's not a chick anymore, and all she could tell me is that there were no guarantees about what would happen."

With her index finger she gently stroked Buddy's head, the little creature waking up from a slumber to quietly coo at her mother hen.

Pam added, "I'm not going to let some circus group kill Buddy just because she grows up. What's fair about that?"

Chickens die every day by the hundreds of thousands

in the name of food, big chickens, small chickens, young chickens, old chickens. There was nothing fair about it, but it was life. Still, this kind of outlook would not have been well received, so I kept my mouth shut on the topic. Actually, what I said was "You'll find just the right place" and headed upstairs to take a shower.

*   *   *

Ends up, "just the right place" wasn't so easy to find, although please don't accuse me of cynicism if I harbor the sense that maybe Pam wasn't looking all that hard. She would set out with Buddy in a box to visit area farms. She would come back with Buddy in a box, only mildly disappointed with the news that the farmers wouldn't add an outsider to their flock, what with the potential for diseases and all. The fear she saw in my eyes prompted her to keep trying.

She made calls. I heard them. She sent e-mails to various farmers and groups. I saw them. She even reached out to her old veterinarian school contacts and to the author of a book about backyard chickens. She hit one wall after another, and it never seemed to particularly bother her.

All the while, Buddy grew—and fast. Her yellow feathers were turning white. The once cavernous dog crate began to look tight. It didn't matter to the kids, who continued to cradle her in their arms, sit her on their laps as they watched TV, play with her on the kitchen floor, and generally fuss all over her. In truth, I kept waiting for the appeal of Buddy to wear off, to the point where she'd be sitting unnoticed for long swaths of time in a lonely crate and I could make the argument that life wasn't being fair to her anymore. That did not happen.

One early summer evening I arrived at Pam's house after work to find Buddy and the kids in the yard outside, the bird tentatively high-stepping around the lawn, picking at the grass with her beak, the kids delighting in her every maneuver.

"Brian," Caroline called out in her squeaky voice as I got out of my car, "Buddy loves it out here. Look at her. She loves it."

Abigail swooped Buddy up in her arms, thrust her toward me, and said, "Pet her."

"I'm not going to pet the chicken," I said, reflexively stepping away.

"C'mon, pet her," she said again, holding the chicken closer.

"Abs, I'm not going to pet the chicken."

Abigail got a delighted look on her face, mischievous at the same time, and called out, "Awww, great big Bwian is afwaid of a lil lil chicken. That's too bad for Bwian." Bwian, she said, like it's spelled.

Caroline started chiming in. Buddy was squawking. I looked up and saw Pam in the door laughing.

It was four on one, unless you include the two dogs, Baker and Walter, who were trying to jump on me, but they weren't really taking sides. They just wanted me to throw the ball for them. So I reached my left hand out and went to pat this bird who, on the occasion of our last physical contact, had bitten me. As my fingers got close to her downy, increasingly white flank, she let out a long, loud guttural sound that basically said, *Touch me and I'll peck your eyes out.*

I stepped back, probably quicker than I intended. The kids laughed—at me, not with me. Pam was smiling. The joke was on Bwian. And I was just starting to get a very clear idea of the extent of it.

"Brian's a bigger chicken than Buddy," Abigail said. Before she even finished her thought, young Caroline let out a little chicken squawk.

*   *   *

Dinners and work and all that kind of stuff kept me in the city for a few nights, so when I finally found myself back in suburbia, it was Friday evening, the kids were at their father's again, and Pam's house was very quiet when I arrived. We headed out for a suburban dinner, meaning something extraordinarily mediocre, invariably involving too much cheese. But the food didn't matter. Much as I adored the kids, it was always nice getting a good, healthy dose of Pam alone. We talked, we laughed, we drank a little bit, and when we got home, I didn't notice anything different at all.

The next morning, getting ready to head to the field

with the dogs, I saw there was no crate in the living room, meaning there was no Buddy in the crate. My heart lightened. Whimsical thoughts danced through my brain. Pam had finally come to terms with the fact that Buddy should be at a farm, needed to be at a farm, and everyone involved was the better for it. For the life of me, I couldn't believe she hadn't told me about it the night before or when it happened. I mean, we only talked on the phone about ten times a day. She must have been holding it back as a surprise.

I tried to control my joy, thinking that was best in this situation. Pam was in the kitchen when I casually walked in.

"Are we missing something here?" I asked. Keep your voice straight, Brian. Straight.

She looked at me quizzically.

"Buddy," I said. "Where's Buddy?"

Pam was still wearing her trademark surgical scrubs and a heavy sweatshirt. It could be ninety degrees and that was what she wore to bed, unless she was feeling particularly risqué, and then it was a T-shirt and surgical scrubs. Her hair was tangled. Her eyes were sleepy. I was expecting her to take a seat and start telling me a long story about her sad kids, who had finally realized that they had to let Buddy be the bird she can be, and the nice farmer who'd agreed to take her in.

But no, that story never came. Instead, Pam said, "Oh, she's in the garage."

Although it wasn't the answer I'd been hoping for or expecting, it was certainly something I could work with, an improvement over Buddy as living room–based pet. The move to the garage, at the very least, was a strong signal that the women of Checkerberry Circle were starting to get sick of their chirping bird. I had to assume, happily, that we were a halfway house to a farm.

"When you take the dogs, would you mind letting her outside?" Pam added casually, pouring herself a cup of coffee.

The three of us made for the front door, the two dogs bouncing with excitement about the tennis ball–fetching session that was about to come, the human endlessly curious about what he was about to find in the garage. I pulled on the door, but it didn't budge. I was basically the last person in suburbia to understand that that isn't how anyone opened garage doors anymore. I figured it out, opened Pam's SUV, which was parked in the driveway, and hit the door opener.

I walked into the dank space filled with old furniture spread everywhere, dried-out leaves on the floor, and garden tools and the like lining the walls, and saw nothing that even resembled a bird. I poked around the kids' bikes, their scooters, a giant stuffed horse, but still nothing.

"Buddy?" I said quietly. "Buddy, are you here?"

I was really hoping to find her sitting in a small cage by the trash, but I knew that was too much to ask. Sharper now: "Buddy?"

I heard a soft, guttural squawk. I saw something out of the corner of my eye, something that was actually above eye level. I looked up, surprised, and saw Buddy sitting on a shelf in the rear of the garage behind a mess of mismatched and otherwise useless furniture. My God, Pam had her on a shelf. This woman/bird love affair was finally, decisively over. Common sense wins again. Next stop: poultry farm.

She squawked louder now, and I asked if she needed a hand.

"Buddy, you poor thing," I said, my point being to press the point that she certainly appeared on the outs, a far cry from the bird who'd lived on the living room floor curled up with a stuffed animal in her likeness and free constantly to watch TV with two adoring girls.

I started pushing through furniture to get to her, when she did something that I'll never forget: she stood up on the shelf and leaped effortlessly down upon an old dining room table right beneath it, the surface of the table covered with discarded beach towels. She walked purposefully across the dining room table and leaped upon a chair, similarly covered in a sheet. From the chair she floated casually to the ground. The whole journey took about twenty seconds. Once on cement, she strutted proudly through the garage door to the great outdoors to greet the new day.

Left behind, I noticed that there was a nest of quilts and blankets on the shelf that was serving as Buddy's bed. I think the top one was angora, but I could be wrong. It couldn't have been cashmere, right? Jesus. I followed her outside to see a much livelier Pam walk out the front door carrying a cereal bowl filled with oatmeal, shredded cheese, and cracked corn. She spread her arms wide and excitedly talked to Buddy in what can only be described as her chicken voice, telling her how pretty she was, how smart she was, and how much she'd love her breakfast. The bird cooed along as though she were trying to sing a song of thanks. And then she pecked ravenously at the contents of the bowl.

Later that morning, Pam and I were heading out to look at houses. Buddy was high-stepping around the lawn.

"She's okay here?" I asked, starting my car.

"She's fine," Pam said, settling into the passenger seat, peering across the dashboard at the bird.

"She won't go anywhere?"

"Where would she go that's better than here?" Pam asked.

As I backed out, Pam rolled her window down. "Hold on," she said to me. Then, to the bird, "Bye, Boo-Boo. Have a good afternoon!"

Boo-Boo? The bird had a nickname? People, let alone Pam, don't give away animals with nicknames. Later that night, Buddy took the reverse route to bed, hopping onto the chair, then the table, then the quilt-lined shelf. After dark Pam shut the door to protect her from coyotes, which, by the way, had become my new, favorite, nondomesticated animal, such that I made my screen saver at work an outsized photograph of a coyote who was shooting a look at the camera that basically said, "Don't you worry, I'll take care of everything." The food chain is a vital part of our natural world.

"Good night, Boo," I heard Pam say from the kitchen.

And no one ever spoke of getting rid of Boo again—well, no one not named Brian.

>10<

As a kid, I was given what almost seem like unfair advantages in my life. No, we didn't have a lot of money, though I imagine we had enough. My first memories were of our apartment on the bottom floor of a two-decker house on a crowded one-way street in the Boston neighborhood of Roslindale. It was pure bliss. My grandparents, who owned the house, lived upstairs. I slept on the upper bunk in a bedroom with my sister Colleen, who would tell me ghost stories that I didn't want to hear on our way to sleep. My other, more maternal sister, Carole, slept in the refinished attic.

The front yard was so small you could reach every corner by standing in the middle, but it didn't seem to matter. I'd build snow forts as my grandfather, a retired Boston police sergeant, watched from the sun porch on the second floor. One day a paving truck showed up and covered the whole backyard, such as it was, in blacktop, because my grandmother had grown tired of my grandfather's failure to mow it. When I got home from school that day, it was as if Heaven itself had paid a visit to our house; we could now bounce balls and draw with chalk and not get yelled at for being in the street. Everything was in walking distance, whether it was Boschetto Bakery or Ashmont Discount or the Rialto Theatre in Roslindale Square, or the Cumberland Farms a block away. Healy Field, a huge park with baseball diamonds, was just behind our house. Everything was crowded and loud and busy, meaning it was perfect.

Then one day we moved. I remember the truck slowly meandering down our street, the neighbors shedding tears, my sisters too distraught to talk for the entire ride down the highway to the nearby suburb of Weymouth, where my proud parents had bought our own house, with our own grassy yard, where I would have my own room. I was eight years old, and pretty much everything I knew was gone.

I was surprised to discover that Weymouth was great for many reasons: the people, the schools, the teachers, the parks, the basketball hoop in our narrow driveway, the bedrock normalcy of it all. There was nothing stuck up about it. Parents worked hard. Kids got jobs. Nobody lorded over anyone with new cars or nicer clothes or built-in swimming pools. I was able to play sports, make good friends, find part-time work. The real advantage I had, though, was two wise and wonderful parents.

Yvonne and Leo McGrory knew the rare times to hover but mostly when to pull back. They gave me the freedom to think, to experiment, to make mistakes, which is something I didn't see nearly enough of in the girls' world of contemporary suburbia. I often came home from school to an empty house, which was great. I had to find my own rides to work. When I graduated from college, my father proudly handed me a $35 golf putter as a gift and said, "Congratulations, you did exactly what you were supposed to do." Nobody nagged me about getting my homework done. Of course, if I showed up with anything but As and Bs on a report card, I caught holy hell.

These days, every game, every recital, every pageant, is a capital-E Event, parents in suits and dresses jostling for the best seats, cameras whirring, kids constantly looking from the stage or the court for their family in the stands. There are Brazilian supermodels who aren't photographed as often as a typical kid in the year 2012. In my entire childhood, I'm not sure I ever made it to video.

For all their wisdom and strengths, my parents, however, had one basic shortcoming: they weren't dog people. They didn't get dogs, didn't want dogs, and were forced to spend an outsized amount of their time battling my pleas to get a dog.

Like so many other kids, I had a fantasy of what it would be, me and my dog. I saw us sleeping together, eating together, walking together, playing together. I saw the dog doing great things for me and me doing great things for the dog. We would be best friends, inseparable soul mates. People would say, Wow, they even look alike, this boy and his dog. He'd be the one I'd confide in after a particularly tough day at school or a bad loss on the Little League diamond. I'd be the one he'd come to if his paw was ever sore or he had a sour stomach. It would be two as one, me and my dog.

Miraculously, when I was eleven or twelve, I wore them down. I don't know what put them over the edge or whether it was just the constancy of it all. But one day, my father told me we'd take a drive to the Weymouth dog pound to see what they had. I didn't know much then, but I certainly knew this: a father doesn't take his son to the pound and come away empty-handed.

The Weymouth dog pound was at the end of a dead-end street next to the town incinerator, back when towns had incinerators. We walked inside, and I realized it was nothing more than a glorified garage with hard, unforgiving floors and unromantic cages lining the walls. I'm not sure exactly what I had expected, but it wasn't that. In those cages were dogs—big dogs, small dogs, silent dogs, loud dogs, young dogs, and old dogs. I paced every cage, analyzing every dog, taking note of who approached the metal wire and who hung back in the shadows, who seemed hyperactive and who seemed calm. There was another variable that kept entering my mind: who was particularly adoptable and who wasn't. To that last point, I kept focusing on a mangy German shepherd mix who simply sat alone in a cage with a vacant look, so skinny you could see every one of his ribs. As I methodically made my rounds, I kept coming back to one thought: if I didn't take the shepherd, nobody would. Every kid that age lives a hero fantasy. That dog would rescue me from a life of boredom, and I would rescue him from a life of confinement.

"Him?" my father said, surprised, when I pointed to the skinny, gangly mutt.

"He's the one," I said. My father swallowed hard, signed a form, and we were off, me and this reticent dog sharing the backseat for the short ride home.

It was the Saturday of Easter weekend, which meant I could spend that entire first day doing nothing but tending to my new dog. It was pure bliss, or at least mostly bliss. Sure, he might have been a little aloof, even skittish, but those things would pass. He'd get comfortable. He'd accept what I was offering. It would be everything I imagined, and more.

Sunday came, and we had to leave for Easter dinner at my aunt's. It broke my heart to leave him, even if he didn't really seem to care. The return home couldn't come soon enough, and I was the first to rush from the car into the house, and it was there and then that I saw my world, my future, in tatters in front of me.

My mother was the next one to come inside. "Oh my God," she said, oddly calm in her delivery. My father came next. I could actually see his jaw drop. My sister Colleen just kind of snickered and slipped off to her room.

The dog, my dog, had somehow opened the cabinet door to the trash barrel under the sink. I knew he was smart. He'd dragged the barrel across the kitchen and into the breezeway, where he had knocked it over onto the blue rug. There he had proceeded to eat whatever was edible, and tried to eat what was not. The result was a room strewn with half-consumed trash, bile, vomit, and feces. For good measure, the dog had also ripped a gigantic hole in the rug.

My mother simply began crying. My father began picking up. The dog cowered in a corner, even though no one was saying anything to him. The next day, over my muted objections, he was gone, back to the pound. My parents worked hard. Money was never plentiful. Time was always valuable. I understood why he had to go, even if I didn't like it.

We never talked about another dog again, but in that silence, my desire only grew more intense.

* * *

Animals and kids generally like me. Maybe I'm supposed to say something different. Maybe I'm supposed to act coy about it. But it's been the way of my life.

My oldest sister, Carole, had her first child when I was in high school, an utterly delightful kid named Matthew whom I took under my wing when he was just a few weeks old. By the time he was a toddler, I was tossing him in the backseat of my beat-up Toyota Corolla and merrily lugging him all over town—on errands, to pickup basketball games, just hanging out with friends. When he was ten years old or so and I was in my twenties writing for a newspaper in New Haven, Connecticut, he came down and visited me for a weekend and I bought him a set of golf clubs with money I didn't actually have, starting him on a lifelong pursuit.

My first trip to my ex-wife's grandmother's house in Pennsylvania, there was a cousin there with a particularly problematic son. "A nightmare" is how one relative described him. He threw constant fits featuring shouts and tears. During one of those loud sessions, when the tired, frustrated mother simply shut him in a room away from everyone else, I slipped in and asked what was wrong.

"Nobody ever listens to me," he said.

I doubted that; he didn't really give anyone any choice. But I said, "I am."

He looked surprised, as if he didn't know what to do, until I suggested that we read. I pulled out a book called *The Berenstain Bears,* and as I read the words aloud, I quizzed him on the pictures.

"El—e—phant," he was saying slowly when his shocked mother opened the door and saw the two of us sitting together on the floor.

Then there are animals. I pretend not to like cats, but as a boy growing up in the proudly working-class suburb of Weymouth just south of Boston, my parents wouldn't let me have another dog, so cats were what I had. I had one tiger cat, Kitty, who used to follow me to school many days, hang around outside biding time, then follow me back home. Calico, my all-time favorite, disappeared for months, only to return quite a bit chubbier than she'd been before she left. We all assumed that she had been in the company of a kindly person with a heavy hand on the Meow Mix, but that notion was put to rest on the early summer morning when she laid down beneath the bushes next to our sun-splashed patio and delivered nine kittens, each a soaking wet ball of fur. Then, one after another, she took the kittens by the scruff in her mouth, waited at the side door for me to open it, and purposefully walked through our small Colonial, up the front stairs, into my room, and under my bed, where she deposited her offspring before heading outside for another. She kept them there until she couldn't care for them anymore, which is when she gave me a look that said, "Get these things out of my life."

Then there was the first golden retriever I ever had, even if he was never actually mine. My first job at the *Globe* was on the South Shore of Boston, in a small suburban bureau about thirty minutes from downtown. I loved it, even as I spent all of my energy working as hard as I possibly could to get promoted to the city room. I loved seeing my name in the paper I'd grown up reading. I loved covering the area of the state that was part of my soul. I loved fulfilling what was pretty much my only career ambition, to write for the *Globe,* even as I wanted to go higher and higher up the writing chain. The first Sunday morning I had a story in print, my parents woke up early, turned the pages to find my byline, and cried.

I also loved the fact there was a store called the Docktor Pet Center about two minutes from the office in the Hanover Mall, where I'd head every lunchtime to look through the plate-glass window at the dogs in their depressing cages looking back at me. When I wasn't trying to be a big-time writer in the main newsroom, I was dreaming of walking a dog of my very own around my fair city.

One dog in particular caught my attention, first and foremost because of his breed—golden retriever—and second because he didn't seem to be going anyplace fast for reasons I couldn't comprehend. The dog was absurdly handsome, with dark, reddish, slightly curly fur and an expressive face that stared out the grates of the cage, begging me to take him home. I showed up day after day to see him, communing through the glass, until one afternoon the manager of the store asked if I'd like to play with him.

"Love to," I said, more than a little startled. "But I just want to warn you, I can't have a dog now. It's in my lease. I don't have the time—"

I would have still been there stammering out excuses, but he cut me off and said, "No worries, just play with him for a bit. You'll be doing us a favor. Poor guy has been stuck in there a lot longer than he's supposed to."

The nice man led me into what was called the "Love Room," a small square with linoleum floors, bare walls, a small dog bed, and a couple of folding chairs. It felt more like the visitation room at a medium-security prison. "I'll be right back," he said.

I stood, inexplicably nervous, waiting. A moment later he popped back in with the puppy dangling over one arm and placed him gently on the floor. It was like meeting someone famous whom you had seen only in pictures or the pages of newspapers or magazines. You knew what they looked like, but you didn't know what they were really like, and when they came to life right in front of you, it was a jolt. I had stood outside the glass six, maybe eight, possibly ten different times just gazing at this wonderful creature. I had spent that time imagining life with me and this dog, the walks we would take in the mornings, the evenings that we would spend on some vast and empty field, the time we would while away together, the people we would see, the places we would be, always him and I, together. But I'd always had the glass separating us, just as I always had reality keeping my dreams at bay, and now here we were, able to reach out and touch each other.

"You perfect little boy!" I said, as soon as the manager retreated to the main part of the store.

That perfect little boy wasted no time. He could have acted aloof. He could have gone and lay down on the bed, thinking to himself, *Finally, a comfortable place to sleep outside of the goddamned metal grates of that punitive cage.* What he did, though, was urgently scamper to me, jump determinedly up onto my leg, and make every possible effort to climb into my lap.

I lifted him up, laughing. Apparently he was having similar thoughts looking at me as I did looking at him. Once on my lap, he burrowed his face into my chest. He kept burrowing and burrowing, as if he were trying to reach my heart, until there was no place else to go, and then he went completely slack. He was heavier than I had imagined, and stronger. The manager came in with a stuffed dog toy, which he tossed on the floor. I whispered into his ear, "What's that?" and he popped his head out, saw the toy, and retrieved it. We played for half an hour or so, him fetching, then resting on my lap, until I had to get back to my job.

We did that almost every day for the next few weeks, my time with my sort of dog. He'd be staring toward the door, seemingly looking for me, when I walked in, pawing at his cage the moment he saw me. I'd almost be running to get into the little room for my twenty minutes of dog Zen. We did this as he outgrew his small puppy cage and had to be moved to the larger cages normally reserved for the shepherds and Saint Bernards. We did it on Saturdays, when I'd make a special ride to the suburbs to see him. We did it until the day I walked in and my curly, red-furred friend wasn't in his usual spot.

I walked up and down the aisles, slowly, trying to be calm, peering into all the other cages, wondering if they had just moved him to clean his spot, but no. I poked my head into the empty puppy room to see if they had put him there ahead of my arrival, but again, no. I stood there staring blankly at my reflection in the glass, convincing myself to be happy that my dog had probably been bought by some kind owner with a big yard and a happy family but not exactly thrilled that I'd never gotten the chance to say good-bye. All around me, I suddenly noticed the harsh sounds of the pet store—exotic birds squawking, the water in the fish tanks gurgling, dogs barking. I was standing there when the manager approached with a grim look.

"Someone bought the golden?" I asked, trying to sound upbeat. I wasn't sure of the answer I wanted to get back.

He shook his head, his expression still flat. "He's in a crate in the back. He's been diagnosed with a skin condition called seborrhea. We're not going to be able to sell him, so we're sending him back to the breeder."

Breeder? First of all, that was a joke. Anyone and everyone knows that pet store dogs come from rancid mills in the Midwest, where there was pretty much a 100 percent chance that they would kill the dog within the hour he arrived, if, in fact, they were even sending him there.

"What do you want for him?" I asked. My heart started beating faster as the question came forth.

"If you want him, just take him," he said. Before I could say anything else, he was already walking toward the back of the store, as if he had been waiting for my visit. He returned with the fat, happy puppy in both arms, grabbed a leash off a wall rack, and handed them both to me.

"Good luck," he said in a way that indicated he knew something I didn't. I clipped the leash to the dog's collar, and we walked out of the store into a hot June Friday. It occurred to me, from the way his snout went high into the air, taking in every possible smell in the parking lot, to the way his feet barely touched the ground as he clomped along like a Clydesdale horse, that it was the first time in his entire life that he had been in the great outdoors.

I took him straight back to the office, where I needed to finish a story on deadline, and he sprawled out beside me on the soft blue carpet, seemingly in disbelief over his sudden good fortune. I took him in the car to Pennsylvania that night to visit the woman who would later become my first wife. I took him up all five floors to my studio apartment, him pausing on the landing to give me a look that said, "This is nuts."

Then I worked the phones. I rang up friends, acquaintances, anyone I knew, and told them I had an amazing dog that needed a great home. Spread the word: a $600 dog for free.

Almost immediately, I got a call back with interest from two married reporters from another newspaper with a bunch of sons who had been begging and pleading with them for a dog. I took my unnamed puppy down to their house, a nice place a block from the ocean with a fenced-in yard, and they fell instantly in like—so much so that they wanted him right there and then. I asked for a few moments to say good-bye.

"You're going to love it here, you good boy," I whispered to him as the parents and kids probably looked on from the window. He seemed to sense that something was strange and locked his eyes on mine.

"And if you ever need anything from me—anything—I'll be here in a snap. Just bark."

Which is exactly what he did as I walked out the gate, the mother gripping his collar with every ounce of strength she had. He barked. He cried. He lunged. He couldn't believe what was happening, and as I looked back, neither could I.

Two weeks later, I got a call from the mother. I sensed a tinge of desperation in her voice as she invited me to come and visit "Tito," the name they had apparently given him. "I think he really misses you," she said.

I got there that afternoon. The boys were playing Wiffle ball in the yard. Tito was on a chain stuck to a tree, just out of reach of the game, lying down in the dirt, bored out of his brain. When he saw me, he charged in my direction until the chain snapped him violently back. When I took him down to the nearby beach, nobody really seemed to mind.

This scene repeated itself just about weekly, until I got another call from the mother months later. She didn't sound desperate this time but hesitant. "We're going to have to bring Tito to the pound," she said. "We just don't have time for him with the kids."

"I'll be right down," I said. And not for the first time, it was me and Tito, together, on a moment's notice. It wasn't the family's fault. They just didn't know what they were getting into, and in my more honest moments, I had to admit that young Tito, with his single-minded devotion to me, may not have been the easiest dog on the planet.

And devoted he was. He ignored the world to focus on me. He liked nothing more than to walk beside me down a city street. At the beach, if another dog approached, he'd chase him away in a flurry of barks and growls. He would allow nothing to get between us. So this time, I was a little more selective with offers and careful with placement. A friend of a cousin in Newport, Rhode Island, was in the market. I took him down. It was encouraging. Their house was beautiful, with a rolling lawn and a shop on-site that was the family's scuba gear business. The family said they would install an invisible fence. They said the dog would have free rein. They said there would be someone there virtually every moment of every day, including their six-year-old son, who had been begging for a dog. I left him there after another long hug and the same whispered promise: just bark and I'll be back. This time he didn't. I think he may have been too shocked.

Weeks later, I got another call, and when I heard the new owner on the other end of the line, I girded for more bad news. "You've changed our lives," the wife said. "We love him in a way we never knew we could." The next summer, I was driving through Newport and my car naturally found itself on their street, in front of their house. There was Tito, renamed Chips, sprawled out on the crest of the lawn, watching the world around him. I stopped. He stared. I walked. His tail thumped. I got to within ten yards, and he exploded in my direction, blinking, whining, flinging himself at me. We played for half an hour, and when I left, he couldn't have seemed more content to stay. He lived another twelve years, a wonderful life with wonderful people.

While Chips was still alive, I moved apartments in Boston. I married. My job became more stable. Then I got Harry, the single nicest warm-blooded creature I will ever know. All of which is a long way of saying that I've always gotten along famously with dogs. I've done great with cats and even do all right with kids. There wasn't a reason in this world to believe that this wouldn't, couldn't, and shouldn't continue.

> 11 <

In retrospect, perhaps I took it for granted that Pam's kids and I would quickly settle into a fun, familiar relationship, one of easy jokes and advice or just a little bit of sanctuary from the stresses of modern day childhood. I pictured them accompanying me on errands, driving around in the cart when I played golf, happy to go to the movies or for ice cream or just to the coffee shop, the atmosphere around us always light and free. I didn't want to be their father. They had one of those already, a very good and involved one. I wanted to play a role that, twenty years from now, they'd look back at and thank their lucky stars that they'd had.

And why wouldn't it become this? History said it would, given what I had with nephews and friends' kids and the animals—especially Harry. A good relationship with Pam's kids seemed more destiny than uncertainty. Add the fact that they were terrific kids, outgoing, scary smart, opinioned, adorable—they were no wallflowers with constantly runny noses just looking to bide their time.

But a funny thing happened on the way to stepparenthood: reality. Take, for instance, Memorial Day weekend. I've always loved Memorial Day for what it's come to represent, which is, ironically, beginnings, the first true weekend of the blissful summer season, warmer days, longer nights, hot dogs on the grill, the cold water of a hose cleaning sand off the bottoms of your feet. I suggested to Pam weeks ahead of time that we load the kids and the dogs into the car and spend the upcoming Memorial Day weekend at my little house on the southern coast of Maine. It sits a mile or so from a wide, soft-sand beach with calm water and minnows and many darting crabs, perfect for little girls exactly that age.

"That sounds great," Pam said. "Let me just get the kids on board."

When I was a kid, we were simply placed on board, but I was quickly learning that that's not how it works anymore. Life with children is one long lobbying campaign, not only on the hard stuff like homework and household chores but also on what should have been the fun stuff. Some kids have so many appealing options these days that they need help getting excited about anything anymore.

I heard nothing, then still nothing, and I hesitated about asking. A few days out, Pam, harried, told me on the phone, "The kids really want to have a relaxing weekend around the house. I think they're so sick of running back and forth between their father's and here, they just want to stay put."

I knew, Pam knew, that the kids could have had an exquisitely relaxing weekend in Maine, only with the ocean thrown into the mix, and clam shacks and cool breezes and sand castles, as well as an outdoor shower and freeze pops on the back deck overlooking the woods. But how do you convince a couple of vocal, strong-willed kids of something that they don't yet know? And how do you prevail upon their mother, by nature a conciliator, not a dictator, to take matters into her own hands? The answer, if you're me, meaning the outsider in this closely held group, was simple: you don't.

"We don't want to hold you up," Pam told me sincerely. "If you had your heart set on Maine, you should go. You've been under so much pressure at work, you could use the time up there."

All that was true, right down to having my heart set on Maine. But I wanted to demonstrate my commitment to this new life, to show that I was capable of thinking of something outside my own skin, as aberrant as that was for me. So I stayed put, determined to make the best of it and not think about my vacant slice of Nirvana to the north.

There was something else at play in my decision to stay, something as real as it was difficult to grasp. I would regularly bemoan all that those kids—and many, many others like them—were given in this life, whether it be sizable houses or virtually every toy that they momentarily desired or vacations to exotic places and luxury resorts. Hope, ambition, gratitude, and wonder lose proportion when you have so much so young. But there was a burden they carried on the other side of life's ledger and that many of their friends did as well, a burden most from my childhood didn't have to confront: divorced parents.

Both girls were reasonably cognizant when their mother and father parted ways. Suddenly Mom was in a house ten minutes away, and soon enough, that rental house became one of their two homes. They were old enough, and certainly astute enough, to see that Mom and Dad were two very different people who didn't get along particularly well. Still, I have no doubt that they harbored the common view and dream of a joyous reunion, everyone together again in the old happy home. My presence, of course, ruined their ability to dream that dream. I was, despite my best efforts, an inherent part of the confusion that must have been unfolding in their minds. Add to that the daily complications of being the products of divorced parents. There were complicated schedules that baffled even me in terms of who was where on this Wednesday or next, or which house on which Monday holiday, or the number of back-and-forths over the annual Christmas-to-New-Year's break. There were different rules in each house, different moods, different expectations. Every few days, they were moving, packing bags, kissing animals good-bye, bidding their mother teary farewells. No wonder they wanted to stay put.

On the Sunday of Memorial Day weekend, there was near-record heat. It wasn't just a little hot but blistering hot, a shock to your system, which was more used to the cool spring temperatures of New England. Young Abigail awoke hell bent on fishing, and there wasn't a cuter kid, or a more inspiring vision, than that nine-year-old in tall rubber boots and shorts, a ballcap pulled low over her head, explaining the new casting strategy she wanted to unveil that day. She tied her own knots. She handled her own worms. When she caught a fish, she gamely grabbed it in her two hands and pulled the hook out of its mouth.

So we were off after breakfast, in pursuit first of bait and then of a place to cast it, adults in the front, the kids in the middle row, and the two excited dogs panting from the back of Pam's SUV. If any vision of Chevy Chase in the movie *Vacation* entered my mind, I quickly batted it out. The day took us farther into exurbia, to towns I had never been in before, and I thought I had been just about everywhere. We stopped at gas stations looking for bait, sporting goods stores, and finally at a massive Walmart superstore, where we found success. The two kids and their mother returned to the car not only with a Styrofoam container of worms but also with directions to a fishing hole that had garnered rave reviews from the knowledgeable people inside.

"It's going to be the best fishing we've ever had," Abigail announced.

Not that I was keeping track, but we had already been in the car for an hour—just enough time to have gotten us to the Maine border. The nameless pond was supposed to be about twenty minutes away, so off we went.

About forty minutes later, we were still looking. The kids were getting hungry. The dogs, in the way back, were panting up a storm. The driver was getting (uncharacteristically) frustrated. The mother was trying to hold everything together. "Perfect weather for fishing," Pam said.

Finally, mercifully, we came across a body of water upon whose shores some older men were sitting in folding chairs holding rods and reels. I swerved to the side of a relatively busy road. The dogs were agitated, thinking they were going swimming. The kids, particularly Abigail, were hesitant, theorizing that the lake didn't look as though it held much promise. The sun was pounding down. Cars were flying by.

"It's beautiful," I said, my gaze looking past the discarded soda cans and candy wrappers that had been tossed into the water by obnoxious motorists. "Let's just give it a little try," I said, and I swear, I think my voice might have cracked from the pressure.

Mercifully, everyone agreed. I calmed the dogs down. Pam walked the kids across the street, looking adorable with their rods slung over their little shoulders. We found a stretch of shore that seemed to have a little less muck and litter than anywhere else, Abigail and Pam tied worms to the lines, and they cast.

It was amazing to me how insects so large, so bulbous from feasting on human blood, could fly so quickly and sting so sharply as the omnipresent mosquitoes and greenheads that seemed to be having a convention at this roadside pond just west of nowhere. Abigail gamely continued to cast, the hook pretty much coming within an inch of my eyes on every toss. The traffic seemed heavy for a holiday Sunday. And Caroline began to have a meltdown about twenty minutes after we got there, which was actually fine, because I was at risk of having one myself. The fish, not for nothing, were all somewhere else.

I was trying my level best to live in the moment, to revel in exactly where we were. But it was suffocating. I actually felt short of breath, and my mind kept roaming north, to Maine, to the soft fields and wide open stretches of Goose Rocks Beach. Had we left this morning at the same time we had embarked on this fishing expedition, we would not only have been there, but we also could have changed into our bathing suits and been standing knee deep in refreshing ocean water, a salty breeze whispering through our hair.

"Owwww! Shit!" That was Pam, smacking her palm against her neck to kill an insect so heavy it actually made a sound when it fell dead to the ground. Caroline had her head down, basically accepting her miserable plight. Somebody beeped from a pickup truck and yelled, "You got a fishing license?"

"We need to get some food in you," Pam said to Caroline, her hand absently rubbing her back, and just like that, after a ninety-minute ride, after no more than thirty minutes of fishing, we packed up the tackle boxes, the cooler, the worms, and the rods and trudged through the heat back to the car. I started to wonder, with no small amount of fear, what was on tap for the next day.

"It's all about blood sugar levels," Pam explained in the

front seat as Caroline balled up in her car seat behind us. "Kids need to eat constantly, or the levels plunge and they crash. It's my fault for not bringing more food."

Next stop was a Bertucci's about ten minutes down the road. If there's a more depressing place than a chain pizza restaurant in the middle of a ninety-five-degree afternoon on a holiday weekend, I hadn't been there yet, though I was sure I'd see it soon, maybe even tomorrow.

The waitress was perky. Caroline was despondent. Abigail was frustrated about not catching fish. Pam was apologetic. And I was doing my level best not to scream for help, for someone, anyone, to take me by the hand and show me the way back to my once straightforward life.

One thing I was slowly learning is that as quickly as things unravel, they can come back together all over again. Best I can tell, tantrums and episodes leave no residue. As Caroline got food into her system, her adorable face began to rise. She was coming back to life, and it was kind of amazing to witness.

"Hey, Abs," she said, chewing on the piece of bruschetta that she was waving in her hand. "We should have thrown the line out farther into the lake. That's where the fish are."

Abigail agreed, providing her veteran analysis on why the fish hadn't come close to shore: they had undoubtedly been avoiding all the litter that clogged the little dirt beach. Maybe next time we should rent a canoe, or even a little motorboat, to take us farther out and into more fertile ground.

"Maybe we can go again tomorrow," she said, Caroline

nodding, as if everyone had had a perfectly wonderful time.

When we finally got home that afternoon (we could have been tucking into soft-serve cones at the Goose Rocks Dairy in Maine), the kids leaped from the car, shouting, "Buddy, Buddy!" as the bird bounced down from the front stoop and greeted them in the yard with every one of her clucks and caws.

"You were so good to wait for us," Caroline said.

"We love you, Buddy," Abigail told the bird.

Ah, to be that bird.

After I lugged Pam's air conditioners up from the basement and we wedged them into the windows, after I told two exhausted kids a bedtime story about a magic beach ball that floated from Maine all the way to Greenland, I sat in Pam's kitchen mindlessly spooning Brigham's chocolate chip ice cream into my sunburned face. Pam walked in, quietly, sleepy-eyed, wearing her trademark scrubs and T-shirt.

"Not what you had in mind for your Memorial Day weekend, I know," she said.

She was absolutely right, but there was no polite way to agree, so with uncharacteristic tact, I remained quiet.

"Sometimes this is just what it is to have kids," Pam said. "You go with the flow, even when it's not flowing anywhere you would normally want to be." She paused to push her hair out of her face and added, "Believe it or not, the kids had a fun day today, because they were with us, and even if they don't say it, some part of them appreciates the fact that you were there for them."

She kissed me softly on the lips and headed up to bed, leaving me in the netherworld between the old and the new, between selfishness and selflessness, between what I had and what I wanted. The next day, we would get up and do it all over again, and the day after that, and the week after that, and the year after that.

Was I ready? Were they?

I staggered over to the couch, stretched out, and imagined that the window fan was an ocean breeze in Maine.

>12<

I pulled up to Pam's house one summer's eve to an all-American scene—well, an all-American scene plus a pampered chicken. The kids were trotting and galloping around the front yard, leaping over miniature painted horse jumps set up along an elaborate course. The two dogs were sprawled in the grass, taking stock of another hard day of being canine. And Pam was cradling Buddy in her arms as she ran her hands up and down her feathers. Something in the way she was looking at Buddy—inspecting her, really—made me ask if everything was all right, and I tried my level best to hide any hint of hope in my voice.

"Go look at the note from the cleaning lady on the top of the refrigerator," Pam replied, her voice as flat as a board.

In an otherwise clean house, I found a barely legible, three-line note written on the back of a discarded envelope that said, "We fed some cheese to your rooster. Hope it's okay. Back in two weeks."

I pushed open the screen door and sat on the stoop beside Pam, just far enough away that the bird couldn't peck my eyes out. "I don't get it," I said. "I thought Buddy liked cheese."

Pam shot me a look of mild annoyance. Then she lowered her voice so the kids couldn't hear and said, "The rooster part. Didn't you see she called Buddy a rooster?"

I hadn't noticed, but what's the big deal? To some people, probably to most people, the words are interchangeable. Rooster, hen, chicken, dinner—they're all an unholy mess.

"They don't know the difference," I said.

Pam may well be the smartest person I have ever met, with an outsized brain on constant overdrive tucked inside a very attractive head. If her mind were a lightbulb, it would actually be a floodlight. She graduated near the top of her class from the University of Pennsylvania. She graduated near the top of her class from the University of Pennsylvania School of Veterinary Medicine. But what was most impressive about her, what set her apart from any other person I've ever met with that kind of intellectual wattage, was that she was well aware of what she didn't know.

That became apparent yet again when she said, "The cleaning lady is from Brazil. Brazilians know the difference between roosters and hens."

As she spoke, her hands kept traversing the very happy bird, feeling the comb on his/her head, his/her wattle, his/

her narrow frame, and—good God—his/her private area. "Chickens have all their genitalia on the inside, so it's impossible to tell," Pam said matter-of-factly, still in a low voice.

"She's never crowed in the morning," I said.

"I know. That's good. But maybe she just hasn't started yet. Now I'm thinking of every little sound she makes, these strange little barks I've heard lately." She paused again, held the chicken slightly away from her as they gazed bizarrely into each other's eyes, and said, "The kids will be devastated."

Yes, they would. I could already picture the scene: Abigail and Caroline giving good old Buddy one last kiss on the side of his manly little face as Pam placed him in the car and drove off to Happy Acres Poultry Farm, where he would live out his life exactly as he should—in the company of a couple of hundred other chickens, eagerly performing his roosterly duties in the name of commerce and the future of the flock. The kids would cry. The bird would be clucking. I'd have to tell everyone that he's going to have a great life with all his little chicken friends, then I'd help wipe away the tears, bring them inside, and heat up some chicken fingers for lunch.

"Why are you smiling?" Pam suddenly asked.

Huh? What? "Oh, I, uh, was just thinking about all the good times the kids have had with Buddy. I'm sure they'll go on for another fifteen years."

"God, I hope so," she said. And she said it like she meant it, the scariest part of all.

"How do you find out about the sex for sure?" I asked.

Pam put Buddy on the ground. She stared at me for a long moment and let out an aggressive-sounding squawk— the bird, not the girlfriend. Then she turned around and trotted off toward the kids in that side-to-side dinosaur gait that she had.

"You wait and see if she starts sprouting a crown and begins crowing, which could be any day now. Or you do a sexing test."

I didn't even want to know.

*   *   *

It's not every day that a chicken struts into the refined environs of the Back Bay Veterinary Clinic on fashionable Newbury Street in Boston, what with its exposed beams and espresso-colored walls and doctors who look as though they could be starring in a weekly television drama on Fox called *Cats and Dogs*. Pam's clinic has had its share of exotic animals and other assorted pets with unusual problems, ferrets, pythons, a macaw, an iguana that swallowed its master's underwear. But a chicken, even a Rhode Island White that could have been on the cover of *Martha Stewart Living*? No, a chicken was breaking new ground for this city clinic.

Pam loaded Buddy into the car that morning, which was not difficult because Buddy had become something of a fan of Sunday drives—or any-day-of-the-week drives, for that matter. She would settle on a pile of quilts that Pam had placed on the front passenger seat for the dual purpose of making her comfortable and giving her enough height to gaze out the window at the shocked and amused motorists in the other cars. Buddy probably didn't even care what people were honking and pointing at.

At the clinic, the vets and the techs cooed at Buddy far more than she cooed back at them. She peered around suspiciously with a look that said, *What the hell am I doing here?* Pam carried her back to the prep room, where an uncommonly capable doctor named Beth Waisburd and a smart and gentle technician named Kali Pereira were waiting with a textbook opened to the section that explained how to draw blood from a chicken. Ends up, the book explained, you have to hold the chicken upside down by the legs to make sure it doesn't move or variously peck, and then insert the needle into its wings.

Okeydokey. Kali whisked her up in her arms, grabbed hold of her skinny, rubbery legs, and there she hung, shocked, confused, and defenseless as Beth found just the right place on her feathery wing to insert the needle. Just like that, it was done. The bird squawked. The staff smiled, and Buddy got a fresh bowl of cracked corn, which she ravenously pecked at on the floor of the clinic.

The blood was then carefully placed in a tube, which was tucked into a ziplock bag, which was placed into a padded overnight envelope, which was shipped to a laboratory in Canada that would determine whether the sample came from a male or a female. I'm betting some poor bespectacled guy in a white lab coat would be as baffled about receiving a tube of chicken blood for a sexing test as I was in having a chicken sitting near me on a couch while I watched preteen television shows with two tired girls.

For weeks after that, Pam waited. She would check her computer numerous times each day to see if IDEXX Laboratories in Canada had reported back. It was the first thing she did in the morning and the last thing she did before going to bed at night. In between, she constantly gave Buddy the once-over, looking for any new signs of gender: soft crowing, mild aggression, or the slight desire to, say, lay an egg. But Buddy held her cards close to her chest, and the nice people at IDEXX were taking their sweet time. Nothing short of Buddy's future was riding on the results. If Buddy was a hen, it meant she was good to go as a lovable lifelong pet, pecking around the yard, squawking at the door, and being fussed over by two adoring kids. The girls wouldn't bid it farewell until they were turning to leave for college, where they would smile constantly as their roommates and friends repeatedly asked, "You have a what for a pet?"

A rooster? That was an entirely different story—perhaps a better story, depending on your perspective. Roosters were loud. Roosters could be aggressive. Roosters might hurt children and bug the living hell out of neighbors. Roosters didn't quite fit into a regular house in a standard suburban neighborhood, all of which meant that Buddy might find himself living a more—how shall I say it—

traditional rooster life. Think of a distant, rural town, a farm populated by many other creatures that looked and acted just like him. I'm not so sure he'd like that, which somehow made me like it even more.

Days turned into weeks. Weeks became a month. I was wondering what business IDEXX was actually in when Pam's cell phone rang. The young woman from Pam's office had no idea how much anticipation had been built up, the hope and fears riding on this one piece of information, and simply announced, "You've got yourself a rooster." And there you have it. Brazilians know their birds.

When Pam called me at work, I could vaguely make out the word "rooster" through the sniffles and tears. "The results came back?" I asked, seeking clarity.

"Yes," she said, slightly annoyed now. "Buddy's a rooster."

Do not smile. Do not laugh. Do not attempt a rooster joke.

Do not shout. Do not sing. Do not weep with joy.

I told her calmly that things would work out. Everything would be all right. That night, Pam sat the girls down at the kitchen table and informed them of the news. Abigail was the one who'd brought Buddy into this world. She was the one who'd had the idea for the science fair project. She was the one who watched Buddy more closely than anyone else, who drew Buddy pictures at school, who could cluck like Buddy, walk like Buddy, capture Buddy when she ran and hid under a table or chair because she realized somebody was going to make her go back outside.

She was also the one, on that night, who promptly burst into tears, opening the way for her mother and sister to cry as well. That was the scene I walked in on as I arrived at their house after work.

"Guys, I'm so sorry," I said, doing my absolute best to act it. "But you've got to know, Buddy's going to be really happy for many, many years to come, happy with all his chicken friends."

"Tests can be wrong!" Abigail kept repeating through her tears, her words a mix of anger and sadness. "It happens all the time. They get the test wrong."

* * *

For a while, it was dead chicken walking—though the chicken didn't actually know it. No, the chicken was getting even more of the royal treatment than he was used to, and I don't think either of us thought that was possible.

The kids were constantly summoning him inside, positioning him between them as they watched television, stroking him as he clucked around the floor, allowing him to peck at a bowl of corn in the kitchen as they ate their own macaroni-and-cheese dinners. "We love you so much, Boo-Boo" became the refrain of the day, often said in chorus. I just kept waiting, never saying anything, knowing this was headed—perhaps not as fast as I'd expected—toward an inevitable departure.

One morning I woke up in suburbia at what seemed

like first light. The kids were at their father's house for the weekend. There was an odd sound floating into the bedroom window from the garage, something between a moan and a bark, like a space alien missing his home planet a thousand galaxies away.

"The hell is that?" I said, mostly to myself, but Pam, wide awake beside me, answered.

"Buddy's finding his voice," she said. She said it without seeming particularly upset about it, not sad, not frantic, not anything. Actually, she was kind of clinical in the way she can sometimes be when she gets into Dr. Bendock mode.

Come to think of it, the gloom that had engulfed the Buddy situation in the first hours and days after the results came back seemed to have lifted, until it suddenly disappeared. The renewed urgency in finding Buddy a home had drifted toward complacency. Shortly after the news, Pam began burning up the phone lines again. In desperation, she reached out to the local author of a book titled *Tillie Lays an Egg,* Terry Golson. Terry trained her hens like dogs, set up an elaborate backyard system of protected pens, and fired up what she calls a HenCam, allowing visitors to her website to watch her chickens frolic in their home. For Buddy, though, she had foreboding news. She told Pam she couldn't take an outside rooster into her flock and it would be very unlikely that anyone else would, either. There were too many disease risks and too high a chance that a sexually jacked-up newcomer could change the dynamics of any situation. It sounded like college.

Terry was right. Drumlin Farm, the Massachusetts Audubon sanctuary located about ten minutes from Pam's house, said no dice, as did Codman Community Farms, a perfectly wonderful place located nearby. Somebody at one of the farms went so far as to say, "You should probably just put the rooster down." That person, quite obviously, didn't know Pam.

But as I said, the sadness, the hand-wringing angst, it all just kind of dissipated, and in its place was Buddy doing what he always had: frolicking in the yard, moseying through the bushes in search of ticks and other bugs, pecking at the door when he thought there might be something better going on inside, which was quite often. And as always, at the end of the day, he headed to the safety of the high shelf in the garage for a good night of sleep. The kids didn't seem so mournful. Pam wasn't bringing up the topic with me nearly as much. It got to the point that when the actual sex certificate—I wish I could get one of those someday, by the way—arrived in the mail, declaring Buddy to be a full-fledged, hen-loving rooster, they posted it on the refrigerator door. Their worst fear was now a proud proclamation.

As I headed out with the dogs that morning, I hit the button on Pam's truck for the garage door, then stepped inside. The first thing I noticed that I hadn't seen before were the dark, heavy beach towels covering the three windows, undoubtedly to block out sunlight that would cause him to crow even earlier. I took a closer look at them and saw that Pam had actually nailed them to the walls. She meant business.

Buddy jumped from the shelf to the table, from the table to the chair, from the chair to the floor, in his well-practiced morning ritual. As he walked by me in his self-important way, he made a feint at a bobbing sidestep, then decided I wasn't worth it and marched out the door into the light. As I gazed at him waddling toward the dogs, an odd emotion washed over me, something that I imagine wouldn't be dissimilar to how a workaholic father must feel when he one day looks at his son and realizes he's not a boy but a young man, with stubble on his face and a deep voice, and he has no idea how or when that must have happened.

Buddy all of a sudden looked a lot like a rooster, and I don't believe I had ever seen a live, up-close rooster before. An agrarian I am not. But gone was the demure, henlike creature with the soft, rounded head and tentative gait. In its place was a minimonster with a broad chest, a cherry red comb sprouting atop its snow-white face, and a walk that oozed the kind of confidence a star lineman would have on his way across the field before the big game. Holy shit, I thought to myself, I may really and truly be stuck with this creature for life.

On more than a couple of occasions, I had come across Pam in the dim light of her computer screen at the end of a long day, staring at stories and journal articles about roosters. The life of a working single mother is nothing short of physically and emotionally exhausting. The children want her undivided attention. They are constantly scrambling and seeking more and more of their mother—more of her touch, more of her emotions, more of her time, her help, her words of praise and encouragement. Work, as in her veterinary clinic, is constantly in need of her, with veterinarians looking for input, the manager looking for insight, vet techs looking for guidance or time off, clients looking for her support and advice. Then there's me—let's go to a Red Sox game, let's have dinner, let's head to Maine. Of course, there's also herself and the need everyone has to spend some time in her own mind, sorting out the often frantic events of the moment and contemplating where it all goes from there.

I'd find her bleary-eyed, her blond hair mussed up, wearing her pale blue surgical scrubs just before bed, peering at a science journal discussing "rooster aggression" or on a website called My Pet Chicken reading a discussion about crowing roosters. I had assumed all of that would only further convince her that Buddy had to go, that it just wasn't normal, or even possible, to keep a crowing, growing rooster in a suburban house. I mean, hens were weird enough. Now, playing the silence over in my mind, the beach towels on the windows, the lack of gloom over Buddy's gender, it was becoming obvious that I was reading things all wrong. The tide had turned in Buddy's favor, and nobody had told me to pick up my beach blanket before it got all wet.

But don't panic. Never panic. That particular morning, I played fetch with the dogs. I got coffee. I had a few Dunkin' Munchkins in the car on the way back to Pam's house. It was a beautiful, summery day, one that carried endless possibilities, and I wasn't going to let it be shrouded by the fear of a loud, obnoxious animal hijacking the last remnants of normalcy in my fading urban life. Still, I needed clarity. I needed to understand my new reality. Only facts would allow me to create and assess options, and I was good—by dint of my career—at uncovering facts. When we pulled into the driveway, the dogs and I, Pam was sitting on the front stoop reading the morning paper. Buddy was sitting right beside her. As we walked toward her, Pam smiled and Buddy stood protectively, letting out a long *"Eeeeeeyowwwwwww."*

From a distance we talked about what we wanted to do that day, whether it was worth driving up to Maine, whether there were errands we should run, any open houses we should see on Sunday. That's when I reached inside myself and pulled out the obvious and inevitable question that needed to be asked: "What's the deal with the bird? I haven't heard you talk anymore about where he's going to end up."

Pam petted his feathers for a moment, her eyes away from mine. She said, "Nobody's going to take him, and I'm not going to put him down. And if you really think about it, why should we get rid of him in anticipation of a problem when those problems haven't come up yet?"

"What if he goes after your kids?" I asked, leading with my best cards first.

She looked up at me and said, without hesitation, "If he does, he's gone that day. You know I'm not going to mess around with that. But I've been researching roosters, and everywhere I look, it says that when you handle them a lot as chicks, they're far less inclined to be aggressive when they grow up."

Well, the three Bendock women certainly had the handling part pretty well covered. There are newborn babies that don't get handled as much as that bird.

"His bird poop?"

"It washes off. And it's great for the lawn."

I went in for the final thrust. Pam, you see, may be the most considerate person on the planet, which is probably why we do so well together—they say opposites attract. Anyway, she would never, ever intentionally do even the slightest thing that might anger or annoy or frustrate anyone else. So I asked, "What about the neighbors?"

The neighbors, as in the people living next to the crowing rooster, the people who may not be Boo-Boo friendly, people who would logically ask what on God's green earth we were doing keeping a screeching farm animal in the middle of a residential town. Couldn't she picture, in the neighborhood she lived in now, and after we eventually moved into our new house, the inevitable knock on the door, the neighborhood petition, the furious demands that we keep the peace? I had read about such people in stories in my very own newspaper, angry neighbors who took exception to the burgeoning backyard chicken movement, and those people were upset over hens. A rooster? Seriously, imagine having a rooster next door? Those people, aka my salvation. All I needed one was old curmudgeon. Or a young one. I'm not picky.

Pam paused. She looked at Buddy, then at me, and said, "We'll see."

*   *   *

And did we ever see. We saw Wendy and Lisa, Pam's across-the-street neighbors, come over constantly and play with Buddy. When they didn't come over, Buddy would sometimes stand at the edge of Pam's lawn and holler to them for attention. We saw one next-door neighbor constantly talking to Buddy along the fence. Pam arrived home early from work one day to find a young boy and his nanny in her backyard feeding Buddy bits of cheese, which, knowing this bird's luck, was probably imported.

The nanny told Pam that the boy barely communicated with anyone but every afternoon would say to her, "Buddy. Go see Buddy." When they met, Buddy would gently take the cheese as the boy talked up a storm to him, telling the bird about his day, his life, his dreams, Buddy clucking along in response.

Traffic gradually increased on Pam's street, which was bizarre, given that it was a dead end—or a cul-de-sac, as they call it in towns like hers. Drivers would slow to a near halt outside her house, searching for the snow-white bird with the red accessories. Sometimes he'd be sitting on the stoop. Other times he'd be pecking through the bushes. Still other times he might be napping on the lawn. Regardless, he was becoming a mini–tourist attraction, a local destination, a neighborhood mascot. Word of his presence filtered all through town, and not in a negative way.

Who was it who told me chickens were supposed to be stupid? Look at the size of their head, never mind the marble-sized brain within it. But as I was watching him, I had to say to myself, Here is one evil genius. He pecked at the door when we were inside, knowing full well that if he was annoying enough, he would inevitably be let in. When nobody was home, he'd just sit and wait on the front steps for someone, anyone, to get back. Whatever room we were in, he would stand outside the window and squawk. He would come when called, typically sprinting across the yard in his dinosaur run if it was Pam, whom he worshipped. He followed her around like a dog. He would eat out of a bowl, careful not to knock it over. And, most disturbing, he was always a total hamball for the right people, meaning the female people, and put on this calculated, goofy, adorable show. Of course, it only became more apparent how he felt about me. By midsummer, I had abandoned all hope of a valiant curmudgeon coming to the rescue. And despite how my script read, Buddy wasn't acting aggressive, at least toward Pam and the kids, and nobody in the house was losing any interest in him in the way that sometimes happens with pets.

"You know," Pam said, "Buddy has allowed us to get to know the neighbors. Without him, we just wave back and forth over long distances. With him around, we all talk. It's just another thing I love about him."

Oh, you little feathery doll. One day, when Pam was out doing errands and the kids were in the basement playing horses, I went online and Googled: average life span of a rooster.

Peck, peck, peck, peck.

All sorts of chicken websites spewed forth—chicken this and chicken that, farm journals, discussion groups, chicks-for-sale sites. My eyes were wide open at this whole new world that, like it or not, I was now part of.

Peck, peck, peck, peck, peck, peck, peck.

Buddy was knocking on the front door to get inside. It was growing louder as he grew impatient, longing for some more time with the kids.

He wasn't going to get me, though. I continued my search, smiling to myself, clicking open a site, scrolling to the part about roosters and longevity. That's when I almost keeled over: "A healthy, well-cared-for rooster can live to be 15 years or more."

PECK, PECK, PECK, PECK.

No, this can't possibly be right. Please, someone, somewhere, tell me this isn't right. Fifteen years? A chicken? What about the food chain? What about all those hawks that fly in the suburban sky? What about the coyotes that are supposedly taking over the state?

Please? Please!

PECK PECK PECK PECK PECK.

I had my head in my hands. I heard the girls' voices emerging from the basement, one of them exclaiming, "Poor Boo-Boo, c'mon inside." Then I heard the satisfied squawk of an entitled chicken in the front hallway.

This was not going as planned.

>13<

I'll never forget the only thought that rattled through my shocked brain the first time I walked down the rough-hewn path that snaked between a couple of weathered cottages and through the sand dunes, then stood on the white sands of Goose Rocks Beach looking out at the calm, crystal blue waters of the Maine coast.

Holy shit.

I'd never seen anything like it. There were no stones, no trash, no crowds, no blaring boom boxes, no Skee-Ball machines, no amusement park, no hot dog carts, no nothing except for powdery sand that squeaked underfoot, acre upon acre of firm, khaki-colored ocean floor revealed by the retreating tide, and a long sandbar that took people out to the wooded environs of Timber Island.

Experience would soon teach me that the only sounds in the early morning were the distant hum of lobster boats traversing the bay to pull up more traps, that the late-afternoon breeze always required a fleece, that you could walk a hundred yards into the absurdly clear—and cold—water at high tide and still be no deeper than your waist. It was a far, far cry from anything and everything I'd known as a kid, which was Nantasket Beach in Hull, Massachusetts, where Paragon Park and the 25-cent arcades were the backdrop, or Wessagusset Beach in my hometown of Weymouth, which was constantly being shut down for high fecal counts. I was, instantly and eternally, in love.

I was there courtesy of a close college friend, Peter Kelley, whose parents had the uncommon wisdom—and money—to buy a ramshackle cottage across the quiet street from the beach in 1961, then never let a renovator or designer anywhere near the place. He brought a group of us there the afternoon we graduated from school, so the "holy shit" moment was in every way a collective one.

My college friends and I would come to learn all the charms of Kennebunkport, most important and especially the back deck of the Arundel Wharf, the single nicest bar in America, where we would sip gin and tonics and ice-cold beers as whale-watching boats and fishing vessels navigated the tidal river at the day's end. We would stand there while the fizz of the tonic water tickled our sunburned wrists, until light gave way to dark, until polo shirts gave way to jackets, until there was barely a square inch of our legs that hadn't hosted a mosquito, all the while talking about the triumphs of our past and the dreams of our future and wondering how it could ever get any better than this.

It did, for most of us. There were marriages and promotions, births and successes, all recounted year after year when we got together on those same spots, whether the sands of Goose Rocks or the forgiving fairways of the Cape Arundel Golf Club or the welcoming environs of the Wharf, where the bartenders truly did know our names—and our favorite drinks. Somebody's wife or girlfriend once joked, "I don't know how you guys ever have any new stories to tell when you stand around all the time and talk about your past." But somehow there always were new stories, which only got better and funnier in the retelling.

I couldn't wait to introduce Harry to Kennebunkport back in the day. I didn't think it was possible for anyone to love Goose Rocks any more than I did, but he somehow topped me. He would dig in the sand, plow through the small waves, wade in the crystal waters, and sometimes just pad along the shore next to me with a ridiculous smile on his unfailingly handsome face. His presence led me to stay, year in, year out, for every summer of his ten-year life, in some of the most dated rental cottages along the beach, the only ones that would take a dog, but it didn't matter, because it was me and him in Maine and that's what counted most. We would be on the beach early in the morning. We would be back on the beach in the early evening. The women with us may have changed, when there were women with us at all, but we stayed the same. Always damp, he would ride shotgun in my car, nose out the window, breeze in his ears, lying in the doorways of stores in

Dock Square as I ran through whatever errands invariably poked into my days.

That last summer, August 2004, was at once the best and worst. I never knew joy and sorrow could be so intricately entwined. Harry was sick and getting sicker. I rented a beautiful new house about a mile or so from the beach for the whole month, a contemporary farm with a sprawling back deck overlooking forest and fields. We slowly walked Goose Rocks every morning, Harry merrily trudging beside me, a smile on his face, eyes squinting in the early sun. I don't imagine dogs can recall the past, but maybe so, and if they could, he was thinking of all those times from years gone by when he would be ripping across the sand, leaping to catch a long toss on the first bounce, swerving into the surf, paddling through the river, digging holes so deep that the only thing you could see was his tail and the constant whoosh of sand. He was such a different dog now, gray around his whole muzzle, mature beyond his years, drinking in the scenery, smelling the salt that filled the air.

Then we would sit in the soft sand by the dunes, Harry and I, in the warming sun. He would gaze toward the water, eye the younger dogs that were loping through the surf, make a feint at digging a hole but then quickly stop and look at me, somewhat amused, as if he were saying "Remember when?" If he could have said "Thank you," he would have. I could, so I did, hugging him close, his damp fur against the grain of my weathered polo, nuzzling his ear. "You're the best friend I'll ever have," I'd tell him again and again and again.

By the second week or so in Maine, I basically stopped doing anything else—no golf, no midday trips to the beach when he wasn't allowed, no long dinners out, no nights at the Wharf. I knew then what I know now: there would be a time, too soon in this life, when I would give anything I had to reach back and spend another hour with this incredible dog. I wanted to savor what I had left, and I wanted to be there for him after all the being there he'd given me.

One day, my mother and sister Carole, two of Harry's favorite people on the planet, arrived for a visit. When they walked through the French doors into the house, Harry literally dived under the coffee table and refused to move. My mother started to cry, thinking it meant he was about to die. My sister was shocked. I could only laugh. Harry wanted exactly the same thing as me, which was time for just the two of us together, and he looked at them as intruders who might take him away.

We lived out our month in solitude, the beach in the morning, the back deck every afternoon, Harry sprawled on the wood, me tapping at my laptop, and at night, we'd drive into town for a plate of fried clams, then head back home to read, the Red Sox playing on the car radio amid their remarkable August surge on the way to the World Series. That last evening on an empty beach, we both lingered until all the light had drained from the sky. We sat in the soft sand down by the far river. I did a few sit-ups to try to create the veneer of normalcy. Harry licked my nose, as he always did. I looked at his gaunt face and said, "Harry, I don't want you hanging around for me. I know you're in pain. When you want to go, just let me know and I'll make sure everything is just right." He looked at me as I spoke, and then he looked away.

An old Bill Clinton quote kept coming to mind: "It doesn't take long to live a life." And a dog's life comes and goes far too fast.

Walking off the beach that night, I knew Harry would never see it again. He had watched me packing a couple of hours before, so I suspect he knew it as well. Still he came, reliably, readily, bravely. What mattered wasn't so much where we were or what we were doing but the fact that we were together. Harry was calm until the end.

When Harry died about a month later, back in Boston, I thought, maybe even worried, that my love of Kennebunkport would die with him. But it didn't. The next year, I bought the house where we had spent his last August. I placed a photograph of him sitting on the beach, soaking wet, tennis ball in mouth, prominently on the living room wall. Morning walkers on Goose Rocks still asked about Harry. I can still see him in the water, smell the beach on his fur, picture the breeze blowing his damp ears. Those memories, the many things we shared, make Maine even more vital and ever more tranquil a retreat for me—my favorite place in this world.

On another August afternoon, a few years later, a rooster named Buddy made his virgin trip to the house, and the Maine I knew would never be the same.

*   *   *

From the moment Pam lifted him from the soft blankets that covered the passenger seat of her Toyota SUV and placed him gently on the terra firma of the state of Maine for the very first time, young Buddy was a bird in distress.

It didn't take a member of the Audubon Society or a third-generation poultry farmer to see why. His beady little eyes darted around the perimeter of my yard with a mix of fear and scorn. What he saw was a vast forest, sprawling fields, and quiet meadows dotted with wildflowers. What he didn't see was a fence or nice neighbors who would bring him corn and imported cheese. He didn't see one lawn flowing into another. He didn't see simple ornamental bushes that provided safe and vital shade. No, he didn't see any of that.

If you're a human, which I am, the fields and forest provide a respite from the crowded concrete of the city, an opportunity to commune with nature, a tranquil massage for the mind. It is quiet but for the cackle of the occasional hawk and the nighttime howl of the distant coyote. It is remote, and it is peaceful.

For an overly domesticated bird, specifically a chicken, and especially this particularly pampered chicken, every inch and every moment of this unfamiliar setting represented a monumental threat to his increasingly self-important life. The woods where I saw nature, he saw predators. The fields where I looked for clarity as I typed on my computer keyboard, he saw as spawning grounds for beasts that would eat him alive. The clear blue skies over-head, with their regular display of nighttime stars, were the perfect habitat for flying monsters who could swoop down and carry him off in one jaw-clenching bite.

So what Buddy did, once he quickly calculated the score, was draw a deep breath into his puffed-out chest, hold it there for a moment, and then let out a crow so deep, so long, and so loud that it all but shook the needles from the ancient scrub pines that made up so much of the surrounding woods. And then he did it again and again and again, until his pointy little head seemed ready to explode off his fat neck—and so did mine. He did it until Pam finally leaned down and cheerfully said, "Poor Boo-Disk, you're not used to it up here, are you?" Buddy clucked a soft acknowledgment to her that, no, he wasn't used to it up here, didn't particularly like it, and preferred to let people and creatures know about his feelings. And then he went back to warning the rest of the natural world not to mess with him.

I looked at him a little nervously, thinking, Okay, he's going to calm down. I mean, he's got to calm down. It's impossible to keep screaming that loud without putting yourself into a state of total exhaustion. "You'll be okay, Buddy," I said, trying to sound sincere. Of course, the thought occurred to me that maybe his enemies really were lurking lustily in the woods. I could only hope. God, I love the state of Maine.

As I listened to Buddy's incessant crowing, something else, some blur, some frantic, foreign motion, caught the corner of my eye and seemed equally alarming. I whirled around to see Pam emptying out the back of the car of bikes, special blankets, pillows and dolls, scooters, coloring books and craft kits, coolers filled with unusual foods, grocery bags, and, of course, luggage, many pieces of colorful nylon luggage. Christopher Columbus didn't pack this heavily when he was in pursuit of the New World.

Buddy screeched through it all. Pam was stacking everything in neat piles by the stairs that led up to the deck as if Buddy weren't even there at all. The happy kids were dragging horse jumps they had brought across the lawn I had just mown, leaving divots in their wakes. The two dogs were looking at me as if the world as they knew it was coming to an end. And it was—their world, my world. I just didn't know how to explain it to them or to admit that I had invited this on myself.

The dogs and I had arrived in Maine a day earlier to get things ready for our vacation. I did yard work. I opened all the windows and let the house breathe, watered the flowers, took a long sunset walk on the beach with the hounds, sprawled on a teak lounge chair on my beautiful deck and read a book to the quiet sounds of nature, grilled a ribeye for dinner, watched the Red Sox, and fell into a deep, satisfying slumber. It was my life, or at least one part of my life, okay, maybe a fading part of my life, and I loved it.

And now here were Pam, her kids, Buddy and—look what else!—the two rabbits, which Pam began lugging upstairs in their cumbersome cage. "I know you wouldn't want Dolly and Lily to be all alone," she said, flashing a smile that she knew I couldn't resist. My old life was crashing into my new life or, more accurately, being overwhelmed by it, here on my favorite stage set, which is Maine. I looked at the kids excitedly jumping around the yard, shouting to their mother "We want our bathing suits!" I heard Pam cooing to the rabbits "You girls will love it up here!" I watched the rooster crowing his guts out. I thought about the past and the future and told myself— really, convinced myself—that that was the way it should be, the good and the bad. I grabbed a pile of Pam's luggage and began the monstrous task of taking it all upstairs.

*   *   *

Buddy, it ended up, had a strategy for dealing with nature: he did everything in his power to avoid it. That meant he wanted nothing to do with the lawn, which undoubtedly contained a veritable buffet of delicacies for him, things like worms and ticks and various other delicious bugs. He went nowhere near the growth that ringed the yard. He wouldn't so much as look toward the fields that I thought might have helped him discover his true chicken.

No, what he did was climb up the half-dozen or so steps to the mahogany deck that spanned the entire back of the house and try pecking his way through the glass doors that led into the living room. He pecked and pecked and pecked, pausing only long enough to defecate on the flooring that I was so irrationally proud of you would think

I had nailed it together myself, big black-and-white gobs of feces that hit the wood with a cringe-inducing splat. When he wasn't pecking and splatting, he was screaming at the top of his lungs, warnings to predators lurking in the woods and pleas to the girls inside to protect him from the ruthless dangers of this godforsaken place.

"Come on in, Boo," Caroline, the younger, said, opening the French doors. He proudly walked inside, left another gift on my hardwood floors, and hopped up onto the white couch to join them for a quick show on TV before the beach. When I finished lugging their belongings upstairs, I sputtered at the unfolding scene. The chicken eyed me warily, and the girls basically ignored me. Actually, Abigail tossed her arms around his neck and proclaimed, "Poor Boo-Boo's not used to it yet."

The girls, being exactly that, were easily distracted, and moments later they raced outside to ride their scooters and jump their horse jumps and shout again to their mother that they wanted to get ready for the beach. Buddy sat on the couch, suddenly looking a little less comfortable, with me but a few feet away.

"C'mon, pal," I said, trying to lure him back outside through the open French doors. He looked at me as though I had absolutely lost whatever tiny mind I ever had.

"Come on, Buddy, seriously," I said. No movement whatsoever, except for his little head twitching. Maybe I was imagining things, but his eyes were trained on the television set as if he weren't quite done watching the show. I walked over to the closet and pulled out a broom, which made him leap through the air and scurry beneath the kitchen table, squawking all the while. The kids were playing on the driveway. Pam was upstairs unpacking. I pulled one chair out, and he hid beneath another. I pulled that chair out, and he moved into the corner, clucking and barking. I had no idea what I was going to do, but finally, mercifully, Pam appeared, took measure of the situation, and calmly declared, "Buddy, out!" He dropped his head and waddled back out the French doors he had entered, softly cawing his protests but doing exactly what she asked.

My sense of victory was fleeting. Once outside, young Buddy resumed his crowing regimen, never stepping on the grass that we had wrongly figured he would love. Chest full, chest empty, beak to the sky, beak to the ground. It was as if he were a windup doll you'd buy at a joke store to annoy the living hell out of someone you truly didn't like.

"Why don't we just drive down to the beach?" I said to Pam, unable to hide my exasperation.

"We can't now," she said. "Let's let Buddy settle in. I don't want to leave him when he's this emotional."

Emotional? Emotional! Try tyrannical. But either way, the impact was the same. I was trapped in a hell of my own making. My tranquil getaway house, this place where I used to laze on the deck for hours at a time with music softly wafting through the doors, where I used to come on brilliant autumn weekends to escape the noise of the real world, where I would quietly write columns for the *Globe*, was suddenly a bad Sartre play: No Exit.

"Hey, Brian, can we use the paint in the basement

to draw some lines in the driveway?" That was Abigail, giving me a somewhat urgent and breathless look as she popped her head in the door. I looked out the window and saw several cans sitting in the grass, Caroline about to pull the lids off them. I also saw a bunch of logs spread out over the lawn. How could an entire state suddenly feel like a shoebox?

"Abs, no on the paint. And what are the logs doing in the yard?"

"They're our jumps," she said proudly before bolting back outside.

Pam shut the doors to keep Buddy from getting back in, which in itself was odd for me, because I liked everything wide open, nature as part of my living room and my living room as part of nature. If I sound like a Crate & Barrel catalog, so be it. The doors, however, only spurred Buddy to scream louder and longer. I stood there frozen in my own kitchen for a moment, almost disoriented. The day before, every door and window had been open. Colorful butterflies had fluttered across my deck and I could all but hear their wings flap. The dogs had been wet, exhausted, and content. The yard had been quiet. My mind had been at ease. The only real tension had involved whether to head into town for dinner or grill steak at home.

And now this: kids dragging logs across the grass I'd worked so hard to grow; rabbits defecating in a cage on my second floor; a rooster screeching bloody murder outside my door; a girlfriend telling me I was basically a prisoner of my own chaotic house. I looked at Baker, who looked back at me, and we both seemed to have an identical thought at the exact same time, that being "How did this happen to us?" But what should I do? Should I get in my car under the guise of running errands? Should I pull a Harry Angstrom and never come back? Should I throw a tantrum to let people know who's really in control? Should I put up with this lunacy until everyone returns home and then take the appropriate steps to make sure it never happens again?

As my mind was working a hundred miles an hour, my gaze fell upon Pam, who had picked up the stray broom and begun absently sweeping the floor before placing it back in the closet. A thick strand of blond hair was matted across her tan forehead, making her look at once exhausted and beautiful. And as I looked at her, the thought occurred that she couldn't help any of this, all the luggage, all the animals, the demands of her kids, the cloud of chaos that sometimes followed her around. She might not necessarily be proud of the cacophony, but she was certainly not going to feel regret about all the wonderful moving parts comprising it. She is an unapologetically caring woman, and with that, there is accumulation. She undoubtedly knew that none of this was easy, not on her and definitely not on the people like me whom she wants in her life. But the kids, the bird, the bunnies, the bedlam, it was what her life was made of, and without it, she wouldn't be herself. What about my life? Would I really rather have constant order and total silence, everything where I wanted it when I wanted it there? Is that really how you live a meaningful life?

I recalled Pam once looking around my Boston condo, where precious little was ever out of place, and saying "Everything is always exactly where you left it. Doesn't that ever start to feel old?" I didn't have an answer because I didn't know any other way.

As I listened to Buddy screeching, I even thought of something else: he, like me, was out of sorts, him in a new environment, me in a new world order. I was probably shouting too, just not aloud. We had more in common than I thought, though I had the ability, even the predisposition, to keep it all inside. So I took a very deep breath, as if I were filling my lungs with perspective, and did something uncommonly—or maybe it's uncharacteristically—magnanimous. I went out on the deck, Kindle in hand, and reclined on a lounge chair to keep the screaming bird company.

"You and me both, Buddy," I said. "We'll get used to it."

He didn't seem particularly heartened by my pearls of wisdom or my presence. Rather, he came sidestepping over like a boxer in an old movie, stutter steps followed by furious maneuvers with his beak, ominously close and then closer still, until I jumped up with the chair between us, exclaiming "What the hell are you doing?" The damn bird wanted me dead—or at least bloodied. We probably had that in common too. Tonight's dinner dilemma? Solved: roast chicken. That was when Pam walked outside, once again to the rescue. "You guys not getting along?" she asked, innocently.

I was about to accuse her bird of attempted murder, but

she picked him up in one easy swoop and stroked the side of his face as he quietly cooed his approval.

Caroline raced up the few steps and asked in that tone of exasperation that kids use better than anyone else, "Can we just go to the beach now?" Pam met my gaze with her clear green eyes and replied, "In a few minutes, Bear. I just think everyone needs a moment to settle down."

*   *   *

That evening, after a jarringly early dinner (it seems more like lunch when it's still light out), I announced that I was taking the dogs to the beach for their nightly walk and offered my standard-issue invitation to the girls to come along. I expected the typical and immediate rejection— "No, thank you, *iCarly*'s on," or some variation of it. Instead, Abigail looked at Caroline, Caroline looked at the dogs, and a moment later, there were two kids and two golden retrievers vying for space in the back of my well-worn little SUV, giggling and panting. Pam waved from the top step of the deck and said, "Make sure you come back with everyone you left with."

I had gone on hundreds of evening walks on Goose Rocks Beach, often with Pam but even more often in the sole company of my dog or dogs. On almost every single one of those walks, I'd see men of about my age playing Wiffle ball or beach bocce or touch football, with groups of young boys and girls. Sometimes it would just be a father and his son out for a swim at dusk or playing a simple game of catch like my father used to do with me. Every time, every night, every scene, I'd feel a flicker of regret, nothing overpowering but very real, as if I had missed something that I could never get back, and much as I might have loved Harry or, later, Baker, it would never be the same.

That evening was different. The girls sprinted for the edge of the water and immediately started to play a game they described as "Jump the waves." So did I.

"Brian, you've got to jump higher!" Abigail exhorted me. So I did.

Then they ran along the shoreline chasing the dogs, which quickly transformed into a game in which the dogs ran along the shoreline chasing them. And then we all played a game of "Red light, green light" at my suggestion, spreading out along a wide stretch of hard beige sand on the increasingly empty beach.

When I announced a red light, they would screech to a stop, prompting me to put my face right up to theirs in inspection. If they laughed, they were sent back to the starting line, and Caroline always did. We took turns. We shouted commands. We pleaded for mercy. For that hour, as the light faded from the vast sky, I felt myself living the life I had watched from a distance all those years ago, and it was nice—better than nice, actually. Well, I was living it until Abigail suddenly announced, in no uncertain terms, "I'm bored."

"Me too," Caroline said. A moment before, they had been giggling up a storm.

So the five of us made for the car and headed home, the girls complaining now that the sandy, wet dogs were leaning against them. At the house, they ran inside as if they hadn't seen their mother in years, so quickly that they left the car doors open and the dogs looking at me confused.

"How was it?" Pam asked them.

"It was okay," Abigail said.

"I'm hungry," Caroline added.

Pam looked at me for some hint of what had happened. I offered a modest shrug and said, "Well, I thought it was great."

*   *   *

That night, after the girls were asleep, Pam told me, point-blank, "I'm putting Buddy to bed in the basement."

Oh, God.

A word about my Maine basement: immaculate. Some other words: sanctuary, simple, soothing. There are a couple of others as well, such as pristine and uncluttered. You could eat a gourmet dinner off my basement floor. A Massachusetts General neurologist would feel comfortable doing brain surgery down there. It has all the usual basement accessories, such as a washer and dryer, hot-water heater, furnace, and all that, all the accessories completely accessible—and precious little else, which is exactly the way I like it. In my real life, my city life, I didn't have a basement. I didn't have a lawn either, which is why my Maine basement and lawn made me feel so, well, adult. City life is complicated, messy, cold, and sometimes hard. I wanted my country life to be its restorative opposite. That explains why I like to cut my own grass, apply my own fertilizer, and keep my cellar lovingly unburdened of all the junk most people acquire and hide, never to be used again. I wanted the lawn thick and the basement sparse. I specifically remember Pam telling me she was putting the bird in the basement, and I explicitly remember her seeing the look of horror and annoyance on my face. She said that everything down there was washable and she would clean it herself.

I just didn't appreciate the immediate, real-world implications of the maneuver.

At dawn's first light, I came to realize that Buddy had somehow positioned himself directly under my first-floor bedroom—to be more specific, the clever little guy got directly under my bed. When he awoke, he was undoubtedly filled with questions, such as *What the hell am I doing here, and where is everyone else?* So he let out a thunderbolt of a *cock-a-doodle-doo* that slammed through the bedroom floor like a jackhammer, blazed through the mattress, and sent me just about hurtling skyward toward the ceiling fan in an *Exorcist*-like stunt. I could actually feel myself hit the bed again, which only seemed to cause him to screech anew. Was his beak in my goddamn pillow, pecking at the insides of my brain?

Slapped awake, I found myself inexplicably breathless, as if I had just gone on a long bike ride in extreme heat. The room was mostly dark, though through the windows I could see the very first drops of light in the morning sky. I looked over at Pam, but there was just the vacant expanse of white comforter. She was gone or, more likely, had never been there. The last I had seen of her was when she said she was going upstairs to see the kids off to sleep. She'd likely fallen asleep beside them or between them, exhausted at the close of another long day.

The bird's screeches made me wonder about the quality of my flooring. There didn't seem to be anything between me and the monster's voice box. I needed him to stop, desperately so, but I sure as hell wasn't going down there, not after the porch scene the afternoon before, when he'd seemed as though he wanted to take me down, and not when he was this agitated. I lay in bed amid the avian screams, hoping, praying that Pam would again take charge. I mean, she had to hear him upstairs. Hell, my friends in Boston could probably hear him.

Finally I heard merciful footsteps on the staircase, the opening of the cellar door, and someone descending the steps. Then I heard Pam's voice, muffled by the floor and choked by sleep. "Boo-Boo, you poor guy, all unsettled. It's okay. You're safe down here."

He gave her a long, explanatory caw, the two of them

continuing this interspecies dialogue. Next thing I knew, Pam was falling into bed beside me, still wearing the same shorts and T-shirt she'd had on the day before, her hair a tangle of wisps and knots.

"He's just getting used to things," she said, kissing the side of my head. I was about to respond, but she was already snoring softly. She hadn't moved an inch when I got up an hour or so later to take two excited dogs to the beach for their morning romp in the sand and waves. Afterward, standing inside a delightful store called Cape Porpoise Kitchen, where I always got my morning coffee, the nice young woman approached and as I said, "The usual," she pulled out a small bag for my muffin. My cell phone rang. "Excuse me one second," I said, stepping away to take the call.

It was Caroline's squeaky voice on the other end of the line. "Brian, where are you?"

"At the store, cutie. Where are you?"

"Um, I'm at home. Hey, can you get me a cinnamon muffin and a toasted bagel, and Abby wants a blueberry muffin."

"Of course—"

"And Mom wants an everything bagel."

"I'm on the way," I said. "How's Buddy?"

"He's loud."

And the phone went dead.

I told the young woman what I needed, which was much more than I usually got: half a dozen muffins, a couple of bagels, another cup of coffee for Pam.

She smiled. Maybe I was reading too much into this, but it looked like an admiring smile, a smile that said, *Hey, maybe this slug isn't just in it for himself.* "Full house?" she asked.

I nodded. "Kids, dogs, woman," adding under my breath "rooster."

"Excuse me?" She looked legitimately surprised.

"Toaster," I said, quickly. "Would you mind throwing the bagels in the toaster?"

* * *

Ends up, this was a rare time that Pam was wrong. Buddy never did settle down. For hours at a time, he stood at the doors peering in with a pleading, desperate look on his twitchy little face. He constantly fouled my deck. He bolted through the door whenever anyone slipped it open for any brief period of time. He charged my legs so often that I took to carrying a rolled-up newspaper in my back pocket, though that only convinced him of his relevance and pushed him to keep charging and pecking.

For days at a time he did nothing but crow, to the point that even when he wasn't crowing, I could hear it. The sound was stuck in my mind, maybe forever.

Great vacation. I couldn't even hear myself think, not that I'd want to, because the only thing I was really think-ing was a string of vulgarities mixed in with fifty ways to kill your chicken. Where the hell is Maine's famous wildlife when you need it most? I didn't need a herd of anything, just one little fisher cat.

"I'm really sorry," Pam kept repeating over the screeching. "He's just so scared." When I barely responded, she added, "It's my own fault. I shouldn't have brought him up." She knew full well that I couldn't take the dejected Pam, so I would invariably give in and halfheartedly say, "It's not all that bad."

"What?"

Louder now, over the crowing: "I said it's not so bad."

Buddy wasn't eating the cracked corn that Pam put on the grass. He wasn't eating the chicken fingers—yes, I know, it's bizarre—that she diced up and piled in a bowl on the brick walk by the driveway. The poor bird was starving himself out of fear. It hit a point, when he slipped through the door and raced through the house squawking with exhilarated relief before being carried back outside by one of the kids, that I actually started feeling bad for him, which I hadn't thought possible.

And then something happened that was beyond the pale. The kids were getting ready for bed, and Abigail went into the cellar to grab her pajamas from the dryer. There was an urgent squeal. Pam raced downstairs. I heard crying. Then I heard Pam shouting in a way that she hardly ever does, "That's it, Buddy. Now you've done it. You've gone after my kids. You're out of here. See if you like living in the woods. Let's see how aggressive you are out there!"

I walked down the stairs slowly and quietly. I'm not

sure why. Abigail was sobbing but, in truth, completely unharmed. It was the shock more than the beak that bothered her. Pam was crying softly as well. Everybody's nerves were frayed. Buddy was standing in front of them on the cement floor, his head down, clucking forlornly. It was as if the whole tense, often miserable vacation had come to a head in the basement of my house that night: the fear, the anxiety, the constant screeching.

In that moment, looking at Buddy staring at the floor, making guttural noises that I had never heard from him before, I felt legitimately sorry for the bird. He was out of place. He was frightened. He probably wasn't sleeping. We knew he wasn't eating. And in a moment of uncertainty, he had pecked at Abigail, hurting her feelings more than her physical being—but still.

"Listen," I said, and I couldn't believe the words coming out of my mouth. Everybody turned to face me. Buddy even looked up, surprised. "He didn't mean to do anything bad," I said. "He's just really anxious about everything right now. And because of that, so are we."

Me defending Buddy. It was the start of something odd.

*　*　*

Later that night, as I sealed up the house before bed, I saw light seeping from the crack between the cellar door and the floor, so I returned to the scene of the crime to check on the feathery criminal.

The only problem was, he wasn't there—not in the basement, not in the cold storage room, not on the blankets that Pam had spread as his bed across the floor, not behind the furnace or the hot-water heater or anywhere else I looked.

"Buddy," I said in a loud whisper again and again and again. "Buddy, where are you?"

I checked the door to make sure it was locked. I had bizarre images of Buddy, so despondent over pecking at Abigail and losing Pam's trust, wandering into the dark night clucking that he wasn't worthy anymore.

"Buddy, c'mon, where the hell are you?"

And that's when I heard it, a soft cackle, not really anything that comes out of his beak, but something that starts and stays in his throat, kind of like the roostery version of a human humming. I whirled around toward the washing machine and dryer, the seeming source of the sound, but didn't see anything.

"Buddy? Buddy, are you there?"

That same noise, faint but real. I walked over to the appliances, figuring he must have wedged himself in behind them, and that's when I saw it: his little red comb sticking out from the tub of the washing machine. It was a top-loading washer; the lid was open; and Buddy had somehow either fallen or jumped inside.

"Buddy, what the hell are you doing in there?" I asked.

By now I was standing above him and he gave me a look that said, *What difference does it make, moron? Get me out of here.* I went to reach my hands in, tentatively, but he clucked and poked in my direction with his beak. Even then, vulnerable, needing my help, he wouldn't accept it.

I thought about leaving him in there for the night, but something stopped me, something beyond the obvious fact that he'd be defecating in my washing machine. I didn't want him breaking a wing or having a panic-induced heart attack or—and I can't believe I was thinking it, but I was—just being completely uncomfortable for the night. So I went upstairs, to the second floor to get Pam, who, as usual, had fallen asleep with the kids.

She opened her eyes slowly as I gently touched her shoulder. "It's Buddy," I said. She bolted upright, her eyes wide, panic spreading across her tired features.

"He's okay," I said, "but he's stuck."

She maneuvered between her kids and climbed out of bed in the dark room, followed me downstairs, and burst out laughing as she came across Buddy sitting in the tub of the washing machine, his head sticking out but his body concealed within. She reached down fearlessly, pulled him up, and pressed him against her chest as she exclaimed, "Oh, Boo-Boo, you fell in the washing machine. You poor guy." She kissed his face as he cooed his appreciation.

She poured him a small bowl of cracked corn from the feed container, placed him gently on his blankets, and sat down for a moment beside him. Not that either of them noticed, but I headed for the stairs.

It had been a long week, which is not how my vacations usually felt. There were thousands of crows, constant anxiety, and death wishes from just about everyone involved.

And that was just the first day. It got worse as the break went along. And at the center, there was this simple comedic bird who was only trying to fend for himself in what he suddenly saw as a menacing world. The good news, I hoped, was that Buddy had surely seen the last of Maine—and Maine had seen the last of Buddy.

As I hit the top step, I heard Pam calling back to him on her way up, "Don't you worry, Buddy. You'll be with us forever."

>14<

To all of those who say the United States has become little more than a nation of hardened skeptics and unwavering pessimists, ladies and gentlemen, I'd like to present to you the institution of marriage.

At least one out of two of them fails, and those failures result in shattered hearts, staggering legal bills, unwanted time apart from kids, forced moves, long nights alone wondering how it all came apart, and longer days alone wondering how some semblance of a life will be stitched back together. No one in their teens and twenties ever imagines themselves forty and divorced, the tang of failure all around them, cooking for one, awkwardly reentering the dating pool, yet that's how it too often is.

But we keep getting married—young people, middle-aged people, old people, those who've never been married before and many who are wading in for a second or third try. It's who we are. It's what we do. Ours is always going to be the marriage that ends not in family court but in death, preferably not involving a weapon and hopefully a long way away, immortalized by our children and grandchildren, who will strive their whole lives to have the kind of relationship we had, or at least they believe we had.

Against this backdrop of hopes and dreams, there was me, carrying around so many fears and failures. Everything in my life seemed to be in flux, as if you could take all the disparate pieces that made up my identity, toss them into the air on a breezy day, and see how they might fall. The *Globe,* my employer for the better part of two decades and an institution I happened to love, was facing the darkest days in its long and storied history, though fortunately, it seemed to be emerging intact. The *New York Times,* our corporate overlord, had threatened to shutter us in April. A couple of months later, the *Times* threatened to sell us. Meanwhile, it was cutting the hell out of us. Besides that, I think it really liked us. Luckily, the closure or sale never came to be. The economy rebounded, advertising bounced back some, and we cut staff and raised the price of the paper. Suddenly we were profitable again, nowhere near what we had once been but enough to turn out a damned good report most days, and the *Times,* to its considerable credit, kept the resources in place for us to do it.

I made the decision to go from being a deputy managing editor overseeing our local news operation back to writing the metro column I had for nearly a decade before. Managing people was deeply satisfying and mostly fun because they were good people, talented people, hardworking people who made a vital difference in the communities we covered. But ultimately I missed searching for the story that wouldn't otherwise be told, sharing an opinion that might occasionally have impact here in my native city, and having my own name on my own column. I also missed having some semblance of a life. The editing job required me to be in a glass-walled office in the *Globe* newsroom morning, noon, and night, which wasn't really my style. And when I wasn't there, I was on call and constantly being called. When I went into management, I struck a deal that I would try it for two years and ended up doing it closer to three. The editor of the paper, Marty Baron, whose calling card is his integrity, was kind enough to hold true to his promise and give me my old job back when I asked.

That was the professional side. The personal side was more daunting.

I had lived alone for so long that I didn't even have to talk to myself anymore, I was that comfortable. It was me and Harry, and then me and Baker, constantly on the go, a perfect, seamless pair. But it was getting old, and so was I. By the time I was looking down the road at fifty, the routines and lifestyle that had had so much appeal when I was in my thirties and early forties were starting to seem just south of dysfunctional. The fun uncle who was jetting around the world chasing stories, staying at great hotels, always aware of the best restaurants—make sure you ask for Felix and tell him I sent you—suddenly looked as if he'd stayed at the party a couple of scotches too long. I'm sure there were more than a few conversations about whether I would ever change. Hell, I didn't know the answer to that myself.

But in truth, that wasn't the reason why I wanted to get married, just the backdrop. I wanted to get married because Pam, quite simply and honestly, was the most remarkable woman I had ever known. When she first expressed interest in the form of the tie, I was adamant about not getting involved. She had two daughters. She lived in the distant suburbs. She drove a big SUV. She had a scientist's mind. She was a fully formed, responsible adult with people who depended on her every step of the way on every single day. I was a city-dwelling writer with a dog. It was never going to work. But one thing led to another and then another, and then it was, Holy shit, I can't get this woman out of my mind. Next thing you know, I was out there nearly every evening, never quite sure of what I was going to get, happy girls who wanted to show me their newest drawings of horses named Misty or Snowflake or agitated girls who would stare silently at the television when I walked into the room or, worse, would sit in a corner until I left. What are you supposed to do with that? I didn't have a good answer, so I kept plugging along, but through it all I kept my sanctuary apartment in Boston. It wasn't always easy, not for me, not for Pam, but it's never easy melding two established lives. At one point we even went our separate ways for no short period of time, convinced that it wasn't meant to be. But eventually, slowly, we found our way back to each other, and when we did, neither of us ever wanted to let go again.

Which brings me to Christmas Eve 2009. I had bought a ring a few weeks earlier. Now, mind you, shopping for a diamond engagement ring might be the most profoundly unsatisfying mission any man will ever undertake. You are spending an obscene amount of money on a tiny object that is inherently imperfect from the moment you buy it— an SI1 in terms of clarity or an H as far as color. There are no straight As and number ones in the diamond business, not for the regular guys anyway. Beyond that, you can't drive it, change the channel on it, inhabit it, or sit on it. But somehow, the Diamond Institute of America has successfully positioned it as the symbol of true and everlasting love and the initiation fee in terms of a life of happiness—or at least normalcy.

That day, Christmas Eve, I poked through my desk drawer in my small hunter green study and found the tiny rectangular scrap of paper saying "Thank you for making me smile." A sentimentalist I am not, but something at the time told me to save it, even when I believed it wouldn't add up to anything more than a distant memory. I put the cherry red ring box and the tiny scrap of paper with the note in my jacket pocket and only checked it three or four hundred times during the day to make sure they were still there. Pam arrived at my apartment a little after dark, a little harried from the typical last-minute rush of Christmas preparation for two kids. Her girls were with their father that night, arriving at Pam's at midday on Christmas, and our plan was to spend the evening having a leisurely meal in a downtown restaurant. On the way, I would ask her to be my wife—Mrs. Pamela, well, Bendock.

It was cold out that night, and the charming streets of Back Bay were illuminated by the old-fashioned street-lights. It was strikingly quiet, prompting thoughts that my frozen fingers would drop the ring down a sewer drain at the critical moment or we would be robbed. I dismissed those as the irrational thoughts of someone about to embark on a barely rational journey. As we walked down the Commonwealth Avenue promenade, glowing with white holiday lights strung through the ancient trees, Pam slipped her arm into mine, and it didn't seem cold or ominous anymore.

We took a right and found ourselves on Newbury Street, all exactly by design. We arrived on the same side of the same corner where she'd said she saw me patting Harry so many years earlier. I waited for the light even though there didn't seem to be a car within five miles. She waited with me, and God only knows what must have been going through her head. I said, probably awkwardly, "Hey, isn't this where you got the idea to send me that tie?"

She smiled and, without missing a beat, said, "I was right over there, at the outdoor café. You two were right here, exactly where we're standing now."

My mind, surprisingly, or maybe not, flickered on Harry for a moment, Harry and the utter effortlessness of true love. And then it was back to Pam, whom Harry had led me to and with whom I was fumbling for the right words. I had been practicing this moment in my mind every day for the past several weeks, but everything just kind of left my head right when I needed it most—the witty entreaties, the smooth lead-ins, and definitely my meaningful and scripted narrative. It was as if someone took a bottle of Wite-Out to my simple little brain. Silently I fumbled for the piece of paper in my pocket and handed it to her, still all folded up. She looked at the paper, which closely resembled a gum wrapper or some minuscule piece of litter, then looked at me as though I were completely off the wall, out of my mind.

I nodded toward it. I wasn't entirely sure, but I might have lost my ability to talk.

Say something, Brian, anything. For chrissakes, speak. Years from then, Pam's children and grandchildren would retell the story of how I had proposed to their mother or grandmother, and they'd keep going back to the irrefutable fact that the slug with the ring couldn't actually get any words out of his mouth.

Pam slowly unfolded the slip of paper, read the words "Thank you for making me smile," and now was completely sure that I was, in fact, nuts. She looked at me a little confused, though, in typical Pam fashion, trying to mask the confusion until she figured out my play.

Again, there were lines I was supposed to recite here, lines about how it had ended up that it was she who had made me smile for all these years, millions of smiles that I otherwise never would have had, smiles I didn't think I was capable of having, smiles when she was right in front of me, smiles over her kids, her rabbits, her dog, smiles at the mere thought of her when she wasn't even there. But I didn't have those lines anymore, because what I had was the ring in my hand and a lump in my throat, and I pulled it out of my pocket and croaked out the question "Would you marry me?"

She looked at the ring for a moment and took it, and before she even put it on she looked at me, her skin pink from the cold, her hair wispy from the winter breeze, her eyes suddenly shiny from the moment. She put her pretty face next to mine and kissed me. And then she said, simply, never one to dramatize things, "Yes."

She said yes. And from there on in, it would be me and Pam. Well, me and Pam and her two kids. Actually, me and Pam and her two kids and their two rabbits and our two dogs and perhaps a couple of Maine coons that I didn't realize were on the way and the frogs hidden in an upstairs bedroom and of course Buddy, who would never have found himself at a loss for words.

* * *

We were in the middle of one of those claustrophobic winter days between Christmas and New Year's. The kids, Pam, and I had played a game of Monopoly. We watched some horse movie on TV. Pam and the girls baked brownies. I give them credit, because it took them until the late afternoon before the two kids started getting on each other's nerves, which is when I quietly announced that I was going to take the dogs for a nice romp in a snowy field. Nobody, except for the dogs, really cared.

The wan sun had already dipped below the bare trees, and the breeze was a little more piercing than I would have liked, but still, the air, the openness, the aloneness, felt like a tonic, fresh, sweet, and invigorating. We walked a big loop around an open park and then another, until the dogs were looking at me as though they couldn't take any more, so we headed back to Checkerberry Circle. I would have killed to be able to convince the kids to go out to dinner to a place filled with activity and humanity, or even just to a movie, but I had no doubt they'd want nothing more than to hunker down at home.

When we pulled back up to the house, Buddy was standing at the front stoop screaming bloody murder—sharp, long, urgent *cock-a-doodle-doo*s, one after another after another. He should have been up on his shelf by now. When I climbed the first of the three steps, he made a move as if to charge me, as though he was protecting the house, and I quickly, literally backed down. "What the hell are you doing?" I blurted out, then, under my breath, "Bastard." He squawked at me in return.

So I grabbed Baker by the collar and put him between me and the bird just to get to the door. Inside, the house was dark but for light I could see spilling out the door of an upstairs bedroom. The sound of sniffling drifted downward, and nothing else.

So we went up, the three of us, with the chicken peering in through the front door and occasionally pecking at the glass. Upstairs, in Pam's bedroom, was Pam, sitting up in her bed, teardrops on her cheeks, staring straight ahead. When I'd left, less than an hour before, everyone had been as happy as you can be when you're stuck in a house on a cold winter's day. But I had learned long ago that when you get three females together, a mother and her two daughters, drama lurks around even the most innocent-looking corners. It's everywhere, waiting to spring forth.

"What happened?" I asked calmly.

"Nothing. It's fine," Pam replied, wiping her cheeks.

"It's not fine," I said. As I spoke, the two dogs jumped on the bed with her, both of them trying to lick her face. Somewhere a rooster crowed. Actually, he was still right outside the front door, but it felt as if he were screeching in my ear.

Through the *cock-a-doodle-doo*s and the anxious dogs and the sniffling fiancée, I could hear the muffled sound of crying—in stereo—drifting in from the upstairs hall. Before Pam could give an answer, I left the room and saw that the doors to Caroline's and Abigail's rooms were shut, light seeping through the cracks beneath.

I knocked softly on Abigail's door and walked in. She was lying in bed face up with her favorite stuffed animal in a tight bear hug against her chest.

"What's going on here?" I asked, trying to sound sympathetic, which wasn't easy, because I didn't know what I was sympathizing with.

"Nothing," she replied sharply. "I'm fine."

"You're not fine. You're crying."

"I'm fine."

"Come on, Abs, what happened?"

For the first time, she turned her head and looked at me with her piercing eyes. "She's my mommy!"

That was more than I could get out of Caroline, who, when I went into her room, rolled herself into a tight little ball under her terry-cloth blanket, and when I playfully poked at her, screamed like she had just been shot. "Okay," I told her, trying to mask my exasperation. "You win. I'll leave you alone."

Back in Pam's room, I asked again, a little more clipped now, "What happened?"

The dogs were still in her bed. The rooster was still crowing downstairs. The kids were still in their rooms. And Pam still gave me a nonanswer. "Don't worry about it," she said. "It's no big deal."

"I'm not worried about it," I said. "But I am in the information business, and I'd like to know. I left here an hour ago, and everyone was happy. I came back, and everyone's in tears. What happened?"

She shifted her gaze away from wherever the hell it was trained, which didn't seem to be on anything in particular, and looked me in the eye. She hesitated another couple of beats, then said, "I told them we were engaged and that we were going to get married."

I smiled reflexively, not a happy smile, not even a sad smile, more like a helpless, holy-shit-what-do-I-do-now smile.

She's my mommy!

What was I supposed to do? Storm out? Shout that almost every other kid I've ever met always liked me, why couldn't they?

No. I couldn't do any of that. It's not easy being a young girl and even less so when your parents are divorced and you're living in two houses and your father's gotten remarried and your mother is about to do the same. What am I? I'm the guy who they think is going to take their mother from them, that's who.

"It's okay," I said. "What are they supposed to do, jump up and down in joy because there's still more change? Because some guy might come between you and them? It's fine. It's just on me—and I guess you—to show them there's nothing to worry about."

Pam nodded. "They know there's nothing to worry about," she said, speaking louder to be heard above the din of the rooster. "They just need to process it all."

We had a moment of silence until I said, "I had really hoped that our engagement would inspire tears in the female world, but this isn't exactly what I had in mind."

Pam laughed politely and went down the hall to convince her two daughters that life, as they knew and loved it, was not coming to an end. I went out and picked up Chinese food. When I returned, the four of us had a completely normal dinner around the kitchen table—though I'm not sure Pam was all that comfortable eating vegetable lettuce wraps with two kids sitting in her lap, arms draped over her shoulders.

>15<

I learned a great deal about life—the suburban version of it, anyway—in our hunt for a new house. I learned what a mudroom is, which doesn't actually involve any mud but sometimes washing machines and dryers, sinks, and elaborate cubbyholes, such that the Boston Bruins could basically arrive unannounced and have a place to hang all their gear. I learned that suburbanites devote their basements to luxurious home theaters and tricked-out fitness rooms with exercise machines that look like there's no possible way they could have fit through the door. In my cellar growing up, we had a Ping-Pong table that was covered with boxes, and I thought, Hey, we've got it pretty good.

"What is this?" I asked on a tour of yet another house I knew I didn't want before we even walked inside. As I asked the question, I was pulling open a glass door that led to a tiled room with a bench.

"That's the steam bath," the nice showing agent said in a tone of voice that suggested I was an idiot. When I bought my eight-hundred-square-foot condo that I proceeded to live in for more than ten years, I felt as though I'd really made it in life because it had a dishwasher that worked most days, provided you slammed the door shut as hard as you possibly could and then turned the handle just so.

I learned that a shower isn't worth talking about unless it has more than one head—and most actually did. I learned that acreage was apparently important, though for reasons I don't exactly understand; I mean, the more you have, the more work it requires. I learned that you no longer open or close garage doors by pulling them up or down, though Pam had sort of already taught me that.

I also learned that every showing agent believes that every house he or she is showing is about to sell within the next half hour, and that if we don't jump on it fast, we're going to lose out on the greatest deal we may ever know. The house could have been on the market for three years. The siding could be falling off. There could be rabid raccoons waving their little paws from the broken second-story windows. Doesn't matter, it's the perfect fixer-upper in an improving economy, and this isn't just the right week for it, it's the exact day.

I also learned that I didn't like most houses out there. Their turrets and gables, pillars and columns depressed me in a small *d* kind of way. They looked as though they should be sitting on the edge of the Black Forest or the side of the Alps, not in another nondescript development twenty miles west of Boston. I kept asking Pam, to her considerable frustration, whatever happened to the center-entrance Colonial? Is that not good enough for anyone anymore? Maybe I just couldn't get my head around being so far from the nearest four-star restaurant or subway stop. But there was something else that was troubling me almost every time we walked inside an available house: as I wandered through the empty rooms, I realized I was becoming my father, without actually becoming a father. Put another way, I realized I was giving up the dreams of my youth for the far more standard dream of American success: love, kids, suburbia, cookouts. Maybe, probably, almost certainly, there was nothing wrong with that. It's the natural order of things. But it was jarring for me because I had skipped—or just missed—so many of the seemingly requisite steps. I'd never had a wife inform me she was pregnant. I'd never seen a child born. I'd never felt cramped in an apartment with an infant and a toddler and longed for suburbia's promise of more space. I'd never needed to move to a town with a good school system. I'd never felt the need to be close to the kids' elementary school.

No, I'd simply fallen in love with the right woman who happened to live in what to me felt like a foreign place. As I walked around each prospective house, it brought home to me all that it required and all that it meant.

"You don't like this one," Pam said to me time and time again as we stood amid family rooms with cathedral ceilings, peered at stone counter finishes, gauged how many years the washer and dryer had left in their lives.

"Not quite right," I'd reply. They never were, and she didn't push.

It happened so many times that I was starting to feel self-conscious about it. So to weed out what I didn't think I'd like, I proposed one clarifying rule meant to propel the process along. My only stipulation in this move to suburbia was that we needed to buy a house on a road that went somewhere. I'm sorry, but this was brilliant. It ruled out the highly coveted cul-de-sacs. It placed a big red X through subdivisions with gauzy names drilled into large ornamental rocks at the entrances—"Willow Estates" or "Brookside Farms." I lived in mortal fear of those places, neighbors knowing every ounce of our business, gazing judgmentally at our weed-saturated lawn, boring the bejesus out of me with constant talk of young Tyler's exploits on the soccer field or in tai kwon do. I wasn't proud of any of my fears and frustrations, but I needed to address them, and Pam was patient as I moved through my ten stages of grief at leaving the urban life behind.

Finally we found it. It was a brand-new house built in the likeness of an old red farmhouse with covered porches and many windows and a family room with a stone fireplace. It was unique. It had never been lived in. It had no media room, no two-story living room, no upstairs catwalk, no palladium window. It was on a main road but a quiet one. It all seemed very Pam, and if it was Pam, then it would and could also be me.

That being 2009, nothing happened easily. The same

bankers who had been sending out preapproved credit cards and home equity lines by the bushel in 2007 basically wanted a gallon of our blood to get a mortgage we could afford in 2009. We lived in that great maw between rich and poor—enough money to put half down on the house but not so much that we could buy it outright. Still, dolphins at SeaWorld don't jump through as many hoops as we did to get our loan.

There was the matter of selling my condominium in Boston. I would get irrationally angry at every person who looked at it and didn't immediately place an offer. I mean, how could they not see what I saw? How could they not know it was the greatest place they could ever possibly imagine? How could they not realize the warmth of this marble fireplace on a January night, the access to the Charles River on a July morning, the ease of walking to Fenway for the October playoffs? Did they not feel the vibe?

Eventually, as things generally do, everything worked itself out—the sale, the loan, the new house. I had come nearly to terms with it all. I was even excited about having a home office with a fireplace and not having to flee Pam's place on weeknights to drive thirty-five minutes into the city to go to bed. I was also ready for the commitment that accompanied the whole deal, and I don't mean just the new mortgage.

* * *

My phone rang in the newsroom one mid-March afternoon. Pam was on the other end of the line. "Will you
make it out here for the birthday celebration?" she asked.

Birthday celebration.

It is nearly impossible to imagine the raw fear, the potential for failure, that I was forced to confront in those
two upbeat words, mostly because I had precisely no idea
whose birthday we would be celebrating that night and it's
not a question that can be easily asked. It used to be so different: I needed to know basically one birthday, my own.
I'd learn and memorize that of my then wife or an important girlfriend. My two sisters would be sure to remind
me of my mother's, and my mother would typically call
me about my two sisters'. I always knew Harry's, though
we didn't necessarily celebrate it because I never felt good
about his getting old. But now there were kids and a fiancée and her extended family, and the whole thing was
ripe for the exact kind of oversight that I was apparently
immersed in at that moment.

My heart sank like a cold stone through hot soup. Birthday. I pictured a crying kid when I arrived absent a gift,
even though there was nothing in this wide world either
one of the kids could possibly need that they didn't already have. I pictured an angry adult, the shocked nanny,
Marsha, who had been with the family forever, a whispered
phone call to my future mother-in-law, weeks of darkness
followed by a pallid attempt at redemption, possibly with
the purchase of a new pony that I couldn't actually afford.
And to think that twenty minutes earlier, I had been bliss-

fully tossing back a bag of Peanut M&Ms while contemplating whether I had the time to get to the gym.

I focused on Caroline, Pam's youngest. Think, Brian, think. Yes, I remembered. There had been a sleepover party about two weeks after Christmas, another one of those affairs when a team of manicurists had set up shop in the living room of Pam's house and a dozen or so seven-year-olds had waited impatiently to get their toes and nails done. That was her birthday. Then Abigail, Pam's oldest. It had been a while, to be sure. Think. For chrissakes, think. Yes, I remembered picking up her cake. I remembered that the Red Sox had been playing that night. It was April. The baseball season had already started. This was still March, so it couldn't be her birthday.

Pam, I knew that one. It was October, among my favorite months.

Who the hell else?

"Of course I'm going to be there," I told Pam, doing my level best to conceal the panic gurgling within. "Don't cut the cake without me."

Walking into her house that night, I carried no gift but a sense of dread. As soon as I opened the heavy front door, I heard Caroline squeal, "Brian's here. We can start!" That was a good greeting, a warm greeting, something that wasn't always guaranteed. Those kinds of greetings made it all worthwhile, offsetting the nights I'd walk through the door and see two kids who wouldn't even look up from the TV to say hello and I'd end up eating cheese ravioli alone while standing at the kitchen sink.

I went into the kitchen, where Abigail was sitting at the table doing homework, Pam was putting away the dinner dishes, and a covered box, from the upscale bakery Icing on the Cake, sat on the counter, not far from a bouquet of red and white balloons. Nobody was messing around here.

"You want to get the birthday boy?" Pam called out to Caroline.

Okay, we had a gender. Pam made a move toward the cake box. She began cutting the taped edges. A door opened and shut in the background. Abigail pushed her homework out of the way and excitedly stood up. I thought my head was going to explode from curiosity.

And in unintentionally simultaneous motions, Caroline walked into the kitchen carrying none other than the clucking Buddy the Rooster in her arms as Pam held up a cake with Buddy's exact likeness in thick white and red buttercream frosting.

"Look, Boo-Boo, it's you!" Abigail announced. Caroline thrust his face right up to the cake, and I'll be damned if Buddy didn't silently stare at it for a moment, as if saying "It better be chocolate inside." One lone candle was lit. The lights went out. The trio of women broke out into a rendition of "Happy Birthday to You."

I was at once relieved and incredibly stunned. I knew they liked this bird, but Icing on the Cake? That thing had probably set Pam back about a hundred bucks. Pam cut a sliver of the cake and put it on a festive birthday plate, which she then placed on the floor. The lights came back on. Caroline let go of Buddy, who let out a loud bark that, if I didn't know any better, could have actually been of appreciation. He poked his beak into the cake and emerged with frosting smeared down both sides of his face, staring at Pam and the girls with a look of unabashed joy. Before they could wipe him clean, he was pecking hungrily at the cake all over again, at the frosting, at the cake part, at the little crumbs on the plate. The girls were giggling loudly, squealing his name. Pam was as light as I'd seen her in a long while. I couldn't help but laugh as well—about the bird, about the kids, about the weirdness of it all.

"One year old, Buddy," Caroline said to a chicken that wasn't really listening anymore. "There'll be plenty of more cakes where this one came from."

It was just a couple of months later, on a warm Sunday afternoon in May, that we got our first, scary hint of how easily that could all come apart.

*   *   *

We were showing my sister Colleen and her husband, Mark, our new house, Pam and I. We were due to close in a couple of weeks, and the builder had been kind enough to give us keys, and we were unveiling it to our families for the first time. Just as we were about to walk inside, Pam's phone rang and her face turned virtually white.

"Okay," she said sharply into the phone. "Okay. Yes. Where is he now? Is he moving? Would you mind staying with him? I'll be right there."

Pam hung up the phone, looked at me with a mix of bewilderment and unabashed fear, and said, "Buddy just got attacked by a dog. I've got to go." Before I could respond, she was in her car, gunning out of the driveway, headed to her house about five minutes across town.

I continued giving Colleen and Mark a tour of the new house, as if I had invented the very concept of suburban living, but something was going on inside of me, something I didn't expect. I had been waiting for more than a year now for this damned bird to meet his demise. I had accepted that he would never wander off on his own because even he knew there was nowhere better to go. That had gotten me praying for hawks and coyotes, to one day finding a carcass on the side lawn, followed by the requisite consolations that he had lived a great life, the kind of life any rooster would have loved to have led.

And now, faced with the distinct possibility of his death, I was unsettled, deeply so. Maybe it was just how hard it would hit Pam and her kids if Buddy no longer was. Actually, I'm sure that was a part of it, but it was something more. As I was showing Colleen how the kitchen faucet had both spray and flow settings (can you believe it?), my mind was on this damn fowl, the little barking noises he made when anyone came out the front door, the way he perched on the front stoop, his impeccable timing at always finding his way into the safety of the garage just before dark, the completely silly, unapologetically joyful look he got on his face when Abigail or Caroline picked him up.

Why was I thinking like that?

Twenty minutes or so later, my phone rang with Pam's name on the caller ID.

"He's okay," she said. "There are feathers all over the yard and a little bit of blood, but I think the blood is from the dog because I couldn't find anything wrong with Buddy—no cuts, no wounds, no signs of trauma. He's just acting a little anxious."

Why did I feel so relieved?

"What happened?" I asked.

"I'm heading back to the house. I've shut him in the garage so he can regroup. I'll tell you when I get there."

I bided time while we waited for Pam. It was one of those beautiful May afternoons, a hint of the summer ahead. Mark was poking around the landscaping, basically recommending things to me that I would soon learn I couldn't afford. Colleen, bored out of her brain, was just waiting to head to dinner. "Well, you almost got your wish," she said.

In fact, I did get my wish. I was just embarrassed to explain why. Pam pulled into the gravel driveway with the crunching sound that would become very familiar. When she got out of the car, I could see that she had been crying but was happy at the same time—her tears, undoubtedly, of fear and then relief and, ultimately, joy.

She pressed her face against my shoulder as I greeted her by her car, shut her eyes, and simply said, "I don't know what I would have done."

"What happened?"

My sister and brother-in-law approached and did a very

credible job of acting concerned about Buddy's well-being. Months later, Buddy would actually chase Colleen down the length of the yard at Abigail's birthday party, pretty much providing the unexpected entertainment for sixteen ten-year-old girls, but she couldn't see that coming yet.

"Somebody was visiting a house down the street with a dog. They took the dog out for a walk, and they're going past my place, and the dog sees Buddy and freaks out."

She paused to collect herself, then continued, "The stupid dog charges Buddy. My neighbor is right next door and sees it all happening. Buddy starts flapping his wings. The dog is trying to bite him, but Buddy's not backing off. He's jumping in the air and pecking at the dog. Feathers are flying, the dog is getting pecked at, Buddy's screaming. I guess it was quite a scene. Finally the guy gets his dog on a leash, and that's when they called me."

"So Buddy basically beat up a dog?" I asked. I have no idea why I felt pangs of pride.

Pam thought about that a moment, smiled, and said, "Yeah, kind of."

She was getting color back into her face and strength into her voice. We agreed to shake it off and go to dinner. On the way to the car, Pam put her head against my shoulder again and said, "I know it's weird, but I love that damned bird."

I wasn't in love, but I was starting to get what she meant.

*   *   *

They say you can't put a price tag on any kind of love, let alone true love, but it seemed as if Pam was giving it a shot. It was a week before we were to move into our new house, a week before the moving trucks would pull up to my place and take all my possessions, and my largely solitary life would slip into that tender world of the past tense.

Pam and I met with the builder of our new house, Adam, for some last-minute tweaks. It's important to understand that Adam basically regarded me as if I had just shuttled in from another planet. I worked not with my hands (unless you count typing) but with my mind, and some people would even dispute that. I didn't own a toolbox. I couldn't pick a wrench out of a lineup of hammers. When I took the kids fishing in Maine, I needed Abigail, aged nine, to tie my lines and teach me to cast. Seriously, picture the scene with a forty-something-year-old guy holding a bright pink Disney Princess fishing rod, a towheaded girl beside him demonstrating when to hold the stupid little button and when to let go. "You can do it, Brian," she'd say. All along, some guy in waterproof Orvis overalls is standing about twenty yards away, every kind of bait imaginable in a veritable steamer trunk of a tackle box on the beach, looking on in shame that I, too, am a man.

Pam, on the other hand, had an innate understanding of how things fit together in the material world. She had a surgeon's hands and an engineer's outlook. She could talk to Adam in a way that I couldn't about cabinetry and flooring and fixtures. Adam tried to be as respectful as humanly possible to me, but in the end it was an obvious struggle, and he inevitably directed most of his attention toward Pam.

On that day, Pam decided that we needed a fence. The only thing I knew about fences was that they cost money—undoubtedly a lot of money.

"What about one of those nice invisible fences?" I suggested. "That way we're not breaking up all the clean lines around the house. The lawn flows to the street. Everything's on an even keel."

They both looked at me as if I were nuts.

"I don't trust those fences," Pam said. "The dogs could still run right through them. We live on a main road. There's no margin for error. We don't want to be taking that risk."

Adam did a lot of pacing around the perimeter and counting in his mind. He scribbled on a scrap of paper. We settled on split rail. Pam asked for wire or mesh between the rails. "It'll keep the dogs in," she assured me. "Peace of mind. Priceless."

As we were getting ready to leave, Adam said to Pam, "You want to talk about the shed?"

Shed?

"For Buddy," she said to me. "He needs a place to sleep. You said you don't want him in the garage anymore, and I don't blame you."

Wow. Suddenly I started feeling as if the pecking order was being established in the new household, and who the hell would have dared imagine this, but I was coming out on top. I had, in fact, made a request that Buddy not sleep in our brand-new garage. The insides were beautiful—shiny, spotless floors, clean walls, the scent of newness everywhere. Buddy would basically destroy it in a night, what with the terraced furniture leading up to a high perch, his excrement wherever he decided to leave it, feathers, strewn cracked corn that would attract bugs and assorted small animals, though none big enough to threaten his survival. Weeks before, I had made a simple request: can't we get him a small hut? Think doghouse—something waist high with a small door that swings shut. There are probably, what, a billion chickens in this world living in that exact kind of domicile. Why not make it a billion and one?

Pam and Adam headed with one of Adam's crew members to a far corner of the yard while I grabbed some things out of my car—boxes of books and the like—to take into the house. As I was putting them into the immaculate basement, the thought occurred about how nice it was to live in a brand-new house. No one had ever died there. There had been no sad moments, no tears shed, no disappointments, no tragedies, no negative vibes. There would be happiness, and it would be ours. The house would be what we made it.

Pam caught up with me in a few minutes, and we drove back to her house. "It's great," she said. "Adam said he could have Buddy's house done in a day or two."

Buddy, just like us, would have a brand-new place to call his very own.

*   *   *

When I pulled into the house the next afternoon with another carload of stuff that probably should have gone into the trash but was instead heading for the basement, where it would remain until my next move, assuming there was one, though maybe not, I heard power saws and the *thwack* of hammers and men shouting instructions to one another over the noise. I walked across the front lawn, around the house, to see the source, and the next sound that could be heard was my jaw hitting the ground.

Before me, in the corner of the yard that Pam had chosen for Buddy's hut, Adam's crew members had wrestled Tyvek drywall siding into place, and it must have risen eight feet into the air. Above the siding, two guys on ladders were banging cedar shingles into the new pitched roof. Two other men were installing clapboard. This little hut was probably the size of my first studio apartment in Boston, though that had been a fifth-floor walk-up and Buddy wouldn't be required to expend that kind of energy to get into his new home. It was nicer than half the houses we had looked at in our months-long search, and much better built.

I stared in silence, my mind trying to get around what all this meant. Adam yelled to one of his workers, "Cut the hole for the transom window right there!" He was pointing above what would be the door. Transom?

He turned around, saw me agape at the proceedings, and said, "My next life, I want to be your rooster. This is the nicest chicken house in town."

In town? There's not another rooster in any of these United States that resides in the kind of splendor that Buddy would come to have in my side yard, including a transom window to make it all aesthetically pleasing and high ceilings to create a sense of space. You have got to be kidding me.

Over the next couple of days, I would watch them install a gently sloping mahogany ramp with toeholds that led to the front of the shed. They hung tall, heavy cedar double doors that fit snugly together at night, with a latch to hold them firmly in place. They built a wide shelf across the back of the shed, which Pam eventually covered with soft quilts and blankets. Someone, I assume Pam, placed a white upholstered chair that had once held a prominent spot in my study in Boston next to the shelf. It all allowed for Buddy to climb the ramp every dusk, high-step through the regal doors, hop onto the chair, then float up onto the shelf, where he would nod off to sleep without a worry in the world. Shortly after dark, Pam or I would walk out and latch the doors shut, leaving him in perfect, protected peace. Come morning, everything would happen in reverse.

As I said, not in America did another fowl have accommodations like this rooster.

On day 3, the painter arrived, efficiently applying a coat of red paint with cream trim that matched our house exactly. Buddy, in essence, had the same crib as I did. Maybe it's irrational to feel you just lost a competition that you're not even sure existed to a rooster who might or might not have been aware of it, but it's how I felt—defeated, and very publicly at that. Half the town was slowing to a crawl as they drove past the yard, probably wondering if it was some sort of illegal rental apartment we were putting up, or maybe a carriage house. They would soon find out. It doesn't help when your two real estate agents, Laura Semple and Beth Hettrich, are leaving you voice mails as they're driving past your new house saying, and I quote, "Buddy's going to need central air-conditioning." I never let Pam hear the message out of fear that she'd think they were right.

There was, of course, a critical question in all this, one I asked Pam on the phone one of those afternoons while the crew of men continued to put the finishing touches on the rooster house. "How much is this costing us?"

"Don't worry," she said. "I've got this one covered. I'm sure he's giving us a good deal."

On the eve of our move, I swung by the house on my eternal mission to unload still more boxes as the guys were stapling wire to the split-rail fence that they had just put up. They were wrapping up, so I went over to thank them. A very nice worker named Ron gave a good tug at one of the wire pieces to demonstrate that it wasn't going to budge. Peace of mind about the dogs, as Pam had said.

"There's no way any predator is getting inside this yard to get at the chicken," he said. And with that, dawn breaks on Marblehead. Of course. That's why Pam wanted a fence to begin with. That's why she didn't like the invisible fence, because it would serve only to keep the dogs in, not to keep wild animals out. That's why she needed the mesh, to really keep the predators at bay. Basically, we had just spent a small fortune—actually, make that a large fortune—to create a safe little kingdom for Buddy to roam by day and a palace in which he could sleep at night. Giving the king a throne would surely assist with the management of his outsized personality disorder.

>16<

It happened, as some of life's important things do, by accident. Pam was putting Caroline to bed. Abigail was sitting
Indian-style on the floor of her own room, biding time
until her mother came in, when I knocked softly on her
open door, walked in, and sat down next to her. The first
good sign was that she didn't seem to mind.

"What are you doing?" I asked.

"Nothing."

"No, you're sitting. You're thinking. You're daydream-
ing or planning or hoping or fretting. You're doing some of
that or none of that, but you're doing something."

She looked up at me, less annoyed than intrigued,
which, again, was a good sign.

I definitely didn't want to ask the next logical question,
which was "What are you thinking about?" because her
likely lack of a response could shut everything down right
there and then, so my eyes darted about the room, looking

for another direction to go in, something, physically, to grab on to.

In walked Baker.

"Here he is!" I exclaimed.

"Baker!" Abigail called out, in the way she does where she lingers on the *r*.

He trudged proudly between us and flopped out on the floor with a loud, laborious groan. Abigail stroked his back while I rubbed his ears and tried to stretch out the moment.

And that's when I saw it: her bookshelf. On it were, ahem, books. Why hadn't I thought of this before? Where was my head? I casually crawled over, scanned through some of the titles, and pulled out a paperback on owls.

"Have you read this?" I asked.

"What is it?"

"*Who.*"

"No, what is it?" she said.

"*Who.*"

"What?" She was annoyed now, which I didn't mind.

"I'm telling you what. *Who.* It's about owls."

She laughed, admittedly not particularly hard, but a nice, sincere little giggle. To me, it might as well have been gold.

"Do you want me to read it to you?" I asked.

She was looking over at the book, scratching Baker's chin, and she said, "You can read it if you want."

"No, do *you* want me to read it out loud?"

She said, "If you want."

Rather than get frustrated, I read. I read about owl habitats. I read about the difference between snow owls and white owls. I read about how owls stalk their prey, about how they see in the night, about how they relate to other birds.

At first, Abigail was noncommittal about the whole exercise, not wanting to give too much away. But as I kept going, reading in an animated voice, she scooched over so she could see the pictures, and gradually we found ourselves sitting on the floor side by side, our backs against her bed, Baker softly snoring in front of us.

"Last page," I said, wondering what had happened to Pam.

"No! One more chapter," Abigail pleaded.

So one more chapter it was. I'd had no idea that owls were this interesting. I'd had no idea that reading aloud was this much fun. Abigail was now engrossed, leaning against me, making comments about the miracle of how far they can rotate their heads.

Finally, I dramatically snapped the book shut. The bedside table clock said it was 9:15, well after the hour she should have gone to sleep, and I theatrically announced, "Bed!"

Abigail laughed again. "Brushing my teeth," she said, scampering from the room. I used the break to slip down the hall into Caroline's room, to see Pam passed out beside her in bed, the two look-alikes fast and deeply asleep. Oh, boy.

I beat Abigail back into her room. Bedtime always involved their mother tucking each of them in, spending time with them until they fell asleep. This would be interesting and I assumed would end with me waking Pam up to send Abigail off to dreamland. And sure enough, as Abigail climbed onto her twin bed in her footed pajamas, she asked in exaggerated fashion, "Where's Mommy?"

"She fell asleep with Caroline," I said. "Why don't I read another couple of pages to you."

She thought about that for a long moment, and I was fairly certain she was about to reject the proposal, until she said happily, "Two pages."

She stretched out. I sat on the edge of her bed. We read four more pages, truth be known, until I could see her eyelids grow heavy and her look grow spacey, and I dog-eared the book where we left off, shut off the light, and whispered good night.

"Don't leave yet," she said.

I didn't. I sat in the dark for five, ten, fifteen minutes of quiet bliss. I sat in total silence until I could hear her breathing grow steady, pronounced, and rhythmic, and then I slowly pulled myself up from the bed without making any noise. Baker struggled to his feet to follow me.

It was a weeknight. I needed to be in the newsroom early the next morning to help make decisions on who might go if we, the *Globe*, needed to lay off staffers—painful decisions that I didn't want to be rushed or out of sorts when I was making. In other words, I needed to get back into Boston that night. So I quietly crept into Caroline's room and touched Pam gently on the wrist. She roused quickly.

I think mothers might be the lightest sleepers of all time, always on the alert even when they aren't.

"I'm taking off," I whispered.

It was dark. Pam was disoriented. She looked at Caroline beside her and then back at me as she got her bearings. She squinted as she asked, "Where's Abigail?"

"She's asleep," I said, unable to prevent a small smile.

"She's asleep?" Pam's hair was tangled. One side of her face was red from being smooshed into a pillow. She looked, in a word, adorable.

"I'll tell you about it later," I said.

I gave Pam a quick kiss. I gave Baker a long nuzzle on his forehead, whispering "You stay here and make sure everyone is okay." He seemed to understand, because as I tiptoed out, he sat down on the rug in Caroline's room and simply watched.

I quietly slipped out the front door into the cool night air for the drive back to Boston. Truth is, I didn't even need my car. I could have floated home.

*   *   *

The next afternoon, at about five o'clock, deadline in full bloom, there were stories that needed to be overhauled, a page-one editor who needed to be sold on our best work, reporters who needed a few minutes of time, and some breaking news spilling forth from the omnipresent police scanners on the city desk. In other words, a typical day in the newsroom. The phone rang in my office. Pam was on the other end of the line.

"It's Abigail," Pam said, a tone of mild surprise in her voice. "She wants to know what time you're getting down here tonight."

I thought of the night before, of her pleas for another chapter, another page, another paragraph. I thought of her drifting off to sleep slowly and quietly. I thought of how good it had all felt, tranquil and purposeful. I also felt another presence and looked up to see two people waiting at my door for me to get the hell off the phone.

"Tell her as soon as I can, but I'll get there by bedtime," I said. "I will."

And I was, and we did the whole thing all over again, a few more chapters, some easy laughs, and an odd and sudden fascination with owls by both of us. With me sitting on the edge of her bed in the dim light of her room, she fell asleep this time without even asking for her mother. It was pure bliss.

And so it was that a routine was born. We read more books in the series, about dolphins and lions and, yes, chickens, all of them checked out of the school library by Abigail. We went on to a serial featuring the lead character, Katie Kazoo, who would routinely be transformed by a magic wind that occasionally blew through her life. We read the entire Puppy Place series, which involves the Peterson family fostering dogs from the local shelter, always successfully finding just the right owners. I found myself regularly haunting the children's section at Barnes &

Noble, studying the shelf that held the Newbery Award winners. I steered Abigail toward the classics, which were probably more riveting for me than for her, but she was good enough to accommodate. Pinocchio allowed me to constantly pronounce the name of the father, Geppetto, with great flair, an Italian accent that I didn't actually have. Abigail smiled at first, until she didn't, which is when she simply rolled her eyes.

It got to the point that I looked forward to our bedtime routine with greater anticipation than I'd had for that nine o'clock postwork, postworkout beer and burger with the guys. It was somehow more gratifying, and much less fattening.

We were just beginning another classic, *The Wonderful Wizard of Oz,* a book that had me especially intrigued. It had been my favorite movie as a kid—and, okay, as an adult. I had read many other books in L. Frank Baum's often overlooked series but not this, the best-known one. The first couple of chapters were a little rocky. Abigail was skeptical of liking something that involved such an evil witch, not to mention graphic death, but we survived that and were introduced to the Scarecrow, and prospects were looking up. Back in the newsroom my phone rang. A friend named Richard was on the other end of the line.

"Picture yourself sitting in the tenth row of the Garden tonight," he said, adding "I'll even buy the beer."

On that particular night, the Celtics were playing the Lakers in the NBA finals, an extension of their storied decades-long rivalry. This wasn't just the toughest ticket in town, it was probably the toughest ticket in the United States that night.

"How the hell did you get a pair?" I asked.

"A customer," Richard said. Richard was a restaurant general manager, one of the best in the city, and people tended to take care of him.

In my head I was already flipping through the highlight reel that would be this night—the ice-cold pregame oysters and smoked salmon at the nearby Oceanaire, the pageantry and celebrity that are the NBA finals, the fraternity of being with a good and old friend, the beer, the action, the view, the whole entire blissful scene of being part of such a critical moment. I had been following the Celtics religiously since I was old enough to heave a basketball toward a ten-foot rim, which was probably around the third grade. I'd spent so much of my youth shooting basket after basket on the hottest summer nights and the coldest winter afternoons in the narrow confines of our driveway, constantly calling the game under my breath, the hero in my running narrative. *McGrory fakes right, dribbles left, stops, pumps, shoots, scores! How does he always do it? How does he have that knack for making every critical shot at every critical time? Ladies and gentlemen, the crowd is so crazy you can't even hear yourself think.*

I played varsity ball for two years in high school. In college, I lived for the Celtics-Lakers rivalry. And now, more than a quarter of a century later, here was the chance to sit in Boston Garden and watch the greatest rivalry in the NBA. I thought I couldn't be any luckier than this.

But then I thought about something else. I thought of Abigail, the look on her face when Pam informed her I wouldn't be around to read that night. I thought of her heading into her room without me, looking at the copy of *The Wonderful Wizard of Oz* sitting on the table by her bed. Would she read it alone, struggling to understand the poppy fields or the actions of the Cowardly Lion? Would she be able to get to sleep? Would she think I'd let her down?

I swallowed hard. I think I had sweat dripping from my brow. "You're not going to believe this," I said to Richard, my tone having lost about 90 percent of its altitude from two minutes before, "but I can't make it."

"Great," Richard responded. "Let's meet at Oceanaire at about six thirty. We'll grab some oysters and IPAs before we sashay into the game."

I was silent. He had heard me perfectly well but was just giving me a hard time. He said, "So you're going in for a vasectomy today?"

"One of the kids," I replied. "Abigail." I hesitated for a minute before completely coming clean, but I knew that Richard wasn't just a father but one of the better ones I had ever met—a guy, in other words, who would inherently understand.

"I told her I'd read to her tonight, and I don't want to go back on my word without any notice."

There was silence between us again. Perhaps we were

both considering the monumental change, how it had gone from what I was to what I am. "You know what?" he said, causing me to gird a bit for what was coming next— that I'm an idiot, that I'm a mediocre friend, that I had completely lost my mind and my way.

"You're doing the right thing. Twenty years from now, you won't remember the game, but you will remember reading to the kid."

That certainly sounded nice—until he added an amendment: "You know what, I'm wrong about that. You actually would remember the game twenty years from now, and I'm not sure you'd remember this specific night reading to the kid. But that's not really the point anymore."

I wasn't completely sure what he was saying, but whatever he meant, I knew he was right.

*   *   *

I arrived at about 7:30 that night because of work and traffic, long past the dinner hour, but in enough time to catch them before they surrendered to the kind of exhaustion that can unapologetically overwhelm girls of that age. They were both splayed out on the couch when I walked in, staring blankly at SpongeBob on TV, a show I happen to dislike for its moronity. Buddy lay between them, oddly calm—just another night watching TV with your pet chicken. The bird was staring so intently at the screen that he looked as if he would have pecked off someone's hand if they reached for the remote control. As it was, his head twitched around just far enough for him to glare in my direction.

"Hello, young children," I said, needlessly announcing my presence in the fading light of the living room. They gave me a hello, neither warm nor cold. I knew better than to disturb them anymore in midshow, so I made my way into the kitchen to find Pam preparing their lunches and snacks for the next day. The work of motherhood, I was learning, pretty much never ends.

"I'd like to get them upstairs and into bed early tonight," Pam said. "They've got dentist appointments before school tomorrow morning."

Sometimes, thinking about what filled her days—the running around, the constant commotion, the fleeting sense of control—my knees just about buckled while my heart raced. I didn't share that. Instead I said, "Whatever I can do to help, just let me know."

Twenty or so minutes later, as we chatted at the table, Pam called out, "Two-minute warning." I heard an "Awwwwwwwww" from the other room that made me smile. Then I heard the rooster give a long, loud protest crow.

"And get him back outside!" Pam called out. "He's got to get to his shelf before dark."

I went in to play the role I imagined for myself that probably wasn't really mine, at least not often enough—that of the facilitator, the go-between who added some perspective and humor to the typical and inevitable parent/ child tensions.

"Buddy goes outside," I said, emphatically, waving one arm in the direction of the door in mock anger. "And you two—upstairs. Now!"

They, of course, didn't budge. Actually, let me correct that. Abigail yawned, and Caroline flicked the channel to a Disney movie that was just starting. "Hey, Mom," she yelled, as if I weren't even there. "*Homeward Bound* is on. Can we watch?"

"No. Bedtime."

"Awwwwwwwww."

The two of them slowly lifted themselves to their feet, sleepy-eyed, grabbed their blankets, and trudged upstairs. The dogs hoisted themselves up and followed, like one long parade.

"Abs, I'll be right up to read to you."

"That's all right," she said absently. She kept walking, her blanket dragging along the wooden stairs.

"No, I said, I'll be right up. We're about to get introduced to the Tin Man."

"I'm too tired," she replied.

I stood there in the landing with one simple thought banking around my brain: I gave up the Celtics for this? I checked the time. It was a few minutes before the opening tip-off. Richard and I would have been settling into our seats right now, clutching our first beer, getting acclimated, drinking in the show that was the NBA finals, Celtics-Lakers style.

Instead, there I was standing in a dim foyer listening to a nine-year-old trudge along an upstairs hallway and—what's that now?—the door to her bedroom softly shutting behind her. I actually started hyperventilating. I wanted to shout to the heavens, please, let me have my decision back from this afternoon. Give me one lousy mulligan. Put me in my seat at the Garden, and let me live the life I was meant to have.

Please.

"Are you okay?"

That was Pam, who was walking toward the staircase to see the kids off to bed, a load of laundry in her arms.

"Yes, I'm fine," I said.

"You don't look so good," she said, squeezing around me.

"Abigail said she doesn't want me to read to her tonight," I said.

"Yeah," Pam replied, "she's pretty tired. We're all pretty tired. Long day, and morning comes early."

I wanted to tell Pam what I had given up, where I could have been, the fun I should have been having, and for what? To be discarded in the foyer of their house as if it or I didn't matter. Calm, Brian, calm. Instead, watching her lug piles of clean clothes up the stairs on her way to get her kids off to bed, I wisely kept my mouth shut.

Still, I followed her up the stairs, gently tapped on Abigail's door, and walked inside.

The lights were off. Abigail was under the covers, her favorite stuffed animal, Who-Hoo, lying with its head on the pillow beside her. I don't exactly know what Who-Hoo was. It looked kind of like a dog but seemed like a puppet. Maybe a puppet of a dog. I asked softly, "Are you sure you don't want me to read?" I knew perfectly well that I was approaching the territory of sounding like an idiot, and in my more honest moments, I was pushing the issue at that specific moment more because of what I had given up than what I wanted to have.

"I'm sure," she said.

I did what I always did at bedtime. I placed two fingers to my lips, then pressed them briefly against the back of her head. Nobody, for good or bad, is ever going to accuse me of too much demonstration. She didn't move an eyelash. I said good night, got only an indiscernible response, and left. If women were a mystery to me at my advanced age, take it as fact that girls were a total enigma.

Downstairs, I checked the time again. It should have been about ten minutes into the game. I was tired. I hadn't eaten. I had a long drive back to the city ahead of me. I figured I'd watch some of the game at Pam's before getting into my car during halftime.

When I walked into the darkened living room and went to turn on the television, I heard a twisted, twirling scream that cause me to reflexively fling the remote in the air. I looked down, and a shock of white was rising from the couch, moving in my direction.

"Buddy, shush," I said.

He walked to the edge of the couch where I was and began making guttural noises, sounds as if he were a kung fu champion preparing to tear me apart. I flicked a light on and saw his wings flapping, his head twitching, and his eyes looking warily at me from the sides of his face.

"Buddy, it's fine," I said.

It actually wasn't. Pam was asleep. The kids were asleep. The dogs were asleep. I sure as hell wasn't going to carry him out to his shelf in the garage, and I knew if I took a broom and tried to push him outside, he'd shout bloody murder and wake up the house and the whole neighborhood. I tried to move to the other side of the couch, still determined to somehow watch the game, but he marched down to that end, warning me with those karate sounds to keep the hell away.

In his mind, his couch, his house, his kids, his woman. I was but the interloper in this group, and judging from everyone else's attitude that night, maybe he was right. Maybe he was telling me what the others didn't have the heart to say directly.

"Screw you, Buddy," I said. I turned off the light. I grabbed my keys from the kitchen table. And as I pulled the front door shut, I could hear that little jerk clucking for joy.

>17<

The morning dawned early on the last day of my old life. I took Baker for a sunrise walk down the banks of the Charles River. We looped through the Boston Public Garden and padded side by side up Newbury Street, his tongue almost hanging to the cement. I thought I'd be morbid, drinking in the scenery as if I'd never see it again, but I had convinced myself of the truth: this was more a beginning than an ending, the move long past due, and not to sound like one of those saccharine kitten-hanging-from-a-branch plaques, but if you don't change, you wither. It was, to use an overused expression that I've never particularly liked, all good.

When the movers arrived around 8 A.M., the crew chief briefly looked around my apartment, stepped back into the hallway, and made a call on his cell phone.

"You told me this was a big move," I heard him say to whoever it was on the other end, the annoyance evident in his voice. "No. There's barely anything here. We'll be done in an hour and we'll have eighty percent of the truck open, so let me know if you want to throw in another stop."

Barely anything here. That's nice. Just my whole life.

He was right about the timing, anyway. They were gone in what felt like a snap, gone with the couch I had bought on a whim at a going-out-of-business sale during a Sunday-afternoon walk with Harry, the leather chair that had been a gift to myself when I got the column at the *Globe,* the desk where I had written novels, the armoire I had claimed from my broken marriage, plates and utensils that had hardly seen any use. On and on, until I signed some paperwork and the crew told me they'd see me the next day in suburbia.

"That's going to be quite a change for you, isn't it?" the burly supervisor asked, as if it had never occurred to me that things might be different.

"No big deal," I replied. "Just every single thing about my entire life." I walked back inside from the sun-splashed sidewalk to an apartment that was barren of everything but an overnight bag and a very perplexed dog.

"Well, Bake Sale, this is it," I said to Baker, who was intently staring at me, straining to understand this seismic event in our lives, all our furniture, our possessions, taken away by those beefy men. He was walking from empty room to empty room, the sound of claws on hardwood echoing from the high ceilings. I sat on the floor, my back to a wall, and he came over and sprawled out beside me with a long, laborious groan, confident that if I was there, things were going to be okay.

My gaze slowly floated around the room, the memories flooding back. I thought of the first time I'd ever stepped foot in the place, a Monday morning probably ten Januarys earlier. It was a wreck, the overcrowded home to a family of four that was finally fleeing for more space, but even amid the clutter, it was love at first sight. I put a bid in by that afternoon. We were done negotiating the next morning. I had no idea I'd live there for more than a decade.

I recalled that feeling after the closing, of walking into a place that's all yours, the anticipation as walls were being painted and floors sanded and rugs ripped up and replaced—everything ahead of you, the overriding hope being that reality can keep up with your dreams. And it did, for the most part—work, books, life, all of it better than I had hoped.

My eyes wandered to the various places in the apartment where Harry used to take his naps—at the top of the hallway, in the study beside my desk, under the left-hand window in the bay as cool air drifted in from the outside. I thought of the warm evenings when we used to sit on the stoop, of the winter mornings waking up to snow, of the Thanksgiving dinners I used to host with Harry wedged tight under my chair because he so disliked crowds. I thought of that September morning when I'd put Harry down and of the afternoon a couple of weeks later when Pam Bendock had knocked on my door.

I thought of how I had done all of that—or most of it—

on my own, built a new life after a rough divorce, moved to Washington, returned to Boston, became a columnist, laughed off failures big and small, every one of them a lesson learned. But most of all, I thought about how a skeptic had transformed into something of an optimist, how my tone had become lighter over the years, my acceptance greater, my insecurities more in check. And I thought about how Harry had had no small role in that, sometimes pushing me, other times making me slow down, always my faithful guide.

My phone rang, and Pam's name popped up. She had known, as she always knows, to give me space on this last night and morning, to let me work through things in my head. It was one of her many gifts, to either be there at the exact right time or not be there when she knew that was what I needed. "So you've canceled the movers and decided to stay," she said lightly.

"I'm a sitting, breathing cliché, here in my empty apartment playing out a highlight reel of my life."

"I hope I make at least a cameo appearance in it," she said. She paused and added, "I'm outside the lawyer's office." She was about two streets away, and we were due to pass the papers on our new house. "How long is this film? Should we start without you?"

"I'll be there in five minutes," I said.

I rose to my feet, gathered my wits and my overnight bag, and informed my anxious dog, "Don't worry, you're coming with me."

In the doorway, I lingered for an extra moment, my gaze floating one final time across the stage set that had been so central to my life. Without endings, I told myself, there are no beginnings, and with that Baker and I were gone.

*　*　*

The papers were all signed and passed, the movers had delivered two housefuls of furniture to our one new home, the kids roared from one room to the next, happily screaming their lungs out, before rushing outside to set up their horse jumps in the yard, the dogs were poking through every corner wondering what it was all about, when Pam turned to me, a wisp of blond hair matted to her forehead, and said, "I'd better go get Buddy."

We weren't quite married yet, but she did have a ring on her finger, I had no other home now but with her, and we had committed to an eternal partnership through that other, most sacred of M words: a mortgage. In other words, I was in no position to tell her, No, I don't want him anywhere near this place.

"He's going to love it here," I said.

"What's not to love?" she asked, jangling her keys in her hand on her way out the door.

Buddy would supply his own (loud) answer soon enough. But first the kids were still galloping around the yard as if they were a few cards short of a full deck. The dogs were hyperaware of every one of my movements. And I was roaming through the house—my house, my suburban house—just trying to get acclimated.

Be calm, I warned myself. You're nothing special. Everyone moves at some point in their lives, often at several points. There were probably tens of thousands of moving vans traversing America's highways carrying countless tons of furniture at that very moment, each and every truck, every single move, leading someone toward not just a new home but a state of uncertainty. And let's face it, this being 2010, many of those moves weren't by choice. I was going from a small city apartment to a real live adult house. I was moving in with the woman I loved and planned to marry. I would be living with two children, who would instill in me a greater sense of purpose and responsibility. It was all new and all different and all part of the grand cycles of life. At the tender age of forty-eight, I, Brian McGrory, was growing up.

So why in the back of my mind did I still have the expectation that come bedtime, I'd be wishing everyone good night and returning to Boston, with all that wonderful concrete and congestion, where I belonged?

"Buddy's here! Boo-Boo's here!"

That was the kids, screaming from the depths of their lungs while they raced across the yard to their mother, who was emerging from her car with a rather annoyed snow-white rooster tucked under one arm. From the kitchen window, I watched the kids stroke Buddy's face from the other side of the fence. I heard him cluck and coo. I heard

Caroline say in her little voice, "You're going to love this place. Everything's brand-new!" I heard Pam say, "All right, I'm going to come in and let him down."

That's when something odd happened; at least I thought it odd at the time. This new house sat on a piece of land that was just a few postage stamps under an acre, almost all of it cleared, and most of that lawn—which meant it was a good-sized lawn, spreading wide and somewhat far. It was an innocent piece of land, fenced in, green, absent any clusters of trees that might be holding predators who were eager to establish the—pun fully intended here—pecking order. So what did Buddy do when Pam walked through the gate, crouched, and set him free into the joyous green environs of his new world?

Answer: he scampered onto the covered front porch as if he were fleeing Frank Perdue. He looked furiously from side to side, then at the kids, then at Pam, then back at the kids, then nowhere in particular, his head spasming atop his bulbous body. Finally, with unparalleled authority, he let out a screaming, screeching *cock-a-doodle-doo* that just about brought down the house. And then he offered an encore.

"Oh, you poor little rooster-boy," Abigail said, climbing onto the porch with him.

For once in his life, Buddy didn't particularly care about the attention. He screamed again, then again and still again, barely pausing to draw in little rooster breaths. The kids eventually got bored and went off to continue their horse jumping on the other side of the yard. Pam went back to her car to carry in some last-minute junk she had taken from her old house. Buddy went nowhere. He followed nobody. I stood in the kitchen, leaning on the sink, wondering how long one animal could continue making this kind of catastrophic racket. If past was precedent, if our experience in Maine was any indication, the answer would prove to be a miserable one. But right then I seemed to be the only one who cared.

>18<

Before the move, I had visions, dreams maybe, of working a day or two a week from my home study or, even better, from the table on our back porch, typing up a column in the summertime sun amid the sounds of chirping birds and the beauty of so many blossoming flowers. In that dream, there were in fact animals, but they had fur and four legs and were lying at my feet, softly snoring in the summery breeze.

Two or three days out in suburbia, I set out to make the dream a reality. Pam was at her clinic. The kids were in their last week of school. I pulled my laptop out onto the back deck, grabbed my trademark legal pad filled with notes from recent interviews, and began to write my next column. Buddy happened to be on the front porch, crowing his little brains out, much of the sound blocked out by the house mercifully standing between us.

Okay, this was working. As I typed, I paused to watch

butterflies flutter in the nearby arborvitaes. The scent was of freshly mown grass. The sun was warm, the breeze was gentle, and the creativity flowed freely from my brain to my fingers. Maybe, I told myself, this suburban thing would work after all. I used to try to write from my front stoop, but the city street, the whole active urban world, would almost always overwhelm my thoughts.

Buddy, of course, kept crowing in the distance, though the source of the noise slowly shifted from directly in front of the house to the front side of the house, steadily moving in the way you can track the movement of a faraway fire engine siren on an otherwise silent night, gradually, subtly, until it's nearby and blaring at you. He was now on the side of the house and quickly coming toward the back, louder, and louder still.

Suddenly he turned the corner. I could not only hear him as clear as cannon fire but also see his white, blubbery body with its red comb bobbing and twitching as he walked straight across the grass and toward the deck where I sat, crowing all the while. He hopped up the two steps, still screaming.

"Buddy," I told him, "for chrissakes, pipe down. There's nothing to be afraid about."

Shockingly, he didn't take my advice. What he did was walk straight toward me, methodically, a bird on a mission, his beady little eyes just about popping out the sides of his narrow head. About ten feet out, the length of a putt I would have been delighted to make, he made a long, angry, guttural sound and charged my leg.

I leaped to my feet yelling "Jesus Christ!" The dogs were laying in the grass nearby, too lazy, surprised, or frightened to come to my defense. I was up just in the nick of time, positioning the chair between me and the bird, but he was a determined little creature.

He did a two-step sidestep around the chair, which I kept between us like a lion tamer. He kept walking; I kept turning. He was squawking; I was telling him to calm the hell down. We continued to circle each other. I finally found myself with a clear shot at the back door, the chair still between me and Buddy, so I put it down and ran for my life. He came scampering after me, fluttering a couple of feet off the ground to try to get up speed. I flung open the screen door, slipped inside, and slammed it shut on Buddy's beak. He stood in the doorway, screeching threats until I shut the main door in his face, and then he continued to scream some more. That was the first and last time I tried to work outside.

I should have known I was being too ambitious, but exhaustion might have been getting the best of me. Every morning began at about 4:30 with Buddy breaking into a crowing regimen from his rooster house, which still didn't have windows because they were special-ordered and hadn't yet arrived. So every morning I would bolt upright. Every morning Pam would scramble out of bed, trek across the lawn, grab Buddy, and carry him to the basement. Every morning he'd start crowing from downstairs at about 5:30 A.M., usually right as I had miraculously fallen back to sleep. Say this about that bird, his timing was impeccable.

Once he started crowing at 5:30, he basically never stopped. He would pause while the kids came downstairs to eat breakfast before school, clucking around the kitchen floor, high-stepping between two wary dogs, who threw me looks that demanded, *What the hell kind of barn are we living in?* You know things are bad when your golden retriever questions the civility of where he lives. But when it was time for Buddy to go outside, he started it up all over again, volcanic, relentless *cock-a-doodle-doo*s that never had an end. Just on and on, the next one louder than the one before. The rare times he took a break, usually to get a drink of water because his little beak had apparently dried out from screeching, the sound still echoed around my head. If I wasn't listening to him crow, I was hearing the residue or girding to hear it again.

And he wasn't just loud but ornery, and not a little bit ornery but your basic beast on two skinny legs. As out of sorts as I was in the new house, Buddy was further gone. Most nights, he refused to put himself to bed in his new house, as he used to do in Pam's garage. Instead he'd huddle in a corner of the front porch, protected by the overhang and taking solace in the knowledge that he was closer to his flock: Pam and her kids. Standing in the kitchen, I'd hear Pam, outside after dark, picking him up, cradling him in her arms, carrying him to the nest of blankets on a high shelf in his own house, telling him "Boo, I need you to get used to all this. I need you to calm down. You're too good a rooster to be this upset." He'd coo back as if he understood every word and meant to honor it, but the next day, the screaming started anew.

As far as I could tell, Buddy seemed to blame me for every ounce of his anxiety, and it wasn't lost on me that I was basically blaming him for mine. He hated me. To be fair, he didn't really understand the point of me. If he was already living on Sawmill Lane, the self-designated head of the flock, what was I doing around? What purpose did I serve? Sometimes, when the kids described it as "Mommy's house" and marched off to bed with nary a good night, I wondered the same thing myself.

Buddy maintained his aggressive posture. He spent his days lurking around the front or back doors, defecating all over the porches in big, wide white-and-black circles that seemed to bother only me. And whenever I came and went, he would lunge, so that I was forced to roam my own homestead with a rolled-up newspaper jammed into my back pocket, or more often, clutched in my hands. Of the many reasons people had to love the *Globe,* warding off one's pet rooster was probably a new one. He'd charge, I'd swat. He'd stagger backward, not so much intimidated as delighted to be engaged, and charge again. Swat. Jump. At some point he usually tumbled over backward, giving me enough time to make for the door. As I raced to freedom, I'd look up, and inevitably some driver going by would have slowed down right in front of the house to watch the entire encounter, man v. chicken, in shock and awe.

* * *

It's not as though I had never been to a suburban restaurant before, though this was my first visit to a suburban restaurant as a full-fledged citizen of suburbia. It was a Friday night. It was late. Well, suburban late, meaning about 8 P.M. We were less than a week into our new house, and the kids were at their father's for the weekend. Pam and I were exhausted when we walked into a restaurant that many people had raved about, even telling me it was as good as any steak house in Boston. The first thing I noticed was that there wasn't a person under the age of forty in the place. Nobody. It was as if they had raised the drinking age by twenty years. It was a warm evening after a beautiful early summer's day, so almost every stool at the long bar was taken by a man in a golf shirt and shorts fresh off the course—or not so fresh. The two bartenders, both men who had a few decades under their aprons, seemed to know every one of them by name.

A hostess who could not possibly have been any less enthusiastic about our arrival informed us that we could seat ourselves in the lounge, so we grabbed the only open high-top table near the bar. It was the first time in a long time that we'd had the chance to have a real, live, uninterrupted conversation, and I noticed that Pam had dark circles under her pretty eyes. I undoubtedly had the same thing, minus the pretty eyes part. How could we not?

"Are we supposed to order from the bar?" I asked

after we'd been sitting for ten minutes and nobody had come over.

"Somebody will come around," Pam said, yawning.

Actually, many people had come around—waitresses and waiters and busboys and the hostess and I think the general manager, possibly the Joint Chiefs of Staff, all of whom had walked right by us without making any eye contact. A couple of times I had even put my hand out in a polite wave, but they had simply looked the other way. I glanced over at the bar and saw the two bartenders merrily chatting with all their regulars, refilling their wineglasses before even being asked and delivering thick cuts of steak bathed in various juices and sauces.

We talked about Buddy. Then we talked about the house and how nice it was, all that space, everything new, the fact the kids had settled in without a speck of hesitation.

"Excuse me, sir?" I said to a server who happened to be walking past. We'd probably been sitting thirty minutes now, and not a person had looked our way. There were guys at the bar who had ordered slow-cooked prime rib after we got there, and they were halfway done with their meals. The server brushed past me, said something to the effect of "I'll send someone right over" and was gone. Apparently, "right over" didn't mean "tonight."

Pam said what I was thinking, which is good, because sometimes you sound like a jackass when you say these things yourself. "You're not used to this, are you?"

I assumed she meant the poor service, the second-class treatment, the fact that I didn't matter to a single person in the place besides, maybe, Pam.

"I don't think I'm used to any of it yet," I replied. She didn't say anything and neither did I, until I realized that I didn't want that to sound more ominous than I intended, so I asked, "Buddy will stop the crowing at some point, right?"

I swear to God, as I posed the question, I thought I could hear him crowing from the dining room; the sound was that ingrained inside the deepest channels of my mind. "He's just getting used to things," Pam said. "It's different for him. We're on a busier street. There's more open space to deal with. His shed, unlike the garage, is away from the house, and I'm not so sure he likes that. I think he liked sleeping under the same roof as everyone else."

It all made sense as she said it—across the open expanse of a completely empty table, void of drinks, of silverware, of menus, because nobody gave a flying damn that we were there.

At that moment a smiling gentleman in his full chef whites came striding around the bar in our direction, stopping to shake some hands with the regulars along the way. He looked jocular, tossing off one-liners that made people laugh, making motions toward their plates, everything light and easy. And here he came toward us, at us—past us. It took me back to the many nights when the chef of some very pleasant Boston restaurant would come out of a much nicer kitchen than this one specifically to see—well, there I go, sounding like a complete jackass. Never mind.

Pam, by the way, seemed to notice none of it, because she was either too tired or too immersed in her thoughts about God's chosen rooster. "It's a lot to get used to for Buddy, especially because he's such a creature of habit," she said.

Then she added, "You know, the two of you have more in common than you think."

With that she slipped off her stool, tugged at my wrist, and said, "Let's get out of here. I'll buy you a pizza and we'll take it home."

"You're assuming the pizza joint will take our order."

On the way out, I noticed the chef with his arm around an elderly man at a table for six, everyone all smiles. I noticed so many waiters and waitresses pushing carts filled with big salads and grilled steaks across the hardwood floors to their destination. At the door, the nice hostess asked, "How was everything?"

"I'm going to tell every person I know about this place," I said.

Pam stifled a laugh. The young woman gave us a big, self-satisfied smile, and we parted ways, never to see each other again.

>19<

I still never knew what I was going to get when I walked into the house, now my house, or partially my house, at the end of a day of work: ebullient kids who would gush about some discovery they had made that day or recite a funny line by their particularly funny friend, Claire, or silent, sullen kids who wanted nothing to do with anything related to me. I'd call Pam on the ride home and casually ask, "How are the kids?" She'd tell me, "Great." And then I'd arrive and they wouldn't so much as look up from their dog-training show on *Animal Planet* to grunt a simple "Hi." Other times, Pam would tell me they were being monsters, and I'd find two adorable kids who would drape their legs over mine as I read them a book on the couch.

During one call, Pam cryptically warned me, and I quote, "Be prepared," which I assumed meant that what awaited on the other end of my long commute was a pair of exhausted kids who would cover their heads with a blanket when I walked into the house. Instead, I got Abigail approaching me in the mudroom before I could even slide out of my jacket and saying with the sweetest smile and in a singsongy voice, "We need to talk."

"Great," I said. "Let's talk. What about?"

She looked at me with her wide eyes, a smile spreading over her smooth face, and announced, "I want a kitten."

I was proud of myself for not flinching, proud that the color didn't drain from my face, proud that I didn't roll into the fetal position and wail, "No *mas,* no *mas,* no more animals in this goddamned house!" I was proud because I had arrived at that point, up to my neck and beyond in the fur and feathers of too many creatures who brought me too little comfort, and I was about one more set of paws from completely cracking up.

Instead, I said, brightly and lightly, "And you know what I want? I want a camel. But the problem is, Abs, we already have more than a few animals in this house, and there's really not a lot of room for any more."

I spoke the truth. We had two dogs, Baker and Walter, Baker being the one I had brought into the household, Walter being Pam's. After Harry died, I'd vowed I would never get another, at least not for a long time. I couldn't take the heartbreak. Three months later, I couldn't take the loneliness, couldn't take the mornings without a long, leisurely walk, couldn't take the nights coming home to an empty apartment, couldn't take the fact that I probably laughed twenty fewer times a day because I didn't have a dog. So I called down to Harry's breeder and had them pick out a puppy from a similar lineage. Before I ever met him, I pitied the poor dog who would live in Harry's shadow, always suffering by comparison. But Baker swaggered into my life without a care in the world. Brilliant? I sincerely expected to catch him on my computer playing video games whenever I got home early from work. He was stubborn. He was athletic. He was small, undoubtedly the runt of his litter, but carried himself large, unimpressed by almost everything going on around him that didn't involve a ball. As a puppy, he had a bizarre fetish for scarves and gloves. More than a few times, some comely woman walking down a Back Bay street would lean down to rub Baker. She'd be cooing at him, when suddenly he'd have her scarf in his teeth, pulling, bringing her with it, the cloth tightening around her neck, her pleading for help.

He was also, to put it politely, a mouthy puppy, playfully biting everything in sight—bare hands, pant legs, once my nose. I couldn't cure the habit, try as I did, so I called in a behaviorist, who showed me a remedy that basically involved violently yanking Baker's scruff as the pup bit the trainer's free hand. Two minutes in, the dog looking at us as if we were crazy, he was cured.

That trainer, Ray, a former member of the U.S. Marine Corps who carried himself as if he had just gotten out of Camp Lejeune, said, "This is one hyperaware little puppy. Let's do some quick exercises."

Baker learned to sit, quickly but skeptically. You could almost see him rolling his eyes at something this remedial. He had a harder time with "Lie down." "It's a more submissive posture," Ray explained, pulling Baker's two front paws out to force him down. "And this doesn't seem to be a very submissive dog."

Then we went outside to start the "Heel" command. Ray put a little training collar around Baker's little neck, and Baker shot him a look that oozed indignation. He proceeded to sit on the sidewalk and refused to move. Ray waved treats in front of his nose. Baker ignored him. Ray started walking, saying "Heel!" in an upbeat voice, giving Baker's collar a quick jerk. Baker lay down and refused to move. That continued for twenty minutes and resumed for the better part of an hour the next week. Normally I like to train my own dogs, but I was curious where this thing with Ray would end up. In fact, it ended up at the corner of Fairfield and Marlborough Streets in the Back Bay of Boston, when Ray handed me the leash to a puppy that had spent the last forty-five minutes sprawled across the pavement in protest, refusing to walk or even rise to his feet. "He's untrainable," Ray declared to me. "No charge for today." When Ray happened to run into us about six months later, Baker padding happily beside me off leash, he looked on in amazement and asked, "How did you do it?"

"I just had to train him at his pace, not ours," I explained.

Walter was pretty much the exact opposite, big, beautiful, and brainless, the Zoolander of the canine world. There was nothing there but the constant and urgent desire for unadulterated affection. He would lean in to perfect strangers, groaning as they stroked him. He liked everyone indiscriminately, except for me. Me he inexplicably loved, which meant he was constantly in my way or panting anxiously as I tried to read or write. Now that we were living together, he saw to it that we never spent a moment apart at home. It was my basic canine nightmare—a thoughtless, anxious, constant presence.

Add to that the two rabbits that lived in a large cage on the kitchen floor, constantly scurrying about, making noise, happily grabbing the food that came their way. Every once in a while, the kids would pull them out to hold and stroke, and one or both would invariably get away, setting off an urgent search-and-rescue operation, the rescue part being for the electric or phone cords that they would invariably chew. Somewhere else in the house, I believe, there were a couple of frogs in a goldfish bowl.

Into this overpopulated world, Abigail wanted to bring a kitten. It was like saying the Brady Bunch sure could have used a few more kids to liven things up.

"But here's the thing," Abigail said, oddly cheery in the face of my initial rejection. "You told me we could get a kitten."

I'd heard that one before. Hell, I'd used a variation on that bluff many times before.

In an exaggerated tone, I said, "I never said you could get a kitten. I probably said, 'Why don't we get you a new pair of mittens?'"

Abigail shook her head, still light and smiling. Something bothered me about it, something I couldn't quite put my finger on. Maybe it was her confidence in the face of my negativity. Maybe it was the fact that, at nine years of age, she had an IQ that was probably fifty points higher than mine. Maybe it was the fact that I was starting to vaguely recall some dumb remark I might have made in regard to a cat many, many long months before. Something I couldn't quite put my finger on. Me saying something.

Or maybe it was the fact that she' was holding something in her hand that she was choosing not to show to me—yet.

"You did say it," she said. "You even wrote it." She held out a sheet of paper, 8.5 by 11 inches, and written across the top were the words "The bearer of this certificate is entitled to one cat of his or her choosing, at a time that he or she desires." Beneath those words was a crude depiction of, I think, a cat, something that a preschooler might have drawn with a beginner's box of Crayola crayons. Beneath that were the words "This certificate expires upon the graduation of the recipient from high school."

And below that was a signature, some virtually illegible scrawl, like that of a madman, and I knew immediately whose it was.

Mine.

Shit.

I looked over at Pam, who had watched the entire scene unfold utterly silently and with a look of bemusement on her face. She flashed me a warm, only semisympathetic smile. From our previous discussions about this, I was beginning to harbor suspicions that she was playing for the opposing team. In her mind, the more animals, the better, and I was living in the physical manifestation of that.

I studied Abigail's sheet like a drug-trafficking suspect inspecting a search warrant at the door of his apartment. Surely I must have been wise enough to write in some escape clause, some technicality to allow for a long stall. I vaguely recalled an eighth birthday, a desperate plea to Pam about what I could get a kid who had everything— every American Girl doll, every imaginable configuration of a stuffed pony, enough arts-and-crafts supplies to last a year's worth of rainy days.

"Well, she really wants a cat," Pam had said then.

A cat, I thought. Okay. I wasn't living with them yet. A lot of things could happen between then and that. It was the afternoon of her birthday. I had no time. I had no ideas. I had only an irrational fear of this one little kid, a fear that I don't think I've ever had of anyone before—not my editors, nor the powerful politicians or the criminals I sometimes wrote about, who were often one and the same. I could only imagine the look if she unwrapped a hula hoop or a badminton set or a board game, as if I was the biggest moron on the face of this Earth. All I wanted was to please her, to have her say thank you and really mean it, to confide in her mother that Brian, swell guy that he is, really does know how to give a good gift.

The day I gave her the certificate, how was I supposed to see into the future? How was I supposed to imagine me and Pam and her kids and a crowing rooster proudly soiling the decks and porches and a dog named Walter panting in my face every moment I was home with a look that said, *You and me forever!* How was I supposed to imagine that the cat promised to the bearer of this certificate could and probably would become my sanity's tipping point?

To tell Abigail no, though, would have turned me into the exact kind of adult that I'd never wanted to become— the untrustworthy one. My job, my persona, was pretty much based on my word. I needed to tell the truth. To that end, I made a point of never even telling any one of my dogs something I didn't know to be completely accurate. I'd never say, "I'll be home in five minutes," if I knew it was actually going to be two hours. I never faked a throw. If you want to have faith in the world around you, you need to give it faith as well.

Of course, to say yes would have meant adding a cat to the barnyard cacophony that had become my life. This was not an easy one.

I looked at Pam again. She shrugged. Never before had I seen her so silent.

So I pulled the ultimate adult stall tactic with Abigail. I told her, "We'll talk about this a little more in the next few days."

And we would have. We absolutely would have, except two cats, one, of course, for young Caroline, arrived before we had time for that talk. At work, I could and would stand up to corrupt politicians. I could and would take unpopular positions in print. At home, though, I buckled in the presence of a nine-year-old girl and her request to turn our house into a glorified petting zoo.

Sure enough, it took me all of about a week to fall completely head over heels for those two cats, particularly the constantly purring one named Charlie. But that doesn't negate the fact that it was just a couple of months into my move, a couple of months into this newfangled family life, and my very name had officially become an antonym for *control.*

*   *   *

A few weeks later, after summer rolled into autumn, I blew out of work at about 5:15 one uneventful Wednesday afternoon with every intention of catching Pam and the kids for dinner. I was learning that I rarely made it home for dinner, though I don't honestly think it was my fault. Young kids need to eat by 5:30 or 6. Newspaper columnists need to work until 5 or 6. Residents of my town have at least an hour's drive during the evening rush hour. The formula, quite simply, didn't work.

Of course, on that particular day, I hit a wall of traffic on the highway that could make the sanest commuter question the meaning and purpose of life, and left me seething in my car. If this epic tie-up had happened a year before, I would have just assumed that there was a cataclysmic crash up ahead requiring a fleet of medevac helicopters to transport many grievously injured victims to area hospitals, perhaps a busload of orphans that had gone off the road. But what I quickly came to learn was that to the average, everyday suburban commuter, it was known as evening rush hour.

I sat in standstill traffic and fretted. I am not by nature a complainer, but it was starting to get to me, this whole thing. I felt as though I spent the bulk of my day scanning radio stations and talking on the cell phone as I drove to and from work. There was, for the record, no easy public transit option, and as a columnist, I never knew where I'd end up on a given day, so I always needed my car. The old Brian, meaning city Brian, had loved long drives because he could use the time to gather his thoughts and regroup. But the old Brian hadn't had a daily list of chores a mile long that had accompanied his foray into suburbia: running the dogs, cleaning the decks, watering the flowers, helping with the kids, feeding the unappreciative chicken. The old Brian hadn't been wracked by guilt—guilt over not spending enough time with the kids, guilt that his dog's life had become boring in the confines of a suburban yard, guilt because he was spending more time commuting than actually working, guilt over never getting everything done to the house that needed to be done, guilt over not being helpful enough with Pam.

I was doing much more than I ever had before, and doing none of it well. Those people with houses and kids and yards and faraway jobs, they are one tough group, all of them scheduled to within a nanosecond of their lives. There was no margin of error.

So I sat in my car on the Massachusetts Turnpike and thought of the way it used to be, the simplicity of city life, the tranquillity of long walks with the dog, the ease of never feeling guilty over not being there enough with the kids, walking to great restaurants with Pam. That very night, for instance, I'd skipped a gym workout to get home, which meant I'd missed the regular group of guys who gather at the bar afterward to watch the Red Sox on TV, which meant I had grown one day more isolated from so many things I treasured about my old life.

My cell phone rang. "Are you going to make it?" Pam asked. She sounded weary. Actually, that's being polite; she sounded completely exhausted. As pressed as I constantly felt, she was infinitely busier, between the demands of her business and the relentless needs of two kids who want to be around her and all over her all day, every day. She also had a whining fiancé in need of reassurance that every-thing was going to end up all right.

"I'm trying," I said. "But I don't know if the million other commuters are going to let me."

She paused and said, "All right. I'm going to go ahead and feed them. They're starved, and we all want to get to bed early."

What was I supposed to say, don't feed two hungry kids because I want to be part of it? No. I hung up, and fifty arduous minutes later, I was home.

If I'd ever imagined suburban life as a fairy tale, me walking through the door like Dick Van Dyke used to do with his son racing out to excitedly greet him, that pretty much went away the first time Buddy leaped up on the front porch in a bid to extricate me from my privates. Pam knew I was trying, and she appreciated it. She knew I was struggling, and she appreciated that as well. When I finally walked in on this particular night, an hour after I'd intended to be there, the house was dimly lit. There was no one downstairs to greet me, no one—besides the dogs— who cared that I had arrived. Pam was on her computer in the family room, checking in on the day's activity at her clinic. She gave me a quiet, bleary-eyed greeting. The two kids were hunkered down on the couch, swaddled in throws, mesmerized by *iCarly*.

"Everyone's exhausted," Pam explained. So I retreated to the kitchen—me, my frustration, and my angst. There I pulled the foil off the plate of ravioli that Pam had made me and heated it up in the microwave. I found the local paper and sat at the counter, mindlessly eating pasta and marinara sauce while reading a story about how excited the new assistant town clerk was to work in a community like mine.

Upstairs, the TV played softly. I heard Pam tell the kids, "Five more minutes to bed." Tigger, the more demanding of the two Maine coon cats, jumped from the floor to the stool next to mine. He jumped from the stool to the counter. He lay down beside me, staring me in the face in the haunting way he always did, just the two of us in the dimness of the kitchen. I stroked his fur and told him he was a good boy, even if he was on the counter. Hey, at least he wanted to share a few moments with me.

"You and me, Tigs," I said. I took another bite and thought about what the guys were probably doing at the bar of the University Club that night, rooting for the Red Sox, giving one another a hard time, eating a dry-aged steak or a plate of oysters. It's funny, because when you're there, all those nights, you assume there must be something better, more meaningful, somewhere else.

And there I was, somewhere else, and it amounted to nothing but a bucket of loneliness. I'd made the big move to suburbia because I'd feared the day that I'd be home all alone, night after night, eating with my dog. And there I was in this new house, surrounded by people and other various creatures, eating all alone with my new cat. I kind of laughed a little bit, quietly, a desperate person's laugh. Suddenly Tigger lifted his paw and swatted at my plate, knocking the uneaten half of one of my last ravioli onto the counter. He grabbed it in his mouth, red sauce dripping down his furry little chin, and plunged victoriously to the floor.

And then it was just me.

>20<

Help sometimes arrives at the most unexpected times from the most unlikely places. In this particular instance, it was an otherwise lazy autumn Sunday morning, the "otherwise" referring to the rooster that was strutting around the front lawn sometimes barking, occasionally crowing, and generally being a nuisance. I was tossing the tennis ball for two delighted golden retrievers. Pam and the kids were inside, starting breakfast and warming up to the day, coming and going from the yard. It was not a bad beginning at our humble house.

I settled into an Adirondack chair next to an evergreen tree at the far end of the yard from Buddy and opened the Sunday papers. If he was going to attack me, he'd have to walk the length of the grass first and I'd see him the entire way. As I read, the dogs delivered the ball to me, placed it on the armrest, and set off in pursuit when I gave a brisk toss. Eventually, they lay down in the dew to contemplate their good fortunes.

We were all immersed in our own routines—I was reading, the dogs were resting, Buddy was pecking at insects—when I heard an unusual sound emanating from the bird, kind of a friendly chirp or a curious caw more than a menacing crow or a happy bark. I looked up and saw him standing near the fence, staring into the street. I followed his gaze and saw a big black sport-utility vehicle at a full stop in front of our house, idling, no more than twenty feet from the bird. That didn't at first strike me as unusual. Buddy had become something of a local spectacle, a one-animal zoo exhibit that seemed to attract visitors from far and wide, drivers who would slow to a crawl or come to a complete stop while kids in the backseat pointed, waved, and even called out his name: "Buddy, Buddy, we love you!" How they had learned his identity and how he inspired such emotions, I had no idea.

But then I watched as the passenger-side window of the SUV glided down. A hairy hand protruded from the inside of the car. The hand held a camera. I heard the quiet click of rapid-fire shots, one after another, like you'd hear at a fashion shoot.

Click. Click. Click. Click.

Buddy continued to stare at the camera with an increasingly delighted look on his twitching face, as if he were posing, basking in the attention that has always seemed to fit him like a suit of custom-sewn feathers. A moment later, the two dogs noticed the visitor and began to trot in its direction. At that point the hand disappeared back into the confines of the vehicle. The window glided up as smoothly as it had gone down. And the black SUV, glistening in the morning sun, continued down the quiet country road, accelerating on its way.

Of one thing I was certain: it had not been a random encounter. Some guy on a leisurely Sunday-morning drive didn't just happen to spot a rooster in a suburban yard and say to himself, *I'm so lucky to have this camera in the front seat with me because my wife is never going to believe it.* For one, he had approached the house slowly. Two, he had spotted the rooster at the beginning of our property. The normal gawkers, and, as I said, we get many, are usually halfway past when they see his eminence strutting around the yard, at which point they slam on the brakes, roll down the window, and shout something creative, like "Cock-a-doodle-doo." Third, the guy took the pictures with a camera, presumably one with a telephoto lens, rather than a cell phone, which told me he meant business. This wasn't a snapshot on his iPhone that he'd pull up at a bar one night to show his friends—look at what this crazy family has wandering around their yard! No. My house had been his destination.

Amid the calculation, I was trying to discern my own reaction, which can probably be best summarized as follows: what the hell took so long? For the last couple of months, I'd been starting to think I might be going crazy. I seemed to be the only person around who thought it wildly annoying, if not outright unacceptable, that we were providing sanctuary to a feathery monster who screeched to the treetops all day, every day, in our front yard. As I've said, Pam and the kids did their level best to ignore it. The neighbors had not complained about it, which stunned me. As a matter of fact, I'd happened across a scene in which Tim, the very nice owner of the house behind us, was having a conversation with Buddy along the back fence. Come on, Tim. If I lived next door to me, I would have hired Colonel Sanders himself to stalk my front yard.

Now, finally, hopefully, some mysterious driver in a jet-black SUV seemed to be taking matters into his own hands. I could picture the scene Monday morning when whatever town official it is that handles livestock complaints arrives in his or her office to find a manila envelope containing a set of glossy eight-by-tens of Buddy staring wild-eyed into the camera, a brand-new house as backdrop. If the owner of the black SUV was smart, the photographs would be accompanied by a noise study or actual tapes of Buddy crowing at various times in the day. I could have kicked myself for not jumping into my car and following the guy. I would have caught up to him in a strip mall parking lot, and he'd have been throwing up his hands and saying "I'm not trying to do anything, I just like chickens." I'd have to tell him, "Relax. We're on the same side here, pal. Let's figure out a strategy together."

I struggled to get to my feet and ambled into the house to tell Pam, "Something happened just now that doesn't feel right." I gave her the blow-by-blow of the scene outside. At the end, she reached the same conclusion as me, only she didn't take it as well.

"He's a rooster," she repeated three or four times. "He's adjusting to a new environment. What do people expect, that he has no instincts? That he's just going to sit quietly and wait for some predator to jump the fence or swoop in from the skies? No, he's doing what centuries of breeding have told him to do, and that's to protect himself in any way he can."

I probably could have told Pam that most neighbors didn't think it was normal to have a rooster in the yard to begin with, but I decided that was not the time to bring it up. "Well, hopefully Buddy settles in sooner rather than later and starts to quiet down, for his own good." And mine.

Pam's never been one to let life happen to her. As a kid growing up with relatively modest means in central New Jersey, she set her sights on an Ivy League School, the University of Pennsylvania, and got there. Once in college, she set out after her lifelong dream of getting into veterinary school, and she achieved that as well, also at Penn. She opened her own clinic in Boston. She juggles that with her two daughters and menagerie of animals and me. Mostly, it all seems to work. So by that day's end, she was walking the dogs around the neighborhood looking for a house that might happen to have a black SUV parked in a driveway. Of course, she found one, on a dead end—rather, a *cul-de-sac*—one street over, an oversized Colonial with an impeccably landscaped yard.

"It's really far away," she groused when she got back home.

"So you couldn't hear Buddy when you were down there?"

"Well, a little bit. Way in the distance. But it was a nice, soothing sound."

That is what I was up against.

I convinced Pam that she couldn't knock on their door, couldn't bake them a pie, couldn't invite them over to dinner—unless it was for roast chicken or chicken pot pie. Instead we waited for the next shoe to drop, assuming there would be one, and while we waited, Pam rededicated herself to the role of helping Buddy settle into his new environment.

More than a few times, I would look out the kitchen windows, the ones over the sink, and get a back view of Pam and Buddy sitting side by side on the top step of our farmer's porch. I could hear her saying again and again in her whimsical chicken voice, "Buddy, you're so handsome and it's so nice here. You don't need to crow all day. Nobody's going to get you. You can be a good, quiet boy." He would, in turn, make appreciative and affectionate little cawing sounds at her, almost apologetic in their tone. I couldn't help but think that he knew one true thing, and that was that nobody else in his life, in his kingdom, understood him—and, in fact, loved him—like the woman sitting next to him on the step.

A week passed, then another, and another still. Pam was spending far more time in the yard, helping Buddy acclimate and having surprising success. The crowing wasn't as loud and didn't happen as often, though, believe me, that's like saying a hurricane wasn't as windy as the forecasters said. He was occasionally still a screaming, howling presence that wasn't making life easy for anyone.

On Halloween morning 2010, I was sitting on the couch with the Sunday *New York Times,* mentally preparing for the Patriots game coming up that afternoon, a pair of retrievers sprawled nearby on the floor, when the doorbell sounded. The dogs went berserk. The cats ran for cover. Buddy began crowing. And I heard Pam and the kids chatting with whoever it was on the porch. I assumed it was someone selling Girl Scout cookies or on some other all-American pursuit.

Next thing I know, I see Pam and a woman in her sixties walking across our lawn, Buddy trailing behind them, heading in the direction of his red-and-cream-colored rooster palace. Through the living room windows, I could see the woman climb the ramp and actually walk into the house—a perfect stranger taking a tour of our obscenely expensive shed. She stayed in there for longer than should be considered normal, not that any of it was normal. In a few minutes she emerged with a big smile on her face, she and Pam chatting and laughing. She walked around the outside of the house, pausing at the front transom window, pointing upward, and saying something that made Pam laugh. She pulled a pink pad out of her shoulder bag, made some notes, tore off a sheet, and handed it to Pam. The two of them walked back across the yard like best friends.

Ten or so minutes later, I heard a car door shut, tires on the gravel driveway, the porch door open, and footsteps inside. That's when Pam suddenly appeared before me, clutching the salmon-colored sheet of paper she had been given outside.

"We passed," she said simply, her wide smile telling me it must have been an important test.

"Passed what?" I asked.

"Buddy. His rooster house."

She handed me the slip of paper, which had the state of Massachusetts seal on top and beside that the agency names, "Department of Agricultural Resources. Bureau of Animal Health."

Great. My old life was roughly two galaxies away. I now lived one that required visits from the farm animal inspector. Below that was a list of specific animals, from cattle (dairy, beef, or steers) to goats to sheep to swine. We fell into the "Other" category, just below equines and rabbits. The nice inspector had written "Rooster—1" on an empty line. To the question, "Do animals listed appear to be free from contagious disease?" she had written simply, "Yes."

It was the next question, though, that I'm sure gave everyone a good laugh: "Are accommodations adequate with reference to situation, cleanliness, light, ventilation, and water supply?"

Adequate ventilation? I assumed that the two screened windows and the cedar double doors probably provided most of that. Light? This certainly was the only rooster in these United States with the benefit of a transom window. Situation? You could fit twenty of Buddy's rooster friends in there jumping up and down on the world's bounciest trampoline, and they'd still have plenty of room. Cleanliness? I think it was cleaner than the kids' rooms.

I looked up at Pam, who was still beaming and about to explain why. "She told me it was the single nicest rooster dwelling she had come across in more than thirty years of inspections."

How about the single nicest rooster dwelling any inspector *anywhere* had ever come across in the history of inspections?

It was nice to see Pam so bubbly about it, but in truth, in her triumph, I was coming to terms with my own sudden sensation of deflation.

"Did she say what brought her out here?" I asked.

"Not really," Pam said. "I was thinking it was a little weird, too, and I kind of asked. But she said she works Sundays because she has a better chance of catching people at home than during the week."

That sounded mildly plausible, but in my heart and in my head, I knew that an inspector doesn't just happen to wander by the house unannounced on a nondescript Sunday morning and knock on the door. The rooster house, first and foremost, looks about as much like a rooster house as I look like an NFL quarterback. She had to have been told that a rooster lived there. And maybe it was my thirty years in the newspaper business that was causing me to connect too many dots, but I imagine the person who began this whole process just happened to drive a black sport-utility vehicle.

The guy with the camera calls the town. The town notifies the inspector. The livestock inspector comes to the house, figuring that the best way to indict the amateur chicken owners is to cite them for improper care of the animal and suggest they get rid of that which they are unable to handle. Then she gets there and, holy Christ, it's the Taj Mahal of chicken coops.

All of which meant that my one government-sanctioned shot at emancipation from this creature had suddenly and officially backfired.

"She did say that this town likes to honor its farming legacy," Pam said, adding "There are no laws, no ordinances, against livestock, and in fact, the community leaders encourage it."

Great. Just great. This bird was rolling sevens everywhere he turned.

By that point Buddy must have heard Pam's voice, because he had waddled to a patch of grass right beneath an open living room window and proceeded to let out a thunderous *cock-a-doodle-doo* that caused even the dogs, who had grown used to his noise, to jump to their feet. The funny thing, though, was that I didn't sense a tone of complaint in his howl but a sense of triumph—Buddy the conqueror. The rooster pretty much had me beat.

>21<

I'll say this for Buddy: he was a more sophisticated enemy than I had ever given him credit for, a devious little devil to the point that I found myself one day Googling "Do chickens have brains?" I knew the answer. I just wanted to understand it better.

I got a ream of feedback in return, almost all of it showing that, yes, in fact, chickens may not have big brains, but they certainly have agile ones, with Lesley Rogers, described in one website after another as a "prominent avian physiologist," concluding that chickens have "cognitive capacities equivalent to those of mammals, even primates." Great. Buddy was as clever as a chimp.

That wasn't really news to me, not, for instance, on the late-autumn day when I walked outside to see Abigail, Caroline, and their friend Claire doing what they loved best, which was running in wide circles and leaping across horse jumps as they videotaped one another's efforts with their mother's iPhone. Buddy wanted in, to the point that he would run all the way up to the wooden jumps, where he would stop and cluck in a frustrated tone.

"Come on, Boo-Boo," Caroline said, urging him, from the other side of the raised pole, to leap over it.

Buddy cackled some more. Caroline offered another dose of encouragement. Eventually the bird walked around the jump and followed the kids along their route. I watched as Abigail nearly tripped over him, bent down, and said sternly, "Buddy, stay out of the way." I can't tell you that he understood the exact meaning of her words, but I will report that he walked toward the dogs, who were lying off to the side chewing sticks, and sprawled out between them. That bird scared me in a variety of ways.

"Good boy, Buddy!" Caroline yelled over. Then she ran inside to get him a fistful of Parmigiano-Reggiano.

It wasn't exactly that way when it was me and him, which is what I mean about his sinister nature.

He developed numerous ways to attack me, like an all-star pitcher expert at changing his speeds. He was so slick, so seemingly knowledgeable about my movements around the yard, where he might trap me, how I'd react, when he would thrust, whether he should parry, it wouldn't have surprised me if he'd sat in his rooster house in the dark of the night studying film.

Interesting that when he's with the dogs, he never looks behind him. And when he's reading the paper, he's essentially blocking his own view of anything in front of him. Look at

how he's lamenting the condition of his lawn in the far corner,
basically trapping himself in an area with no escape.

There was, of course, the blitz. I'm out in the yard,
Buddy says, "Screw it," and charges like a linebacker jacked
up on every imaginable steroid. There was no finesse involved with it, no fakery, no mild chicanery. No, it was just
Buddy sprinting in my direction, usually while *ca-caw*ing
in as menacing a voice as he could muster, his beady little eyes bulging out of the sides of his furious, puffed-out
face. Unless and until you've had a twenty-pound rooster
racing at your legs and midsection at a speed you didn't
think possible for him to achieve, it's hard to imagine the
gamut of emotions involved—white shock, abject fear, a
hazy sense of regret that you may never partake in sexual
relations again.

Then there's the "Wouldn't it be nice to be friends"
approach, where Buddy gradually, casually pecks at the
lawn as I throw the tennis ball for the dogs, slowly coming
closer, closer still, don't-mind-me-I'm-just-finding-all-kinds-
of-interesting-bugs, until, Bam! he's on me, euphorically
going after my legs, the expression on his face scarily similar to Jack Nicholson's in *The Shining*. The dogs give me
a look like *You didn't fall for that again, did you? What a*
waste of thumbs.

There's the shuffling sidestep, or the sidestep shuffle, a
move that should be familiar to anyone who's ever darkened the doors of a boxing gym in South Boston or Brock-
ton: Buddy approaches unabashedly from the side, does a

little two-step, and there I am, engaged in a fight I never wanted.

Finally there's the stand and peck, which, the fatter he gets, the more he falls back on. It basically involves him picking the door he thinks I'm coming out of next, positioning himself near it, often just out of sight, and lunging in my direction the moment he has a clear view. In a variation on a theme, sometimes he hides in the hostas by the side gate, only to emerge the moment I push the gate open on my way in from wherever I've been.

All of which has required me to develop my own defensive strategies. On the blitz, I used to simply turn and run until I quickly realized that a man being pursued by a frantic rooster around the front and side yards of his house caused quite a stir among passing drivers. There's surprisingly little sympathy, or even empathy, apparent. More often it's hilarity. That's not to say that fleeing isn't still a fallback. Sometimes it's just reflex, and the good news is that Buddy generally tires out after a minute or two of running. The bad news is that so do I.

I open doors to the outside slowly. I walk softly and carry a rolled-up newspaper. I peer into the gardens before pushing on the gate. And when Buddy's doing the peck-at-the-grass routine, I slowly, calmly migrate to another part of the yard.

"You have to pick him up and hold him," Pam told me one morning for about the thirtieth time. That time, as during virtually every other before that, she happened to be cradling him in her arms, the chicken loving every minute of it, shooting me a look that said, as the kids so often do, "She's mine."

"If you hold him, it shows your dominance," Pam said. "Here, just take him." She held him in my direction. Buddy let out a loud squawk. I backed away. Pam pulled him back in.

"I'm not touching that thing," I said.

The good news is, he's never really touched me, either— not hard anyway, not like he once did with his chicken sitter, an uncommonly nice guy by the name of Dennis who regrettably fell for the old "Let's be friends" routine one Saturday morning, which left his blood spurting at a ninety-degree angle from his right calf. Our neighbor Tim rushed over with a tourniquet to stem the bleeding. "I'm fine," Dennis assured us when we got home from a weekend away. He said it as he was limping to his car as fast as he could to get the hell away from our house.

No, Buddy and I had engaged in many battles, but they had always ended in a draw, typically with a frustrated chicken undoubtedly vowing to himself that the next outcome would be significantly different. I will say this: in every one of the encounters, Dennis was vividly on my mind. If Buddy struck a vein, if Tim wasn't around to help, if I passed out on the lawn, if Buddy pecked me to death, Pam would surely grieve, but I'm not sure she would have put the bird down.

One day, Pam called out the window in her chicken voice, "You're so handsome out there, you good boy." I didn't have a view of the outside, but I heard him cackle his appreciation in return. She turned to me and said, "You two are getting along better these days. Right?" It was more a statement than a question.

I suppose we were, to a limited degree, though that didn't always seem to be the point, so I said to her, "I don't think you can ever possibly understand what it's like to walk around your own yard, to walk out your own front or back door, to walk through your own gate, to be on the property that you own, that you pay a mortgage on, that you go to great lengths to maintain, that you take great pride in, I don't think you can understand what it's like to feel constantly endangered and always on edge because something that lives there would rather have you dead."

She started to giggle a little, as she often did when I got a little melodramatic, then caught herself when she realized I wasn't joking. In fact, I was in a pretty bad mood, not only because of Buddy but also because of everything. Buddy, I was starting to realize, had come to symbolize, gradually, then suddenly, how unwelcome I sometimes felt in my own reconstituted life.

Pam said, "You know, right, that he can't help what he's doing."

Did I?

Buddy, Pam explained to me, had never met another rooster, never been part of a flock, never even had a brother or sister from the day he'd been hatched as part of the Nixon Elementary School science fair. For all Buddy knew, Pam said, he was one of the dogs that he liked to waddle with in the yard or one of the kids he was constantly searching for through the windows and doors. All he knew was that this space, this yard, this new house was his home, and it was his job, his unwavering instinct, to protect it. It was who he was. It was what he did. He wasn't trying to be obnoxious. He didn't even mean to be loud. He just didn't know anything else.

"Yes," Pam said, "you're a challenge to him. He tries to dominate you because he can't or won't trust you, not yet anyway." She paused and added, "It's your responsibility to improve that relationship, because he's a chicken and you're the guy."

Rather than complain, I needed to take things into my own hands if I wanted to make them better.

It was December. I had been in the new house for more than six months. The bird still wanted me dead. I still had no idea what food was kept in what cabinet in the kitchen. I'd see one of the kids casually pull out a drawer I didn't know existed to grab a bag of chips or pretzels I didn't know we had. The refrigerator was so packed with condiments and salad dressings and various fruit juice drinks that there wasn't a spare spot for me to keep a bottle of Gatorade or water, meaning I had to go down to the cellar every time I wanted a drink. There were horse jumps set up all over the house that the kids were constantly leaping over—and I was tripping across. My brush, the times I could find it, was covered in blond hair. My toothbrush would sometimes be wet before I used it. Every time I walked into the bathroom, like magic, someone was knocking on the door. They had completely taken over the TV I had spent an absurd amount of money to buy.

Case in point on the last one. The Red Sox are playing a must-win game against the Yankees during the stretch run. I've already given up my seats at Fenway Park to be at home. When I go to catch a few innings on TV, the kids are watching something called *The Suite Life on Deck* that couldn't be missed, even though I'm reasonably sure they had seen the exact same episode about three days before. They scream. They hide the remote. They're not joking. I end up in my office watching on a small screen, my dog sprawled beside me. When the bases are loaded and Dustin Pedroia steps to the plate, young Caroline pops her head in and says in her squeaky voice, "Come on, Brian. We're going to bed. Come tell us a story."

I hesitate.

"Come on, Brian. Now."

As I'm walking away, I can hear the crowd roar and the announcer, Jerry Remy, shouting something about the greatest play he's ever seen.

"Brian, seriously, c'mon! We need to get to bed."

And chores. My God, the chores. They started first thing in the morning with a dog walk that was boring because I didn't have the city as my backdrop anymore. The trash needed emptying twice a day. Shrubs needed watering. Litter had to be picked up. Porches needed to be swept. And whatever I did, Pam had to do three times as much, what with laundry, school lunches, snacks, dinners, animals that needed to be fed, the litter box that waited to be emptied. And the dishwasher. That new life, maybe the suburbs in general, was a full-time job.

And still there was bird shit everywhere, baking in the sun or freezing in the cold. Always the rooster lurked. Walter panted nervously at my feet every single place I went. The kids were selectively happy to see me, always on their terms, never on mine. Everywhere I wanted to go, I needed to get into the car, and to get to Boston, I needed to drive a few minutes past forever. Leaving work in the early evening or the gym after work, always in a rush because there was never enough time, I'd look at the lights of the city skyline in my rearview mirror and feel lonely—lonely that I was leaving them, lonely that I was going home to a full house. It made no sense, but it was what I had. It was my new life.

Which is what I mean when I say that Buddy's attitude toward me was representative of a much larger issue: I was the visitor, the interloper. Basically, I was being treated exactly as I felt. Pam and her kids knew the house, they knew the town, they were native to suburbia. They knew that Sundays are the new Saturdays at the supermarket, that you bargain with the guy at the fireplace shop, that you have to accept that everyone is overscheduled and always in a rush. I was just an anonymous presence in a world in which everyone else seemed to be best pals. Hell, the people at the Starbucks, located, of course, in a strip plaza, didn't even know my name. Meantime, Buddy was the best-known resident of my house.

Did I say that to Pam on that gray Saturday morning when the kids were off on a playdate at their friend Claire's—any of it? Of course not. I'm a guy, proudly so, and to bring it up, any or all of it, would be to sound even more like an idiot than I already did, a chronic complainer, which I'm not. Or at least I never used to be before.

Instead, I said, "You're right. I'm just overtired. I didn't sleep well last night. I probably need a vacation. I think we all do."

And I walked out of the kitchen slowly, leaving her behind. I walked into my study, where I flicked on my computer. I wasn't really thinking, I was just kind of typing—typing "The Clarendon" into Google and vacantly staring at my screen as a website popped up with a huge photograph of a beautiful high-rise that I had watched being built next to my gym, thirty-something stories, a perfect location, views to the Charles River, the Financial District, Boston Harbor, and beyond.

The picture showed the tower all lit up at night, glowing, beckoning. Where it said "Condominiums" and "Apartments," I clicked on the latter, and suddenly floor plans appeared on my screen—manageable spaces, big windows, clean and new. I gazed at them, not really thinking about what I was seeing or doing but really looking back into the kind of life I had left.

I imagined the calm, the quiet, the tranquillity, the harmony, which is probably ironic, sitting in the deep suburbs, looking to the city for any of that. But more than anything else, I imagined the familiarity of it all, the control, the sense of self, the blissful absence of constant and seemingly unmanageable responsibility.

As I imagined all of that, somewhere out in the yard, Buddy the rooster let forth with a long, laborious crow.

* * *

I came downstairs on New Year's morning to a sight I didn't expect: two girls in pajamas in our kitchen, their hands out in front of them in full begging posture, pleading "Oh, pleeeeeeeeeeease! Pleeeeeeeeeeeeeeeeeassssssse!"

I looked at Pam, who was making their typical multifaceted breakfast—waffles from scratch, freshly diced fruit, crisp bacon, maybe a mushroom omelet for good measure. I used to get a choice of Quisp or Quake. Pam shrugged at me playfully, betraying nothing about what was going on.

"What's with the begging?" I asked, amused but slightly skeptical of it all.

"Kanani," Abigail said, speaking what sounded like a foreign language. "Kanani comes out today. We want her. Pleeeeasssse!"

"We have to have her," Caroline chimed in with her squeaky voice. "It's, like, not an option."

Pam finally spoke up. "American Girl dolls. I think Kanani is the Doll of the Year, and the Doll of the Year comes out today."

I'm sorry, but this may simply be the most brilliant marketing campaign in the history of American commerce—a toy company that times the release of a must-have doll for seven days after the Christmas rush. I wanted to call the board of directors of American Girl and tell them they are my new heroes—and then suggest that they can kindly go to hell.

The girls were both standing in front of me like two dogs before a butcher. Never mind that they had a roomful—or, more accurately, a closetful—of those dolls that they didn't seem to particularly like or play with anymore. Never mind that this house had basically been carpet bombed with new toys, clothes, games, horse jumps, and other sundry gifts on Christmas Day, a measly week before. No, they needed that doll, and they needed it on the first day of its commercial life.

And they kind of had me, because there was virtually no gambit I was unwilling to attempt in my occasionally pathetic attempts to win the affections of Abigail and Caroline, to prove that I was more than a competitor for their mother's attention, but a decent guy in my own right.

"Okay," I finally said, convincing myself that it could be a good bonding experience—me and the kids shopping for dolls at the mall on New Year's Day, hand in hand, cracking jokes, having the kind of fun we would reminisce about decades later. You look for opportunity wherever you can find it in this newfangled life. "Get your coats on, and let's go."

They looked at me like I was absolutely out of my mind. "No," said Abigail somewhat sternly, her smooth brow suddenly furrowed. "We want you to go get them for us."

What? At first I didn't understand, the request seemed so outlandish. But then it dawned on me: I was to be the glorified errand boy for a pair of four-foot-tall blondes who seemed to share the same entitlement disorder that every other kid does in a town like theirs. I was supposed to run out, plop down a debit card already worn to within an inch of its life from Christmas, and promptly deliver a pair of overpriced dolls.

No, absolutely not. Not only did I have some modicum of pride remaining, though admittedly not a lot, but I also had made a point of never, ever attempting to outright purchase the affections of those two girls. Well, sure, there was the occasional box of their favorite cupcakes on my way out from work. And yes, okay, I all but backed a U-Haul up to their house on Christmases. But you have to know where to draw the line.

It ended up, after some consideration and reconsideration and private discussions with Pam, that the line wasn't meant to be drawn at the new American Girl doll on that New Year's Day. Pam, seeing I was visibly frustrated, explained to me outside of the kids' earshot that they were a little bit sad about their school vacation ending and didn't want to miss any precious time with their mother, which was the only reason they didn't want to accompany me. They were also out of sorts because they were switching houses later that day, from their mother's to their father's. Such is the fate of the children of divorced parents, and that's a tune I'll fall for every time.

So flash ahead an hour, and there I was on New Year's

morning, not at some lavish brunch at a downtown Boston hotel restaurant, preparing for an afternoon of football festivities with friends, or even just sleeping off the effects of too much frivolity the night before. No, I was, by my quick accounting, the only male among the many, many dozens of gleeful young girls who had taken the American Girl store in the Natick Mall by storm.

There was a cacophony of yelling, screaming, begging, and crying, and that was just from the high-strung mothers in designer jeans who were overseeing their daughters. Fortunately, the store seemed to have several million of the newest dolls, each available for a mere $100 or so apiece. Who knew they'd be so cheap? "You should probably get an extra outfit or two to make it really worthwhile," Pam had advised me on my way out the door. That was another $44 a doll, or $88 in total. I was waiting to get to the register, holding two dolls and four outfits, weaving in and out of those Disney-style barriers that make the line appear shorter than it is. Mothers were snapping at their daughters. The girls were pleading for one more bonus pack, another book, a visit to the American Girl salon (?!). I was surreptitiously eyeing all the doll accessories they were buying, making sure I didn't get the completely wrong thing.

At the register, I set my purchases down on the counter and told the middle-aged clerk, "I don't know how you guys make a profit, these things are such a steal." Maybe it was just that she'd never seen a man in her store before, but I've gotten warmer responses from politicians walking out of a grand jury room. "Will you be needing a gift receipt with your dolls?" she asked.

"No, they're for me."

I mean, come on, that's funny. But no laughter, no nothing, except probably a discreet nod to the head of security to make sure they monitored my whereabouts until I was on Mother Nature's side of the door.

When I got back home, the girls were playing in the side yard, allowing me to slip in through the garage and lay the dolls out on the kitchen counter so they would be front and center when the kids walked into the house. Pam assured me that the outfits were just right, though I wasn't as confident. We set them up, and it was like Christmas morning all over again. Moments later the kids raced in to grab leashes for the dogs, skidded to a stop, and screamed, "You got them! You got them!"

Then: "Mom, you got them!"

No, no, Brian went and got them. Brian drove to the Natick Mall. Brian picked out the outfits. Brian looked like the idiot standing among all the little girls. Brian plopped his debit card on the counter so the stone-faced lady at the register could deplete his withering account of a few hundred more dollars.

"Thank you so much, Mommy. We love you!"

"Guys, thank Brian," Pam said urgently. "He's the one who did it all." God bless her.

"Yeah, but you told him to," Abigail replied.

Pam shot me an apologetic look. She was about to say something to them when the two girls, one after the other, in low but sincere voices, said, "Thank you, Brian." Then one of the kids grabbed a piece of cheese out of the refrigerator and shouted to the other, "Let's go feed Boo-Disk!"

And they were gone.

Later Pam would tell me that they really did understand and appreciate what I had done for them and that they loved their new dolls. But given the joking relationship that we have, it's sometimes tough for them to get serious enough to express their thanks.

"I get it," I told her. "I'm just happy they like them. That's the point, isn't it? When you give a gift, it's about the recipient, not about yourself."

It felt good to be traveling along the high road like that. My only fear, being as unfamiliar as I was with it, was the distinct possibility of getting lost.

*   *   *

One afternoon, Pam and I picked the kids up at one of the twenty structured activities that happen on a typical winter's day and were, of course, driving them to another. In that case, it was from horse riding to a playdate that involved some sort of arts and crafts. Our path between the two led right past our house, but there was no time to stop. It was late afternoon, dusk, and as we drove down our street, in front of our fence, Pam quietly told me to slow down, which I did. The lawn was empty of animals, specifically the chicken, but the kids rolled down the rear windows of the car and shouted one of Buddy's many nick-names. "Schnoodle! Schnoodle! Here, Buddy. Here!"

Buddy, I suddenly saw, was in the process of putting himself to bed. Specifically, he was inside his house, on my old Crate & Barrel chair, readying to make the final leap to his raised perch. He heard his name, heard the kids' voices, and frantically whirled around. Without missing a beat, he flew out the double doors, skipped down the wooden ramp, and bolted across the yard toward the fence by the street, his body lilting so much from side to side in his ex-aggerated dinosaur run that every step made it appear he was going to wipe out. All the while he was joyfully shout-ing, "Ba-back! Ba-back!"

A car pulled up behind us, so I edged to the side of the somewhat narrow road. The kids were leaning out the window, asking Buddy about his day, telling him to get a good night's sleep, advising him to stay warm inside his house. The chicken stood at the fence cawing and clucking and barking, absolutely delighted to be part of the mo-ment, this family moment, him and his flock. If he was confused about why they were outside the fence, he didn't betray it.

A truck now rolled up behind me and couldn't easily get past, so I said, "Tell Buddy good-bye. We've got to go."

I accelerated. The kids shouted "Bye, Schnoodle! We love you!" Buddy barked and cackled and ran along the fence until he hit the corner of the yard and was blocked from running any farther. Then he crowed to the heavens.

As the car glided down the country road, Pam looked at

me in knowing silence. I looked straight ahead, knowing that I wasn't going to ruin the best thing ever to happen in my life.

*   *   *

It was breezy and raw when I made my regular trek across the darkened yard later that night to shut the double doors on Buddy's house, one of my last chores of the day. I climbed the ramp and did what I always do, which was to whisper, "Buddy? Buddy, are you there?" I pressed the power button on my cell phone, and the dim light revealed his silhouette. In the inky blackness of his shed, from his perch atop the comforters and quilts on the handcrafted shelf, he let out a low grumble of acknowledgment.

But rather than shut the doors quickly and walk away, as I typically did, I lingered for a moment. That damn bird couldn't be any happier about his place in the world. He had his house. He had his yard. He had his family. He didn't give a flying crow what was happening on the other side of the (expensive) fence, unless he thought it was somehow going to interfere with life within his yard. Much as I hated to admit it, Buddy basically had it all figured out.

"How do you do it?" I asked him. "How are you so content here?" Please accept that, by talking to a rooster in the wind-whipped dark of a cold winter's night, I understood that I had completely lost my mind.

Buddy seemed surprised by the questions. He clucked back, louder than his grumble, and in the dark, I could see that he had pulled himself up onto his feet.

"You strut around the yard like it's the only place that you could ever imagine," I said to him softly, my voice colored by both awe and inexplicable regret. "You look at Pam and her kids like they are the only people who will ever matter to you."

He cackled a little bit more, slowly flapped his wings, and fell silent.

"And it works for you, all of it. You love them. They love you. You love where you are, and it's like you belong here."

He let out his long kung fu sound, a groan more than anything else.

I listened to him. I looked at his round figure in the dark. I thought about him and then about me. My mind dialed back, not weeks or months but years, dialed back to relationships that had begun with hope and ended in pain, a pattern as deeply grooved as the lines that were form- ing on my aging face. Beginnings always led to endings; it was the way of life. I thought about the Saturday after- noon with my ex-wife in our apartment, those hours on the bench in the Public Garden with Harry contemplating the biggest failure I would ever know, and where I might have ended up but for that wonderful dog. He might have been the most vital gift of my life.

And then I thought about Pam and all her accessories. My God, there were a lot of accessories: kids and rabbits and cats and Walter and the need to live in a distant town with this sometimes comic and more often ominous creature named Buddy. The funny part about Pam, the thing that made it different from any other relationship I'd ever had, was that I could never contemplate the ending, could never picture her as an ex-anything, could never imagine running into her on some Boston street on some distant Saturday morning and awkwardly talking about what was new and how we were before continuing on our separate ways. Yes, I had looked up Boston apartment prices. Yes, there were moments, whole evenings, maybe even entire days, when I was frustrated over or frightened about what had become of my tidy little life. But it was never about Pam. It was about me.

On that night, by the way, the sky was clear, the moon was bright, and my eyes had adjusted to the darkness inside the shed, meaning I could see Buddy more clearly now, both figuratively and literally perhaps. He was standing on his shelf, peering back at me, not girding but engaging, offering only little pips and squeaks to keep the conversation going. I pictured, for some odd reason, what Harry would have thought of it all. Actually, he would have loved most of it—living with Pam, a couple of kids, a big grassy yard. The bird he would have tolerated—barely. He would have been sixteen years old at that point, and it wouldn't have been unreasonable to think he could still be alive, even if it felt like a lifetime ago that he'd died.

Then I thought of Buddy crowing outside my window, his beak up, his chest puffed out. I thought of him chasing me across the yard as if he was possessed, which he may well have been. I thought of him sitting around with the dogs, leaning into Pam on the front porch, trotting around with the kids as they played horse on the far reaches of the lawn. I thought of the loneliness he probably felt when there was nobody around and the joy he experienced when there was.

"You don't let the bad overwhelm the good, do you?" I asked him.

He cawed.

"I had a dog," I told him, "named Harry. The best friend I'll ever have. For that reason, I'm not sure he would have liked you—"

"Cluck-cluck-cluck."

"Sorry, I thought we were speaking straight here. But he taught me more than I knew I could learn, gentle lessons about life and looking beyond yourself and about knowing you could get through just about anything if you were comfortable in your own skin.

"And now I've got you," I added. "You demanding that I appreciate what I've got, demanding that I learn my proper role."

Another caw.

"You've got a much different style than Harry," I said, laughing softly.

He cackled in such a way that it seemed to have a question mark at the end.

"Listen," I said in a tone that suggested I was wrapping

up. "I get what you're doing to me. I do. You're right on all fronts. I appreciate you leading by example. So how about a truce now? A real truce. You and me, getting along?"

Total, stifling silence. You could have heard one of his feathers land on the floor.

"No, really," I said, amused.

Nothing. This didn't bode well.

Harry taught me security. He revealed in me a tenderness, a level of emotional attachment, that I never knew was there. He showed me the safety inherent in unconditional love, all of it during one of the most tenuous stretches of my life. Buddy? Buddy didn't fool around with any new-age approach. He was my personal drill sergeant, schooling me in the virtues of commitment, and telling me "Hey guy. You're either in or you're out. Man up." No gray area for miles.

"You're a good boy," I finally said before stepping back down the ramp, pushing the towering doors shut, and fastening the latch to keep them closed.

I stood there in the cold air for a long moment, long enough to hear one final grumble come from inside, then nothing at all. He was probably shaking his head at the idiocy of this guy who was constitutionally incapable of coming to terms with the most basic elements of life.

That goddamned bird really did have it all figured out.

> 22 <

It began snowing in late December of that winter and basically never stopped, all of which would have been fine— actually nice—had I lived in Boston, where big snowstorms had meant that Harry, and later Baker, and I would walk down the middle of Commonwealth Avenue or Newbury Street in the early morning, the city young and quiet and social all around us.

But suburban snow, I learned, was different. Suburban snow came with more wind. Suburban snow led to isolation. Suburban snow meant commutes that harked back to the Donner party trying to pass over the Sierra Nevada.

It came down so hard, so often that winter that my paper, the *Globe,* took to running a Shaq-o-meter to see if we'd clear the great Shaquille O'Neal with our annual snowfall. Shaq is seven feet, one inch tall, and we nearly did, not stopping until we got above his chin.

I reveled in the very first snow of my new suburban life,

big, fat, dazzlingly white flakes falling from a wide gray sky. I pulled out the shovel I had bought on what seemed like my weekly Saturday-morning Home Depot runs and embraced the concept of free exercise, no gym required. If it was good enough for my father when I was growing up, then it sure as hell was going to be good enough for me. I figured I'd have an hour of good, honest manual work, followed by a creamy hot chocolate at the kitchen table with two equally exhausted dogs flopped at my feet and a woman, Pam, expressing her appreciation at my masculine achievement. The kids would probably ask me to light a fire, and we'd all play Monopoly by the hearth on the family room floor.

Then I began shoveling. The snow was heavier than I remembered, and it dawned on me that my driveway from my formative years had been nowhere near this long or wide. What it meant was that on almost every scoopful of snow, I had to walk six, eight, ten, twelve feet before tossing it to the side, then back for another scoop. Scoop, walk, toss. Scoop, walk, toss. It was on one of those walks that I remembered that my father might have had a shovel, but he'd also had me to use it. I'm not sure I recall him ever holding one himself.

An hour in, I was probably no more than a third of the way done, and the pace wasn't getting any faster. The kids came out with a couple of round coasters and began sliding down the minimountain of snow next to the driveway that had risen from my work, giggling as the dogs jumped on top of them when they came to a sliding stop.

They were pushing snow back onto the cleared area, but in my semidelirious state, I didn't really care. Hell, I plunged my shovel into the sixteen or so inches of snow and joined them, the effortless sensation of whooshing down the makeshift mountain, the wind in my face, all of it making me feel like a kid again. I don't think I'd gone sledding in thirty-five years.

We raced, we joked, we laughed. Truth was, it was getting more and more like that between me and the kids, the lightness of being, the shared moments, much of it as natural as I'd always hoped it would be.

Half an hour later, the kids announced in unison that they were cold and tired and wanted to go inside.

"Oh, come on," I said. "Let's keep playing. Please."

"My feet are wet," one of them said.

"My hands are freezing," said the other. They trundled toward the house, the legs of their snowsuits swishing with every step. And once again it was just me and the shovel and the snow.

Scoop, walk, toss. Scoop, walk, toss. I watched private plows speed down our street headed for driveways unknown. I watched the high school kid next door, a nice young woman, open her garage door, emerge with a snow-blower, and clear her driveway in about twenty minutes, the sound of the gas engine taunting me mercilessly the entire time. After she was done, she could have gone inside, cooked dinner in a Crock-Pot, and watched an entire season's worth of *American Idol* on her DVR, and I would still have been shoveling.

When I was finally done some three-plus hours after I'd begun, when I lifted the last piece of heavy, crusted snow that the town plow had deposited at the mouth of my driveway, I hobbled up the gradual hill to my house, so stooped that I looked like I was on my way to ring the bells of Notre Dame. My face was frozen in place. My fingers were permanently gnarled in the shape of the shovel handle. My ears, I assumed, had fallen off a couple of hours before. I'd find them in June, when the snow piles finally gave way to the lawn. As I got inside the door, Pam was standing in the mudroom in her down jacket and a ski cap, pulling on her mittens.

"Oh good, you're finally done," she said casually.

Finally done.

If I could have spoken, I'm not sure what I would have said, but I'm fairly certain it would have been something that I'd immediately regret. Pam added, "Buddy doesn't like the snow, so I need to clear a path to his house."

Buddy doesn't like the snow.

Pam headed out. I staggered to the kitchen table and slowly lowered myself into the chair I had been imagining, dreaming about, for the last hour of shoveling. Like midsummer cherries, it was every bit as good as I had hoped.

From that place of total exhaustion, I had an unfortunate view of Pam in the front yard, lifting one heavy half shovelful after another, creating a path between the porch and Buddy's house, which was way too far away. Pam is basically the type that if a guy can do it, she can too, and mostly she's right, especially when I'm involved. But seeing her outside struggling with the wet snow, I couldn't take it. I slowly lifted myself back onto my feet, pulled my wet gloves on, drew a deep breath of warm air, and headed out the door.

"Why don't I grab that," I said, reaching for the shovel. Uncharacteristically, she didn't resist. Actually, she didn't even stay around to lend her moral support. So there I was, alone again, faced with the utterly and undeniably absurd task of shoveling a path through nearly a foot and a half of snow so a monster bird could be emotionally unburdened and physically at ease as he waddled from his palace of a rooster house to drop copious amounts of personal refuse on the floor of my covered porch. I thought back to a question that a reporter at the *Globe* had once asked me when she saw a bunch of the animal pictures I kept on my phone: "How did this happen to you?"

Presidents do not arrive at the Oval Office on the first day of their presidency with any greater sense of achievement than I arrived at Buddy's red rooster house, my shovel finally stubbing his ramp as I prepared for the final toss of snow. I pushed the snow off the wooden incline, pulled the latch on his big double doors, and swung them open in unison. Buddy sat on his high shelf with an indignant look on his face that said, "What the hell have you been doing all morning?"

"Come on," I said with all the faux cheeriness I could muster, which admittedly wasn't much. I looked at him looking quizzically at the white world outside his door. He stared back at me in what seemed like a plea for help.

He probably would have done that for the longer part of forever if Pam hadn't suddenly shown up at my side and coaxed him in her happy chicken voice: "You handsome Boo-Boo. You come out right now so everyone can see what a good-good boy you are!"

Perfect. I get a *You're finally done* after shoveling an entire driveway, and this obese bird is told that the whole world is waiting with bated breath for him to greet another day after a long night of sleep.

With that Buddy jumped from his shelf, onto my chair, then to the floor, waddled over to the doors, and peered more closely at the snow. For whatever reason, maybe every reason, I'd always suspected that he was a very profane bird within the privacy of his little brain. In this case, he wore his profanity all over his disgusted face.

"Look what we did for you, Boo-Boo," Pam said. "You have a nice little path. Follow me!" And she started off along the cleared area toward the house.

Buddy just stared at her from his doorway as if she were out of her human mind. He cawed. Pam beckoned. He made his kung fu sound. Pam walked farther down the path. Soon enough, he stepped gingerly down his ramp and onto the ground, which probably had an inch or so of snow on top of it because I hadn't wanted to dig up the grass. This he didn't like.

He froze in place as Pam's voice only got higher and more encouraging. His head twitched from side to side, his wattle swaying back and forth with each movement. As Pam continued singing encouragement, he finally

high-stepped past me, a look of beleaguered disappoint-
ment in his beady eyes. He cautiously walked the length of
the path, around the front of the house, and up onto the
porch, lifting each of his rubbery legs high in the air with
every reluctant step. Anyone driving by could probably
have seen only the red comb that sat atop his white head.
Pam picked him up and hugged him, then set him down
in front of his morning bowl of diced chicken nuggets,
oatmeal, shredded cheese, and cracked corn. Buddy let out
a long squawk of relief, or maybe it was admonition. Either
way, shame on me for not foreseeing the next logical step
in that whole grand procession.

*　*　*

Yvonne and Leo McGrory didn't raise any fools. The next
big snowfall, I was ready. Shortly after that first debacle, I
parted with an absurd amount of my hard-earned money
and bought the kind of bright orange snowblower that
looked as if it would have been used by a maintenance
crew at a Colorado strip plaza. It had a headlight, a throaty
engine, and enough torque, whatever that is, to drag me
up the driveway when I slipped and fell down behind it
that first time.

　The truth was, I couldn't wait for it to snow again, and
when it did, I was up early, sending the garage door north-
ward, emerging with my big, mean snow-clearing machine. It took me just forty-five minutes to clear what had

required more than three hours by hand, and then another half hour or so to shovel out all the snow I had blown into my garage and at my parked car. After that I spent a few minutes apologizing to Baker for accidentally shooting so much snow into his face.

It was at that point that I brought the snow thrower around the yard toward Buddy's house, where I would clear a new path from his ramp to the front porch in just a few minutes. But arriving at his palace, something startled me, that something being Buddy's doors, which were swinging open in the winter wind. I noticed deep footprints—of human boots—coming and going in the snow.

"Pam," I called out as I poked my head in the front door of our house. "Is Buddy all right?"

Before Pam could say anything, Buddy answered for himself with a massive squawk that began in the basement, echoed up the stairs, and filled the front hallway. Pam looked at me only half apologetically and said, "He's in the cellar. He hates the snow, it's awful on his claws, and it's too cold for him, anyway. I don't have the heart to keep him outside."

Never in my wildest fears did I ever think I would recall having a rooster in my yard—rather than inside my house—as the good old days.

For the next six or so weeks, men and women all across New England, natives and newcomers alike, complained bitterly about the vicious winter that played havoc with our psyches and tested our souls, the merciless cold, the unrelenting snow, the insulting winds that arrived from the

Great Plains. Through it all, because of it all, I lived with an added, unspoken burden that I'm fairly certain nobody else in the world I live in had to endure: a rooster in my basement, his every crow at the beginning of every morning pulsing through the walls and floors and just about shaking the foundation of the house.

He crowed in the morning at the mere prediction of first light. He crowed in the afternoon to let us know he was still there. He crowed at night because, well, because he was probably just confused. He crowed when he heard us and he crowed when he didn't, and just as consistent was the fact that no one ever seemed to notice him crowing except me. Everyone just carried on with their days, their lives, occasionally to pause and say, "Oh, Boo-Boo." In my frustration and self-pity I began to feel sympathy, even empathy, for this voluble, voluminous bird. Pacing the hard concrete floor of our unfinished basement, Buddy couldn't have been any further out of his element. Night was day, and day was night. There was no soil to pick at, no bushes to brush against, no bugs to eat—at least I hoped there weren't. When I voiced my concerns to Pam, she agreed but said, "What am I supposed to do? There's no farm that will take him. He hates being outside. He'd probably freeze to death in his own house. So am I supposed to euthanize him just because it's a tough winter?"

In my silence she provided the answer, emphatically: "No! In another couple of weeks, it will warm up and he'll be fine to go back outside to the life he loves."

In the meantime, on the days that rose above freezing,

Pam would carry him to the back porch, where Buddy would shiver in the wind on the cold wood, with nothing interesting to hold his attention. He refused to wander off the deck into the snow, so inevitably, invariably, he spent those hours standing at the door peering inside and pecking at the glass.

Back in the basement, he started a new routine. He climbed the stairs, all the way to the top step. Once there, he didn't peck, crow, or scratch. He simply pressed his feathers against the door and fell asleep to the sounds of the household cacophony just out of his reach. It was, figuratively and literally, as close to his flock as he could possibly get. Pam took to leaving a blanket on the step for him to sleep on; the kids would open the door and offer him words of praise.

Admittedly, that got to me, Buddy's attempts to be with the only family he knew in the only way he knew how. It didn't go unnoticed how much the family, in turn, appreciated his efforts. But every time I was on the verge of relenting, ready to declare that maybe, just maybe, he wasn't such a bad creature after all, he would scream his lungs out during a Patriots playoff game or while I was on an important call for the column or simply trying to catch an extra ten minutes of sleep before another day dawned.

February break was especially bad. Pam and I decided not to travel with the kids on principle. Well, all right, principle and the fact that the airlines and hotels jacked their prices through the roof on these school vacation weeks. So we stayed home, with the bird screeching from the basement, the girls getting on each other's nerves, the yard crusted in ice, the winds rattling the windows, and repeats on TV. That might have been the worst move since I'd invested in General Motors in 2009 with the philosophy, It's not like GM would ever go bankrupt.

I don't know how many relationship arguments have begun with the words "I can't take it anymore," but add mine to the list. Otherwise very good kids were uncharacteristically whining; they couldn't have friends over because every other son or daughter of our town was sitting on a tropical beach or in a faraway ski resort. The rooster was crowing. It was sleeting outside. I told Pam I was going for a ride, a ride that would lead to Boston, where I would spend the afternoon. She understood without actually condoning it.

"So much of this stuff is just being there, even when it seems like it would be a whole lot easier to be somewhere else," Pam said to me, not stern but matter of fact, her blond hair streaked across her forehead and an exhausted look in her eyes.

My thoughts, of course, slipped to the creature in the basement, Buddy on the top step, Buddy at the back door in better weather, Buddy always there, all day, every day, because he was exactly where he needed to be.

Pam added, "But you know that already. You know it because it's exactly the way you were with Harry for a long, long time." She paused, then added, "And that's what I thought, or maybe just hoped, you wanted here." And then she casually walked away, back into the kitchen.

But Harry had never seemed like an obligation—a point I was just smart enough not to make to her. But maybe that's exactly the point. Harry hadn't been an obligation because I'd been there whenever I needed to be or should be or wanted to be, which was most of the time.

I thought about Harry. I thought about Buddy. I thought about the kids sitting upstairs, bored and frustrated out of their minds. I thought about Pam, wanting what she had and having much of what she wanted, and if that wasn't the case, she was smart enough to keep it inside. It's called adulthood, or maybe just commitment, and perhaps I was failing my crash course. Or maybe not, because suddenly I felt a little ridiculous standing in the mudroom in a down jacket getting ready to flee a situation in which I should have been doing anything but. Did Buddy ever try to jump over the fence?

So I peeled off my coat and walked up into the family room. I arranged logs in the fireplace and lit a fire. I settled onto the couch with a travel magazine and realized I shouldn't be reading about faraway places, so I put it down and picked up *Golf Digest*. Before I could even read "The Six Things to Know About Perfect Chips," there was a kid beside me, Caroline, asking if I wanted to play a game, something about states and their capitals, all of which appeared on cards that we spread out on the floor.

"I bet I can beat you," she said.

"How much?" I asked.

"If you lose, you have to kiss Nuggy," she said.

Nuggy is one of her dozen or so nicknames for Walter,

a dog she happened to love and an animal she suspected, rightfully, that I didn't.

"And if I lose, I'll kiss Baker," she said. She loved Baker as well. That bet didn't seem fair, but I accepted anyway.

Suddenly Abigail drifted over. "I want to play," she said. They bickered momentarily over the color of their board pieces. I shuffled the cards. Caroline dealt them out. All the while, the cats were nosing up against the score sheets, and the fire kept everyone warm.

I somehow lost the first game. I mean, Jefferson City is the capital of Missouri? Jefferson City? Really? And Carson City is the capital of Nevada? "Wait a minute," I said. "This game isn't fair. I'm getting all the hard ones, and you're getting the layups."

Abigail giggled. Caroline stuck out her tongue in a mocking way.

"Come on, one more game," I said.

The fire made a loud popping sound. Walter was snoring like a rhinoceros. Abigail let on like it would be a burden but replied, "All right, last one."

> 23 <

Seriously, can a grown man really learn from a young rooster?

I'll address the question with a situation. My phone rang just as I settled into my car in a hard-luck city twenty or so miles outside of Boston. I had just finished an interview for a column, and it was Pam on the line, and she sounded awful. "Abigail," she said, trying to hold back tears, "was bucked off her horse. We're heading to the hospital. I think she broke her arm."

It was raining, just after dusk, and the glare from tired storefronts shone on the wet pavement of a Main Street that had seen better days. I sat there for a long moment trying to get my bearings, to collect my thoughts, to determine the best course, one where I would be helpful without being at any risk of getting in anyone's way. My natural impulse was to head straight home to tend to the animals, start some pasta for the kids, and get the house ready for

Abigail's return. What it lacked in impulse it made up for in pragmatism.

But something nagged, and that something had feathers. If I didn't actually ask myself the question What would Buddy do? it's only because I didn't have to. I already knew. The little beast strutted around the yard as if he owned the world, and in his mind he did, his world being everything within that fence. He peered through the doors and windows looking for his flock. He pecked at the glass to remind people he was there. He slept silently on the top step of the basement to feel closer. And he expressed unembarrassed delight when the kids came into his yard.

That's a long way of saying that Buddy would be at the hospital.

It was early November, eight months after Buddy's stay in the basement, eight good months—very good, even. Abigail and I read regularly. We joked constantly. We did homework together. Caroline and I rode bikes across the street, took walks around the neighborhood collecting flowers, and watched movies on TV. I even got them to watch a few innings of the Red Sox from time to time. Were there moments? God, yeah, constantly. That's called real life, and I came to terms with the reality that real life is about trade-offs. What was it that Pam once said, that I was the adult? Ended up, she was right. Usually.

Buddy and I really did form something of a truce. Maybe it was the talk we'd had at the door of his house that night or the fact I had put up with him under my roof for those couple of months. Maybe, displaced in the cellar, he'd taken a lesson from me, just as I had taken lessons from him. But I think I'm getting beyond myself—or at least him.

I even defended him when Pam couldn't figure out who was swiping the strawberries in her garden, only to watch from a distance one morning as Buddy sneaked to the back garden fence when he didn't think anyone was around, hopped over it, ate the fattest, juiciest strawberry off the vine, and sneaked back into the main yard. He's just being a guy, I said.

Traffic continued to slow down as it went by our house, and the drivers weren't trying to get a long glimpse because I lived there. A woman down the street told us that her kids played a game called "Spot Buddy" every day, the winner being whoever saw him first. We live across from the town high school, and so many kids would casually call out, "Hey, Buddy," as they walked by. He'd give them a self-satisfied cluck in response. One afternoon I pulled into the driveway and an SUV followed me in. As I got out of my car, the driver, an older woman, came walking toward me with a slip of paper in her hand.

"I'm the livestock inspector," she said. "I was here last year."

I remembered her, the woman who had crushed my modest middle-aged dream.

She handed me the sheet and said, "Here's your certificate for another year."

I said, "Don't you want to see the bird and his house again?"

She laughed at that, as if in the world of livestock, or at least poultry, I had just said something really funny. "Not unless something big has changed," she said.

"Nothing's changed except for his satellite TV," I replied.

She laughed harder now. "I'm all set," she said. She kept laughing as she got back into her truck. Give me my own act, and I'd kill them in Des Moines.

Speaking of last-ditch hopes, a house just around the corner went on the market, and it wasn't long before a new owner moved in. As I watched the moving truck arrive one morning, the thought struck me that maybe, just maybe, they would be the people who would refuse to tolerate a rooster in their midst. I'm begging them, please.

So on Halloween night the doorbell rang and there were a couple of adorable young girls on the porch, one dressed as a bumblebee, the other as a witch, with a father next to them. We were chatting, and he said, "I'm Tom, your new neighbor. We moved in around the corner."

My face lit up.

"And about your rooster . . ." he began.

The long-dormant organ music cued up from above. Hope had literally come knocking at my door. I thought, for a brief, passing moment, about Susan Orlean's memorable *New Yorker* story about her pet chickens, the one in which she noted that chickens are—her words here— "women's livestock."

"Women and chickens just seem to have a natural harmony," she wrote.

And there I was on my front porch with a guy who was at long last ready to address the utter absurdity and untenability of my situation, guy to guy.

"I love him," he said. "I just love him."

"You do?"

"Oh God, he's wonderful."

"The noise doesn't bug the hell out of you? Oh boy, sorry, girls."

"It's music," Tom said. "If you don't like the sounds of a rooster, move to the city."

Well, there is that.

Quick question: why did I feel more relief than despair over the outcome of that conversation?

So back to Abigail and the horse-riding accident. I strode into the emergency room early that evening and was directed through some double doors, down a hallway, and into a private room. Abigail lay on a bed, her father dutifully perched in a chair on one side of her, her mother and sister in a chair on the other side. I was where every stepanything constantly finds themselves, which is in a place you're not quite sure you belong. I tapped her shoes and told her how sorry I was. She began to cry. Then I pulled out my iPad and said I thought she might want to play the video golf game that she likes at home. She nodded her head, tears rolling down her smooth cheeks.

I stayed another moment and said I'd be in the waiting room just down the hall. Maybe half an hour later, Pam came out and said that the diagnosis was heavy bruising, nothing broken, and that Abigail would be given a sling to wear for a few days. It was a huge relief.

That night Abigail, still hurting, wanted to sleep next to her mother, so I retreated to the guest room down the hall, the one with my bed from Boston in it. It was about midnight, and I could hear Pam in the kitchen making school lunches for the following day. I was reading when a sleepy little figure appeared in my door and climbed on top of the bed—Abigail, in footed pajamas, carrying her blanket.

"Do you want to watch a TV show with me?" she asked.

"Of course."

She pulled my iPad off the nightstand, did some tapping, inexplicably knew my password, and there we were, watching *Wizards of Waverly Place* in the guest room of our humble home. Pam appeared a few minutes later, surprised by the midnight visit. "Do you want to come down and we'll watch the rest of the show?" she asked.

"No, I'm good here," Abigail said.

And she was. We watched until the show was over, until Abigail's eyes were droopy, until I walked her down the hallway so she could get the rest she desperately needed.

And somewhere, the rooster slept.

Afterword

It was a day meant for beginnings. It was a Sunday in May, the start of warm weather. The plants were blooming, the grass was growing, the sun was shining in that kind of way that made it feel like life carried endless possibilities in the soft breeze.

I was driving to get a cup of coffee when my phone rang. Pam was on the other end of the line, as distraught as she had been six months earlier when she'd called to say Abigail had hurt her arm—maybe worse. I could barely make out what she was saying through the panic and the tears.

"It's Buddy," she cried. "Come home."

Buddy.

These last six months, Buddy had become an almost entirely different creature. He had quieted down—not completely, but noticeably. He spent the better part of an uncommonly mild winter lying on a bed of blankets by the back door, watching the world from the vantage of our covered porch and waiting for the hour when he would be brought inside. As darkness fell each afternoon, Pam carried him down to the cellar, to a desk covered with quilts, where he slept in warmth and security. In my point of view, this marked a big improvement, but for Pam this muted behavior inspired watchful concern.

Buddy had begun treating me less as a mortal enemy, more as a harmless, if pointless, nuisance, something he could begrudgingly tolerate. This meant no more surprise attacks, and fewer attempts to castrate me as I flipped burgers on the outside grill or tossed the ball for the dogs. He began regarding me with a look and tone that said, "You're not worth it." You've got to take victory wherever you find it in life, and so this evolution delighted me to no end.

It even got to the point that I—yes, me—learned to carry him between the porch and the basement. If he wasn't tolerant, he was at least complacent. I would don a thick down coat to absorb any fierce pecks and leg scratchings, pull on a pair of heavy gloves in case he went right for the hands, and always follow Pam's wise counsel to never, ever, look him in the eye. I would corral him on the porch or corner him on his desk with an oversized beach towel, so that he looked like Goldilocks with a cape flowing from his head as we made our way up and down the stairs. Quite the pair.

One frigid weekend in March, Pam took the kids to a horse show in some random part of central Florida while I happily stayed home with Buddy. Well, Buddy, Baker, Walter, Charlie, Tigger, Lily, Dolly, and the two rabbits in Abigail's room whose names I could never remember.

When I got in from work that Friday afternoon, I heard Buddy cawing on the back porch, but when I stepped out to carry him inside, cape in hand, there was no Buddy.

I could hear him, but he was nowhere to be found. Darkness was settling in. Sleet was pelting the ground. I knew Buddy wasn't roaming the yard, because he certainly wasn't the type who needlessly subjected himself to unfriendly elements.

"Buddy?" I called out.

"Ba-back. Ba-back," he said in response.

I poked through a shallow alcove on the porch where we kept a small pile of firewood, but he wasn't there. I noticed Baker had climbed off the deck and was now peering under it, into some narrow, dark gap between the side of the porch and the ground. I climbed down and did the same.

Cold pellets of ice kept thwacking me on the head as I crouched on all fours trying to look through the opening. At that point, I could hear Buddy cackling ever more clearly, so I went inside for a flashlight. Kneeling on the wet, icy ground, I shone it into that mysterious little world beneath my back porch.

There were paper coffee cups under there, I assume from the construction workers. I saw a few torn pages of a newspaper. The dirt was dry and coarse, piled in some areas, cratered in others, probably from various scary animals that live in the dark. If Pam met them, she'd undoubtedly invite them inside. Then the light shone on Buddy, standing upright about fifteen feet from me, and staring back into the beam with a look that said, "What the hell do you want?"

"Buddy, come here," I said. Maybe a little too firmly. He cawed.

"Come, Buddy. Come!" He cackled. But he didn't move.

The sleet continued to pound on my head and back, my knees ached, and long icicles hung perilously on the porch roof ready to provide the most wonderful obituary: McGrory dies in rooster-related accident.

Buddy didn't move when I spread diced-up chicken nuggets, oatmeal, and Reggiano cheese at the mouth of the crack. Plan B, trying to prod him toward the opening with a frozen branch, didn't work, and Plan C involved little more than begging, pleading, and, okay, some shouting. I tried squeezing through the opening myself, but the good people of Häagen-Dazs had pretty much wiped out any possibility of that.

I stood drenched and freezing in the kitchen and called Pam, hoping she would tell me that Buddy ducks under the porch for privacy all the time, and if I left him alone, he'll be back up when he's ready.

"He's where?" she asked, shell-shocked.

"Under the porch," I replied, pulling ice balls out of my hair.

"I don't get it. How would he get under the porch? Why would he go under the porch?" Needless to say, she had no creative ideas but was certainly worried. Maybe that call wasn't my best idea.

I sat at the kitchen table with visions of a fox ripping Buddy apart in the early hours of a March morning, and while that would have brought a smile to my lips a couple of years before, now the image made my stomach churn. Forget the fox, I wondered if he'd freeze to death down there. I also wondered how much it would cost when the builder came the next morning to rip up part of the porch so we could reach him. Probably not as much as Buddy's transom window or mahogany gangplank, but hey, this is our beloved family pet.

And that's when it hit me—the window. In the basement, high on the back wall, there was a narrow sliding window that, unless I was spatially challenged, looked into that dark expanse beneath the porch. Maybe, just maybe, I could coax him to the window and get my (gloved) hands on him. Short of that, I could squeeze through the opening, slide along the frozen dirt like a member of the Special Forces, and grab him, preferably without him pecking out my eyes.

I raced downstairs, anxiously climbed atop a step stool, and shone the flashlight through the glass hoping to catch a glimpse of Buddy in the murky dark. I almost fell backward from what I saw: Buddy—about three inches from my face, perfectly illuminated, standing in the well of the window with his beak pressed up against the glass. The two of us had come up with the identical plan at the same time, which was a little more than a little scary.

Of course, he didn't make it easy on me. He never made it easy on me. When I slid the window open, he cawed and pecked until I was finally able to turn him around with a beach towel, grab him from the side, and twist his body through the window. None of this was normal, but when I placed him on his desk for the night and called Pam with the good news, it was one of the most triumphant moments of my life. Buddy and I both slept very well that night, with two floors between us.

Back to Pam's call on that warm Sunday in May. I banged a sharp U-turn and roared toward our house. Buddy, I had come to believe, was invincible. He was seemingly immune to the hawks that flew overhead. He was left untouched by the area foxes and coyotes that wouldn't or couldn't penetrate our fenced-in yard. Here was a bird that had once beaten up a dog.

Beyond that, he was a constant companion to Pam, who found in Buddy things that pet owners rarely, if ever, realize about their animals. He was a playmate to Pam's kids. He was also my unexpected and unusual mentor in terms of leading a flock. In many ways, he was a mascot for all of us, a symbol of an unusual suburban house, full of activity, its owners opting for an unorthodox course. The rooster in our yard sent a message to all: this isn't *Leave It to Beaver* here, folks.

I came up behind some slow-moving Sunday morning traffic, and there was little I could do. I thought of Buddy as a fuzzy, chirping chick sitting between the kids on the couch. I thought of young Caroline proudly showing Buddy the first tooth that she had ever lost. Buddy regarded it for a moment, opened his beak, and grabbed it. Pam spent the next two days searching through his droppings in vain.

I thought of Buddy pecking gloriously at his birthday cakes in the middle of every March. I thought of him sitting on the front steps on warm summer days gazing over his kingdom. I thought of the dirt baths he took in the mulch by the bushes, the holes he dug, the look of unabashed delight he got when the kids burst out the doors to run around his yard. I thought of a moment on Mother's Day, just a week earlier. I had dumped bags of fresh soil into Pam's garden beds, one after the next, as Caroline and Abigail spread it out with metal rakes. Buddy had wandered into the garden, and as I eyed him warily, he simply lay down amid the discarded bags and tools, content to be part of it all.

I swerved into our driveway, jammed to a stop, and leapt out of the car. I pushed open the gate and bolted across the yard toward Buddy's rooster house. His front doors were open, but there was no Buddy and no Pam. Somehow, from the sound of that call, I already knew he wouldn't be there.

I whirled around and saw them, Pam sitting on a chair on the back porch, Buddy in her arms. I saw that he was completely still. His head rested against Pam's chest, his eyes were closed. His clawed feet were in her hands. She stroked his feathers as tears rolled off her cheeks and onto his white wings.

"I opened his doors," she said softly, anguish covering every inch of her face. "He walked outside like he always does. But then he just flipped over into the grass. I swooped him up—"

Pam paused here, collecting herself, her hands never leaving Buddy's feathers.

"I swooped him up, he let out a final caw, and he died."

Pam cried in the shade of the covered porch and held Buddy tighter. I didn't know what to say. I wasn't sure what to think. All these years, all those hopes, all the noise, the frustrations, the fears, and the joy, and this is how his life ends.

"I'm so sorry," I said, my voice catching. "I'm so very sorry."

I sat down and Pam looked from Buddy to me, and then at Buddy again.

"All he ever wanted, the only thing he ever asked for, was to be part of the group," she said.

As I watched them, it dawned on me that I had never seen, or could have possibly imagined, Buddy ever being this still. In life, he was a whir of constant movement, his head spinning and poking, his feathers rising and falling, his voice cackling then bellowing. He didn't just live life; he seemed to define it. Of course, in the last few months, he rested more on the blankets and towels that Pam spread for him in the corner of the back porch, but when anyone opened the door to check on him, he immediately rose, seemingly embarrassed, and got back to the business of high-stepping and clucking around his territory, if not the life of the party, at the very least, the Head Party Planner.

But seeing his body spread across Pam, I couldn't get this single impression out of my head: Buddy looked ancient. His feet, yellowed claws, carried a prehistoric quality to them, scaly and worn. His face, though peaceful in its expression, was physically weathered. His feathers didn't look as bright white as they had seemed even the day before. Maybe all of this, or at least part of this, was what Pam loved so much about him.

It's a cliché, but clichés often carry the mark of truth, that it seemed like just yesterday that Buddy was a fuzzy chick chirping at the television as he sat between Caroline and Abigail on the couch in their house. So much happened to him in these three years. He went from a chick to a chicken, from the house to the yard, from a cage to the garage, from a benign if unusual presence to a loud and occasionally ornery rooster. When we all moved in together, he got his own shed, took over our yard, and became something of a neighborhood celebrity, more popular than I ever would have thought. And through it all, from youth to death, he maintained an unwavering commitment to everything on his side of the fence. Me aside.

Death inevitably makes people think of themselves. Maybe it's a muted form of narcissism, but I think it's just human nature. I thought of my own life and where it had gone over the course of Buddy's time on this earth, not just physically, though certainly that as well—Pam, the kids, the animals, the suburbs, the sense that this was what it all means. My life had changed in ways that I never fully imagined it would.

"I thought he'd be around forever," Pam said, breaking my reverie, "even if I've been worried that he hadn't seemed like himself."

I gazed at her and replied, "Buddy always lived on his

own terms, and he died on his own terms. There was nothing you could have done to prevent this."

In the coming days and weeks, the builder would stop by and say our house looked and felt completely different without Buddy in the yard. Neighbors knocked on the door to offer condolences and to at least say the right things about how they already missed his crowing. Pam bought a big stone planter in the shape of a rooster, filled it with flowers, and put it by the front door. Truth is, in its stillness, it reminded me more of what we were missing than of what we once had. Tom, from around the corner, delivered a bouquet of white flowers with his daughter and asked, as others had, "Will you get another?"

"Buddy just happened," Pam replied. "It was fate. I don't think a rooster is something you go out and get."

Hopefully, she didn't see me furiously fumbling with my iPhone in my efforts to record her words.

Pam would spend more than a little time researching what might have gone wrong, reading and talking to chicken experts at big universities. She came to learn that he was undoubtedly what's known as a "broiler breed," the kind of chicken whose body isn't made to last more than a few years because he was supposed to have been eaten in his relative youth. The reality dawned on us that Buddy lived as long as he could.

That sad Sunday, the kids' father kindly dropped them off at the house, even though it was his weekend. They came walking through the kitchen, out the back door, and onto the porch, tears streaming down their faces as they gathered around their mother and their bird. Abigail kissed his face as she kept saying, "My Nu-Nu," one of her dozen or so nicknames for the chicken that she brought into this world. Caroline rubbed his feet. Pam told them how it happened. I assured them that Buddy loved them very, very much.

The three of them exchanged stories of Buddy's exploits and feats over the years. Pam pulled out some clay, and they made impressions of his claws that would later harden in the oven. I retrieved a shovel from the garage and began digging a hole under Buddy's favorite Japanese maple in the back of the yard, a shaded spot where he had dug many holes before.

I wasn't more than a few shovelfuls in when the kids came over, certain that I couldn't be doing it perfectly enough for Buddy, and took over the job. We all took turns until the hole was deep and wide. Pam wrapped Buddy in a blanket and ever so gently nestled him down into the earth.

"Think of your favorite Buddy memory," she told the kids.

I hesitantly spread a shovel of dirt on top of Buddy, then another, and another. I noticed Caroline staring into the hole as I did this, holding a sprig of flowers she had pulled from a nearby bush. I saw Abigail biting her lip. They weren't little kids now, the little girls they had been when Buddy arrived, but little people, with emotions and dreams and styles that were every bit their own. How far they had come, I thought. How far we had all come, heartbroken in unison over the death of this unusual bird.

As I smoothed out the ground with the back of the shovel, Abigail said, "Buddy must have known he had done his job, so it was okay to leave."

I knew I was feeling emotional, but it didn't seem that truer words had ever been spoken. Buddy had helped bring us all together.

An hour or so later, the kids were upstairs. Pam and I were in the kitchen. Caroline's voice rang out, her squeaky voice, "Hey, Brian, come up here."

So I did. They had their collection of Breyer horses spread all across the room, barns and stables and riding rings and ponies with a dazzling array of complicated names, all of it an elaborate attempt to gamely push through the sadness of an otherwise brilliant day.

"What?" I asked,

"Nothing," Abigail said with a tone of distracted annoyance. "We just want you to watch us play."

So I took a seat, kicked up my feet, and realized quite quickly that there was nowhere else better to be. As they played, we talked a little bit about death and a little more about life, most of it natural and none of it forced.

Outside, it was eerily quiet, the kind of quiet that wouldn't seem normal for many weeks, and in those weeks, I would still see white flashes outside the windows just as I used to hear Harry padding through my Boston condo in the months after he was gone.

But inside, even amid the loss, there was the sense of something gained. Buddy, in Abigail's words, had done his job.

Acknowledgments

This book, oddly enough, rose from the blood of a fellow scribe. One of my very best friends, Mitch Zuckoff, a former *Globe* reporter, now a decorated and bestselling author, came to dinner at my house in the suburbs one summer night with his wife, Suzanne Kreiter. They were accompanied by our longtime literary agent and friend Richard Abate.

We had just moved in, and Buddy, the resident rooster, proved anything but a gracious host. As soon as they strolled through the front gate of our yard, Buddy was on Mitch in a flurry of feathers and claws, his sharp beak catching Mitch's shin in that spot you never want to be hit. There was the oddest wail, an open wound, and probably more laughter than was actually polite. Richard spent the vast bulk of the dinner repeating, again and again, "You've got to write this story."

To his credit, he wouldn't let it drop. Richard helped

me form the idea in my head, pushed me to outline it on paper, and instilled in me the belief that it was a tale worthy of being told. It's impossible to thank him enough, as well as Richard's expert assistant at 3Arts in New York, Melissa Kahn.

Equally impossible would be finding a better home for this story than Crown. I've spent a career in journalism chronicling the deeds and misdeeds, adventures and misadventures, of invariably colorful people, some well-known, others barely known at all; it has been somewhat bizarre to devote this many words and this much time to my own life, or at least this facet of it. But my editor, Lindsay Sagnette, a world-class wordsmith and, whenever needed, a singularly gifted therapist, has guided me along this unfamiliar path with extraordinary vision, empathy, and charm.

So much of Crown is like that, including Christine Kopprasch in editorial, Ellen Folan in publicity, Julie Cepler in marketing, the incomparable Ron Koltnow in sales, and Chris Brand, the art director who spent a memorable day overseeing a photo shoot with Buddy preening from my favorite leather chair. All of them have shown remarkable enthusiasm for Buddy and his namesake book, and beyond that, they are just personable, kind people. It's no wonder that Crown is as good as it is when you factor in the leadership of Molly Stern, whose contagious enthusiasm for this story from its inception gave me the confidence to sit at my keyboard, day after day, and let my memories and emotions pour forth.

In Boston, the aforementioned Mitch and Suzanne were critical contributors, sounding boards and wise counselors, as always. Chris Putala, my other best friend, indulged all my absurd rooster tales with his trademark wit and towel-snapping cheer. Larry Moulter was an invaluable adviser from the very beginning and a key cheerleader as the process spun forward.

Colleen, the younger of my two older sisters, was my first reader, as she was with my prior books, partly due to her insistence but more to do with her insight. I'll never shed the image of looking out the window at Abigail's birthday party and seeing Colleen racing across my backyard with Buddy in hot pursuit; I suspect he had just learned we were related. My sister Carole was just about Harry's favorite person in life for every good reason, not the least of which was that he undoubtedly knew she is mine. She has been endlessly supportive of this project, and for that, has my further appreciation. Then there's Yvonne McGrory, my mother. I flatter myself to think that even a few of her many gifts, most especially her lust for life, have rubbed off on me over the years, but I can certainly hope. There are not strong enough words to express my thanks.

Of course, one of my biggest debts is to the *Boston Globe,* where I've had the privilege of making my writing career for the past quarter century. I don't honestly think I'd trade in a single day. Special thanks to Marty Baron, the editor, who also happens to be the fairest boss and most upstanding newsman I've ever met. Thanks as well to my talented editor, Chris Chinlund, whose enthusiasm for a column I wrote about a young Buddy, long before I ever imagined a book, provided the tacit encouragement to go forward. And without bringing up names, because there are too many to list, my colleagues at the *Globe* have my deepest gratitude and respect. Truth is, they amaze me every day with their extraordinary work, which is critical to making Boston the world-class city that it truly is. We are all fortunate, myself and the entire *Globe* staff, to have the most engaged and enlightened readers that a newspaper reporter, writer, photographer, editor, or designer would ever dare dream.

Lastly, and most profoundly, my thanks to Pam and the kids, Abigail and Caroline, who changed my life in ways I was never creative enough to foresee. Pam wasn't just valuable, but invaluable, in terms of writing this book. It's scary, the things she is able to remember, and it's quite humbling to see her put even life's smallest moments into a larger perspective. A few years ago, I probably couldn't have imagined my life today. Now I can't imagine anything but.

About the Author

BRIAN McGRORY has been a writer and an editor for the *Boston Globe* since 1989 and received both the prestigious Scripps Howard and Sigma Delta Chi awards in 2012 for his twice-weekly metro column. He is the author of four novels and lives in Massachusetts with all creatures great and small.